BURTON BLATT

Director,
Division of Special Education
and Rehabilitation,
Syracuse University

ALLYN AND BACON, INC.
Boston, Massachusetts

EXODUS
FROM
PANDEMONIUM

HUMAN ABUSE
AND A REFORMATION
OF PUBLIC POLICY

*to my wife, Ethel Draizen Blatt,
who encouraged me to engage in
the affairs of the real world.*

Photos: Fred Kaplan

Drawings: Diane Myles

© Copyright 1970 by Allyn and Bacon, Inc. 470 Atlantic Avenue, Boston.
All rights reserved. No part of this book may be reproduced in any form
or by any means, without permission in writing from the publishers.

Printed in the United States of America.
Library of Congress Catalog Card Number: 75–111091

Objectivity is illusion.

Feeling is life:
that's my belief and therapy.

That is why you may find
the pathos is the ethos of this book.

The Theme is From Ecclesiastes . . .

> Better is a poor and wise child than an old and foolish
> king, who knoweth not how to receive admonition
> any more.

> There is a righteous man that perisheth in his
> righteousness, and there is a wicked man
> that prolongeth his life in his evildoing.

> When the Holy One created the first man, He took him
> before all the trees in the garden of Eden, and
> He said: "See how lovely and excellent My works
> are. All that I have created, for you have I created.
> Consider this carefully. Do not corrupt or desolate My
> world. For if you corrupt or desolate it, there is no
> one to set it right after you."

and the Romans . . .

> The Senators are good men,
> But the Senate is a wild beast.

and Abraham Lincoln

> Those who deny freedom to others deserve it not for
> themselves, and under a just God, will not long
> retain it.

CONTENTS

FOREWORD

The great bulk of books should be judged independent of the personality or background of the authors, just as a painting has to be judged
by what it contains and presents. This is not one of those books
because it is a very personal statement and description which can be
misjudged or misinterpreted unless one knows something about its
author. For example, some readers may conclude that Dr. Blatt is a
kind of wide-eyed, naïve, do-gooder who cannot stand evil and injustice,
and has the need (in the tradition of muckrakers) to expose, indict, and
convict. Such a conclusion founders on four facts. First, Dr. Blatt pretty
much knew what he would find in our institutions for the mentally
retarded and, in fact, had pictorially documented the conditions in
Christmas In Purgatory. Second, he is not a journalist but an eminent
member of the educational establishment. Third, he permitted himself
temporarily to head up an entire state program, not because he felt he
had the answers and would right wrongs, but because he felt compelled
to experience the problem in a position of responsibility. In a very basic
sense he wanted to learn. Fourth, and perhaps most important in the
long run, Dr. Blatt was becoming increasingly aware that the problem
went far beyond mental retardation, which was but an instance of
human abuse, witting or unwitting. The fact that he includes a chapter
on his visit to the site of a Nazi concentration camp, and he asks how it
happened and how so many people there today view it as *just* history,
indicates that for Dr. Blatt the problem is far more complex and general
than one would expect if one looked only at the care and treatment of
institutionalized, retarded children. The child-battering syndrome,
racial segregation, the snake pits we call state hospitals, our penal
institutions which apparently cure only heterosexuality—all of these,
and more, testify to the frequency of human abuse and this is what Dr.
Blatt wants us to recognize.

The significance of his general point has come to have deep personal meaning for me. A couple of years ago it became necessary for
me to become acquainted with nursing homes for the aged. As the

reader probably knows, there has been a fantastic number of these facilities built in recent years primarily because of the medicare program. They are very modern, well-equipped settings and many more of them are being and will be erected. Psychologically speaking, however, they are hell-holes in which patients languish until death. From the standpoint of the patient, life is silent and usually in bed. The patient is completely and cringingly dependent on others for all or most of his needs, and any display of anger or complaint is viewed either as a personality defect or the consequence of senility. The actual amount of patient-staff contact, visual or physical, during a day is amazingly slight. These conditions are not due to deliberate human abuse. When one talks to the staff one gets two responses which are identical to what Dr. Blatt describes in the case of those who care for the mentally retarded in our institutions. First, the shortage of personnel is acknowledged (since these facilities are *businesses,* there is no likelihood that more personnel will be hired because that would obviously cut profits). Second, and somewhat in contradiction to the first, it is stated that there is not much one can do for these old people. The self-fulfilling prophecy is always at work!

I was describing these conditions to an undergraduate class, which is not a group one should expect to get personally upset by what happens to old people. They had some kind of intellectual appreciation but it was and could be no more than that. As I said to them: "You get all upset about what you think is wrong with your education—and you should. You have a burning sense of injustice about racial discrimination—and you should. You and others spend a lot of your time tutoring ghetto children—and you should. You demonstrate about the senseless loss of life in wars—and you should. But the aged in our euphemistically labeled nursing homes or convalescent hospitals is not a group you know about or can feel for or have an interest in or towards whom you have the kind of obligation you feel with other groups." This was not said critically but as a statement of fact relevant to something of deep concern to them: man's inhumanity to man. Following this particular class, one of the students asked if he could do his research paper on convalescent hospitals. As luck would have it, he had complete access to a new convalescent hospital and he proposed to spend three weeks there, dividing his time among the three shifts. He was also a photography bug. He did a study which, unfortunately, cannot be published. He presented his data and pictures to the class. What is noteworthy is that although the students were shook up, the student who did the study was far more upset than anyone else. Like Dr. Blatt he experienced the hell-hole and was aware that his words (and even his pictures) could not communicate the depth of his feelings.

There is a saying that war is too important to be left to the generals. In a similar vein I would maintain that the care of dependent children and adults is too important to be left to the professionals, and Dr. Blatt's account amply confirms this. It is not that professionals are evil people or that they do not want to do what is right. It is just that they are people. Their knowledge and expertise notwithstanding, they can be blind to injustice and their unwitting role in it. They can make virtue out of necessity and thereby accept evil. They are torn between personal comfort and security, on the one hand, and the consequences of not conforming, on the other hand. They can pledge allegiance to the symbols of objectivity at the same time that they can discredit an opinion not because of its content but because of the status of the utterer. They may know how power corrupts but not see the process in themselves. Like the rest of humanity the professional person, especially if he is in an important administrative position, needs to be controlled against himself, for his sake as well as for those in his overall care. This control function is not now being carried out in the central administration in our state capitols, or by boards of trustees of our institutions. Although "public control" is supposed to be exercised via boards of trustees or visitors, the fact is they (unwittingly) serve the purpose of window dressing. If my own experience is any guide, and Dr. Blatt's account certainly does not contradict it, boards of trustees are the least knowledgeable about what goes on in the institutions for which they have responsibility.

We have to think of new ways whereby representatives of communities take more direct responsibility for the life of our institutions. There are different ways and bases by which these representatives can be chosen. However, in my opinion they should have one major function: several times each year, and each time at a different time of the day, they should appear unannounced at the institution, have immediate access to anyone and to any part of the institution, make whatever observations they deem necessary, ask whatever questions they think relevant, and following the visit write a report, copies of which should be submitted to those in charge of the institution, central office, and parent organizations, and elected officials. This report should be considered a public document. My suggestion is not meant to supplant any existing mechanism or procedure; rather it is an attempt to develop a mechanism completely independent of the existing structure.

There are problems, known and unknown, with this suggestion. I have offered it here as a basis for discussion. There will be numerous objections to it and they will be of three kinds. The first of these objections will concern the effects of these visits and reports on institutional morale; the second will revolve around issues of knowledgeability and professional expertise; the third objection will involve maintaining that there is nothing basically wrong with present arrangements except for insufficient funds to do what is needed. The first two objections are given no support whatever by Dr. Blatt's account, i.e., morale cannot be much lower than it is, and the performance of our professionals (both as leaders and treaters) is not something to cause us to do gyrations of enthusiasm. As for the third reaction, it is unlikely that one can point to an instance of institutional human abuse for which the expenditure of public monies had other than the most transient beneficial effects, if it had any such effects at all. In all of these instances there have been two major consequences: the system which produced or maintained the human abuse was not tampered with, and many people felt virtuous because it was so easy to confuse spending money with righting wrongs.

But why pick on the professionals? Is it not true, as Dr. Blatt makes quite clear, that professional groups are by no means the cause of the conditions and that in a sense all of us play a role? I agree completely with Dr. Blatt and that was implied in my statement that there is no one problem and no one solution. But I start with the professionals for the reason that by law or administrative regulation our institutions are in the care of various professional groups. They are in the driver's seat but drivers, be they of the real or symbolic variety, must never be allowed to determine the rules of the road.

Seymour B. Sarason
New Haven, Conn.

PREFACE

Now that this volume is, for all practical purposes, completed, I have permitted myself the time to think about why I wrote it. There are many different reasons why people write books, and I had mine.

I hope this volume does some good. I do not expect it to affect my standard of living, but I do hope more than a few people will read it. Why did I write it? I wrote it for myself, which may not be a very good reason, but is my reason. The preparation of this volume has forced me to attempt to understand a little better one of the truly puzzling and frightening aspects of our civilization: the nature and conditions of human abuse. I had become so confused and so frightened by what I had seen and had heard about man's treatment of his fellow man that I could no longer ignore the probability that, unless I struggled to understand inhuman treatment of humans, I would become either insensitive to such treatment (as I believe I had become) or I would not be able to tolerate my own relatively pleasurable life in the face of The Holocaust surrounding those of us unaffected. Therefore, foremost of my personal objectives was the need to give expression to my bewilderment and unhappiness with the very painful and slow progress of the humane in mankind. I wrote this volume to protect myself, to save my mind if not my soul. For this basically selfish act, I do hope that I had other unselfish motivations. That is, I do hope this book will contribute, in its own way, to the alleviation of some pain or suffering for some people and to the clearer appreciation of the concept of human abuse by other people. I do hope that it will be more valuable than, merely, as my catharsis.

Originally, my intention had been to include the term "mental retardation" in the title of this volume. However, as I began to write and to think, I discovered that "mental retardation" is incidental to the purpose of this volume and the pathology it seeks to understand. By this I mean, its subject is not so much "mental retardation" as it is those who offend the mentally retarded. It is not so much about the retarded personality as it is about our retarded civilization. It is not so

xv

much about people who are incapable of changing as it is about public policy which does not permit those people opportunities for changing. Early in the writing of this volume, I realized that its central focus might have been on innumerable groups, other than the mentally retarded, such as: American Indians, blacks, people in jails, possibly even certain college students or ordinary children in schools. I realized that I chose the mentally retarded for, essentially, two reasons: first, I have more interest in mental retardation and more experience in meeting them than other groups; second, the mentally retarded appear to be the "least of the least," the abused of the abused, the least able to advocate for themselves and the most in need of advocates. I will admit that, at one time, my specific interest in mental retardation was much more pronounced than my general interest in human abuse. Now, my specific interest remains deep but my general interest in the nature and origins of abuse has become dominating. Consequently, although some will view this volume as one concerned with the essential plight of the institutionalized mentally retarded, and as one written for the concern of professional workers and parents who must deal with the mentally retarded, I have written it for people who are troubled about our civilization, especially as public policy condones, excuses, and sometimes requires the cruel and inhuman treatment of certain individuals.

In my mind, this volume contains three related, although separate, books. They were begun, simultaneously, in January of 1968 and they were completed, simultaneously, in January of 1969. During that year, I was on leave of absence from Boston University, serving as the Assistant Commissioner and Director of the Division of Mental Retardation of the Massachusetts Department of Mental Health. This volume is not a record of that experience, although it is a reaction to that experience. The volume is not, I hope you believe, about Massachusetts—although it concerns Massachusetts—for it applies to every state. Most emphatically, I do not believe that the Commonwealth of Massachusetts, its public officials, and its concerned citizens should have any more, or less, interest in this volume than other groups and individuals from other sections of the nation. Obviously, my frame of reference is much more often anchored in Massachusetts than in other localities. However, I believe, truly, that this volume is no more relevant for Massachusetts than it is for any other state that I am acquainted with and, most probably, than it is for any other state anywhere. If this volume offends my friends in Massachusetts, I will suspect that either they did not understand or chose not to believe the above statement. I do not want to lose those friends and colleagues in Massachusetts because I value and respect their friendship to me and their concern for the plight of all abused people. I hope they will understand why I wrote this volume and I hope they believe my warm feelings and deep respect for them and for the progress that is being made here in our Commonwealth.

America was discovered long before Columbus set foot on our shores, possibly long before the Indians migrated here. However, Indians discovered America, Columbus discovered America, and each immigrant who sets foot on our shores discovers America. I discovered institutions. I discovered them and conceptualized their being in ways that caused me to think about things I had never thought about before, and to struggle with problems and ideas I had never known to have existed before. With the exception of Chapter 3, Dorothea Dix's presentation to the Massachusetts Legislature, and Chapter 11, portions of a European Diary, Book I is an attempt to present the reality of institutions today and people who inhabit them or serve them. Book I is the raw data, the descriptions of people and their activities and their relationships. Book I is my attempt to present, in some systematic fashion, what I have seen in institutions and how those specific experiences have affected me.

Book II is more than the subjective counterpart of the realism of "People and Their Institutions." Book II is beyond subjectivism. It is illusion. I don't believe we are capable, as human beings, of being very objective. Nor do I believe that illusion is without any objective base. This is by way of saying that I have trouble comprehending what people mean when they use such terms as "objective" and "subjective" when they try to protect and argue for the precious nature of each. During its writing, Book II has meant a lot to me and has helped me to clarify my thoughts and, even, to decide on particular issues and make administrative decisions. I don't suppose it will help the reader in the same ways it has helped me. Book II worries me because I don't know how good or bad it is. I must include it in this volume because it has been good for me and, on re-reading now, it reflects my experiences in the institutions and with the people there in ways that Book I does not express.

Book III might better be titled "The Draft of a Draft of Needs and Values." Having experienced human abuse for so many centuries, it is surprising that we know so little about its genesis and nurture. Little scholarship has been devoted to the problem in the past and few people, even today, are studying it. We have an instructional materials center at Boston University that is devoted to the collection and dissemination, as well as development, of materials for handicapped children and their teachers. Our center is linked to a network of other instructional materials and educational research information centers. While preparing this manuscript, I thought it might be valuable to obtain a bibliography concerned with human abuse or with mistreatment of school children or with malevolence in the institution. Although there are categories in almost every conceivable area of child care, treatment, and education, where one can request and receive a computer-produced bibliography from the appropriate resource center, I was not able to find a single center in this country that has either developed a bibliography on abuse or is inquiring about the subject. I hope this neglect of an area that seems so fundamental to the human condition—and so inexorably related to the possibilities that our civilization will (or should) survive—is more a reflection of the stupidity of bright people than it is of the inability of society's major forces to admit that such abuse exists. I am intimidated by my own feeling that "human abuse" is not a category in the retrieval systems for the same reason that institutions for the mentally retarded, or public school systems for that matter, do not develop centers to study human abuse as part of their organizational commitment. To develop such centers is to admit that human abuse exists, is tolerated, is sometimes encouraged, and is frequently legally permissible, and sometimes legally prescribed. Because we have such a scanty literature on this problem, because we are so new at studying this problem seriously, because I am so newly exposed to the conditions and the issues, Book III is more a beginning than a conclusion. It is a draft that will need many revisions before its last edition is completed. Irrespective of its flaws, however, it is a beginning that is overdue, and the importance of this beginning will not be marred by the imperfections of the author or his treatment of the problem.

There are many, many people who deserve my gratitude and to whom I am in debt for their activities in my behalf during the events of the past year. I hope that this volume is some justification for their faith in me and in our common cause. I will not mention all of the people who deserve to be mentioned now. First, I hope that our prior associations have communicated to these people the profound effect they have had on my life, irrevocably changing me, probably for the better. Secondly, if I mentioned names—there are so many—I would run the risk of omitting people who could only be omitted under circumstances where an unthinking person performs an incredible and unforgivable act. Therefore, I will mention only a handful of names now, knowing that I might well have mentioned at least a hundred colleagues from the Department of Mental Health, superintendents, physicians, teachers, secretaries, students, and friends. Dr. Milton Greenblatt, the dedicated Commissioner of Mental Health for the Commonwealth of Massachusetts, encouraged and permitted me to do what I believed was right or necessary. I hope my gratitude to him and my admiration were communicated in some way and I hope we will always remain friends and colleagues. Dr. Seymour Sarason, Professor of Psychology at Yale University, read this manuscript and helped with its organization and format. Much beyond that, however, for the past dozen years or more he has been a staunch and loyal friend and collaborator and—truly—my teacher. Misses Karen Arentzen, Carol Bennison, Roxann Joseph, Mrs. Louise La Fontaine, and Mrs. Margery MacDonald—who have studied with me, worked with me, and now contributed to the preparation of this manuscript—are rare women, without whom it would have been difficult to get along with this writing as well as I did. They typed sections, read portions with critical and responsive eyes, made observations when observations were needed, found books and papers for me to read that they thought should be read by one writing this kind of manuscript, and were always available for comments and criticism or, when I needed these, moral support and encouragement. I owe a great deal to John Gilman of Allyn and Bacon. His support of the publication of *Christmas in Purgatory* and, now, this volume will always be remembered with gratitude.

In spite of my great fortune in having enormous backing and strength derived from the faith people had in me and this work, it was—nevertheless—very painful to write *Exodus from Pandemonium.* However, I have no doubt that my pain would have been far greater had it not been written.

Burton Blatt
Natick, Massachusetts

1
PEOPLE
AND
THEIR INSTITUTIONS

chapter 1

ANTECEDENTS

By 1956 I had completed approximately seven years of what I considered to be a deep involvement in the field of mental retardation—and had visited a total of two state institutions for the mentally retarded.

My first visit was made during an early graduate year, sometime in 1949 or 1950. It was to a very large state school in New York and was arranged by the professor in mental retardation with whom I was studying. My recollections of that visit are not completely clear. However, I do remember that I was impressed with the beautiful grounds. On the other hand, I also remember that, upon our return home, I complained to my professor about what I thought to be a disgraceful and very distressing etiological conference that we attended there. Patients were presented to our group of about 100; they were seated in a row at the front of an auditorium and, one by, one, were asked to stand and to exhibit themselves to this audience. As each patient was moved and turned and poked, the presenting physician would recount the history, family background, current status, and activities of the patient. I'm certain that now any reader who has had even a minimum experience in state schools knows about these kinds of case presentations. I was forced to sit through all too many of them until—some years ago—I vowed never to subject myself again to a presentation of this kind and, I am proud to report, this is one vow that I have kept.

I do not recollect visiting any institutions for the mentally retarded during the years between the completion of my master's degree and my return to the Pennsylvania State University for the final year of doctoral study. During those five years, I taught a special class for the mentally retarded in a Brooklyn public school and, although I was continuing some graduate work in mental retardation and was very deeply involved in this field, not once did I visit a state school nor, even more surprising to me now, do I remember ever thinking seriously (or, for that matter, casually) about a state school. In retrospect, it is perfectly clear to me that I had, for many years, neither an understanding nor an interest in institutions, their residents, and their problems. Further, and not in any defense of that thoughtlessness, I do not believe that any of my colleagues (i.e. those who taught special classes and were part of "our crowd") and few of my professors were any more knowledgeable or interested in this problem than I. Still further, I do not believe that the situation is very much, if any, different today. Public school special class teachers, principals, and university professors appear to understand little and care less about the institutionalized mentally retarded and the problems confronting those attempting to change the institutions.

During my last year at Penn State (1955), I made several visits to Laurelton State School, an institution for the mentally retarded located twenty or thirty miles from the university campus. Again, I was struck by the beautiful grounds and bucolic setting of the school. As in the earlier visit, I did have negative reactions. These were concerned mainly with the unavailability of schooling opportunities for the residents, many of whom were mildly retarded and, so it seemed to me then, some of whom appeared to be of normal intelligence.

It was not until I completed doctoral studies and began my college teaching career that I became a regular visitor to state institutions for the mentally retarded. After my appointment to New Haven State Teacher's College (now Southern Connecticut State College), I was responsible for the supervision of student teachers in special education, several of whom were assigned to the Southbury Training School and the Mansfield Training School, at the time the two state schools for the mentally retarded in Connecticut. Further, with Fred Finn, then the Director of Training at Southbury, I organized a workshop each summer for teachers of the trainable mentally retarded. These involvements caused me to become a very frequent visitor to the state schools. I attended staff conferences, child study committee meetings, and numerous other activities in these facilities. I visited all of the dormitories on innumerable occasions and, quite literally, became a kind of quasi-staff member, especially at the Southbury Training School.

In 1959, Governor Ribicoff appointed me to the first Connecticut Advisory Council on Mental Retardation. For the first time, I was now required to observe the institutions and to consider their needs from the viewpoint of someone who had responsibility for them and who pledged his commitment to serve them. However, during my years in Connecticut, including those on the Advisory Council, I had a general feeling about institutions that, although not completely positive, permitted me to sleep soundly and not worry about them or about their residents. Obviously, I had visited numerous back wards (although Connecticut did seem to have fewer of these than did other states and did seem to be doing more for its institutionalized retarded than other states) and attended innumerable etiological conferences. Even then, in my naïve, less jaundiced stage of development, I was able to observe all of the obvious and many of the subtle barbarisms that seemed to be perpetrated daily in state institutions. I explained those observations to myself by using stock reasonings: "nature of things in institutions," "the invariant characteristics of the severely retarded," and "we are doing the best we can."

A glimmer of a more mature understanding of the things that are, and the things that need be, began to take hold during the last year of my service on the Advisory Council, just prior to my move to Boston University. Ernest Roselle, the first superintendent at Southbury Training School, articulated during the early 1950's a view of regionalization and community participation in programming that was brought to fruition a decade later by such individuals at Bert Schmickel and Fred Finn. Bert Schmickel, Deputy Commissioner for Mental Retardation, Connecticut Department of Health, and Fred Finn, Superintendent of the Seaside Center, with the approval and encouragement of the first Advisory Council, established a center that began to demonstrate the obsolescence of back wards, certainly, and the inappropriateness of large institutions, probably. We began to understand that the condition we termed "back ward life" is an invention of the nonretarded and a reflection of their character rather than a necessary concomitant to severe mental retardation. As we grew to appreciate the certainty that back wards could be eradicated, some of us learned with ever increasing anxiety and torment how truly evil these monuments to inhumanity were. While we could convince ourselves that back wards were necessary—were, in a way, providing the best care possible under intolerable circumstances—we were able to abide them. With the advent of clear alternatives, our defensive moat—"the nature of things"—crumbled. What was being demonstrated was that the architects of back wards, the progenitors of the feces-smearers, the culprits of this holocaust are normal men and their public policy. This realization did not come to me overnight and, in fact, I am still struggling with it.

In the fall of 1961 I assumed the chairmanship of the Special Education Department at Boston University. Among my responsibilities was the inauguration of a research program sponsored by the United States Office of Education and involving three- and four-year-old children from disadvantaged homes. For any readers interested in our activities during those years, an account of that study and other involvements may be found in my book *The Intellectually Disfranchised,* published in 1966 by the Massachusetts Department of Mental Health. I mention that preschool study for two reasons. First, it embarked us on a series of studies and programs designed to test the hypothesis that intelligence is educable, that it is plastic, that it is a function of practice and training. Essentially, I view the hypothesis undergirding that project as synonymous with the hypothesis that back wards may be eradicated or, as you will read in the chapter on *Jimmy,* every human being is capable of changing and learning. (In fact, when I view in retrospect my research and clinical activities during the past twenty years, it is not very difficult to conclude that practically all of these activities were concerned with the hypothesis that man underestimates his potential and man—all men—are capable of changing.) Secondly, I mention this preschool study because the intervention phase of the program was conducted at a state school for the mentally retarded. Thus, I had an opportunity to visit the Walter E. Fernald State School almost every day for two years.

In the fall of 1965, United States Senator Robert Kennedy visited several institutions for the mentally retarded in New York State. His shocked reaction to those visits brought a storm of protest from many sources. An account of my own reaction to these protests and the eventual decision to produce *Christmas in Purgatory* (a presentation in words and photographs of the horrifying conditions in back wards) are found in the next chapter.

But it is not necessarily easy, once you know the facts, to get them put before the public. Fred Kaplan, the photographer, and I prepared the manuscript and photographs for presentation to publishers. One publisher, William Morrow, turned us down because they felt much more text was needed and, secondly, some of the pictures might be considered offensive. Two publishers, those I have had affiliations with in the past, turned us down without asking to see the manuscript. Both believed this type of book would be unsalable and difficult to produce. Neither the Kennedy Foundation nor the non-profit *Special Child Publications* felt able to sponsor the book. Allyn and Bacon, the publisher who eventually brought out the second edition, turned it down, originally, saying it was an important book but one that presented too many problems to consider sponsoring. We went to the magazines. *Life* was very interested. I'm certain that their editor, Mr. Billings, will not forget me. After viewing our pictures, he remarked that he would not be able to have lunch that day. *Life* wanted to publish a two-part series on *Christmas in Purgatory.* However, they insisted that their editorial policy required the naming of names, the designation of institutions, and the identification of states. For reasons that are brought out in the next chapter, we were unable to agree to those conditions.

Eventually, we decided to publish *Christmas in Purgatory* ourselves and, if necessary, pay for all of the publication costs. Happily, as things turned out, a parent association for retarded children in Connecticut agreed to advance us the money to print the first edition. After publication of the commercial edition, all royalties have been assigned by both Fred Kaplan and myself to that parent association. (Contrary to any possible misbeliefs, neither Fred Kaplan nor I received any royalities from the publication of either the first edition or the second edition of *Christmas in Purgatory*.)

In 1966, at the time we were arranging for the publication of the book, I received a call from Charlie Mangel, senior editor of *Look*. He had heard, through an unnamed source in "high governmental office," that we had completed a study of institutions for the mentally retarded and were having great difficulty in arranging for the publication of our report. After several meetings with him, I prepared an article and it was scheduled for publication in an issue planned for the coming fall. Actually, it was not published in *Look* until October 31, 1967, one year later. Several factors delayed its appearance, including a last minute objection from a very high-ranking official of Cowles Communications, Incorporated, publishers of *Look*. He did not believe that a "family magazine," catering to the tastes of the broad mainstream of America, should publish this type of article, but in the end the article was printed. It drew a phenomenal reaction and, as will be discussed later in this volume, a universal acceptance of the need to expose the conditions we did expose and the need to publish this type of report.

We distributed the first edition of *Christmas in Purgatory* in the early fall of 1966. One thousand copies were sent to a list of those individuals whom we believed would be in the most advantageous positions to support a reform of institutions. The response to this publication was absolutely overwhelming. We received letters from the President of the United States, Mrs. Hubert Humphrey (several letters, requests for additional copies of the publication, and an eventual meeting), practically every United States Senator and practically every governor, and many, many commissioners of mental health and mental retardation, superintendents of state schools, professors of special education or fields allied to mental retardation, presidents of parent associations, and many hundreds of other people from all walks of life who had read the book.

With the publication of the second edition, which was held up so that it could be brought out simultaneously with the *Look* article, reviews began to appear in professional journals and in newspapers. The mail continued to flood in to us and, for about six to ten weeks after the *Look* article, we received request upon request for appearance on radio programs or television discussion shows.

When the opportunity presented itself for us to spend the summer of 1967 in Europe, teaching for Boston University in its overseas program, we accepted this respite from the almost daily pressures and activities that had, by now, become a "normal part" of our lives since the first publication of *Christmas in Purgatory.*

Upon our return to the United States, I found several messages to call Dr. Milton Greenblatt, newly appointed Commissioner of Mental Health. Dr. Greenblatt succeeded Dr. Harry Solomon, who retired the previous spring after a long and distinguished career as Harvard professor of psychiatry and, later, Commissioner of Mental Health. An appointment was made and Dr. Greenblatt quickly came around to his purpose in asking for the meeting. In March of 1967, the Commonwealth of Massachusetts passed legislation reorganizing the Massachusetts Department of Mental Health. For those in the fields allied to mental health and mental retardation, it will be enough to mention that this reorganization was in compliance both with the dissatisfactions voiced in our Commonwealth concerning the care, treatment, and services offered the mentally ill and the mentally retarded, and with the federal guidelines requiring the establishment of mental health–mental retardation regions and areas for states wishing to be eligible to receive federal support for construction and staffing of mental health–mental retardation programs. The Massachusetts legislation was, in my opinion, a landmark, a pioneering achievement. It provided for the utilization of non-medical personnel in high administrative positions. Further, it required the participation of citizens on area and regional boards. It mandated the development of community programs and the provision for alternatives to institutionalization for the mentally ill and mentally retarded. Commissioner Greenblatt asked me to become the first non-medical director of the newly organized Division of Mental Retardation. I explained to him that I was not prepared to leave Boston University or university life. He explained to me that it was his understanding that I was scheduled for a sabbatical leave of absence for the coming spring semester. Why, he asked, couldn't I request a leave of absence, instead of a sabbatical? My first reaction was to refuse the directorship. Probably, the prime arguments for my later change of decision were the remarks made by several people in state government—remarks that I knew to be perfectly valid and to which I had no ready response. Essentially, I was reminded that men of good conscience cannot turn away in the face of their responsibilities to attempt to remediate those problems. I had articulated those problems and aroused a public storm. Here was my opportunity to do more than talk about them. How could I refuse it?

I began this new assignment with the Department of Mental Health on January 2, 1968, expecting to return to Boston University on September 1. Sometime during the late spring and early summer of 1968, after appropriate telephone calls from Governor Volpe and visits from Commissioner Greenblatt and myself to university officials, my leave was extended through the fall semester. In the late fall, a similar "attack" was mounted by various state officials and citizen groups, including Governor Volpe, but without Commissioner Greenblatt's or my participation (we had promised the University that I would return for the spring semester). I returned to the University in January, with a great many mixed feelings—excited and happy to be "back home," and, at the same time, regretting the friendships that must now be neglected, the "action" of the past, and the mission that must now be continued indirectly and without—to use a favorite term of Dr. Greenblatt's—governmental "clout." These were the antecedents. An overview of Book I follows.

In May I was invited to address a joint meeting of the Massachusetts House and Senate on the problems confronting our state schools for the mentally retarded. As matters were presented to me, it was one of the most important and delicate assignments I had ever been challenged with. If we could arouse their interest and support in ways that we have never been able to before, there was a chance that the legislature would take extraordinary measures to relieve the plight of back ward patients and other state school residents. I was acquainted with some of these legislators, a few of whom I admired very much. I was aware that most of the legislators knew of me and knew of *Christmas in Purgatory.* Senator Beryl Cohen, of Brookline, one of the spearheads most responsible for the passage of the Commonwealth mental health–mental retardation bill mentioned earlier, stated publicly that his distribution of our book, *Christmas in Purgatory,* in the final hours of Senate debate of that bill caused sufficient numbers of senators to reverse their earlier stands and tipped the balance to insure favorable passage of the legislation.

I consider that address to the legislature, "The Dark Side of the Mirror," the most important public address I have ever given. It is included as an appendix in Book III. The chapters in Book I by Dorothea Dix and George Albee, written more than a hundred years apart and concerning different times and places, indicate that time passes but times change grudgingly. All three addresses are so strikingly similar in purpose, so plainly clear about a problem that should interest every one of us, and reveal conditions so outrageous, that one wonders what is actually required before things change as time passes. I am optimistic that times will change and things will be better. However, I realize now that we must present with unremitting regularity the raw data of institutions, descriptions upon descriptions upon descriptions of what transpires in those dungeons of hell. The purpose of Book I is to present those raw data, most from my own observations and reactions, with a perspective from Dix and Albee—and hope from Jimmy. Jimmy's story shows both the horror that we permit to exist and the beauty that can be nurtured anywhere.

chapter 2

IN AND OUT
OF PURGATORY[1]

Abandon hope, all ye who enter here
Dante

With a good deal of anxiety, I waited for the white-uniformed attendant to respond to my knocking and unlock the door to hell. And, in America, we have our own special inferno. I was a visitor there during the Christmas season, 1965, while studying five state institutions for the mentally retarded, located in four Eastern States.

As I awaited entrance to the building, which was a residential dormitory, my anxiety belied the ostensible situation. In the 18 years that I had been professionally active in the field of mental retardation, I had been to scores of institutions. I had served on numerous commissions to evaluate or advise such institutions. In fact, the building I was about to enter—and which terrified me now—was no stranger to me. Over the years, and for one reason or another, I had found it necessary to visit this building, never giving it any particular thought; one might say I had visited it thoughtlessly.

However, my fears were not the neurotic outcroppings of an un-

---

1 The original draft of this chapter was completed during the summer of 1966 for the consideration of *Look.* As a result of their severe space limitations, a summarized brief portion eventually appeared in that magazine (October 31, 1967, pp. 96–103). The author believes that this unabridged presentation represents the most complete discussion of his study, *Christmas in Purgatory.* Parts of it are also published in *Changing Patterns in Residential Services for the Mentally Retarded,* edited by Robert B. Kugel and Wolf Wolfensberger, Washington, D.C.: President's Committee on Mental Retardation, pp. 35–49, 173–177.

hinged mind. I had a great deal to be worried about, and my thoughts flashed back to the circumstances that brought me here.

In the early Fall of 1965, Senator Robert Kennedy visited several of his state's institutions for the mentally retarded. His reactions were widely published in our various news media, shocking millions of Americans as well as infuriating scores of public office holders and professional persons responsible for the care and treatment of the mentally retarded. Most of the laymen with whom I discussed his visits reacted to the Senator's disclosures with incredulity. For it is difficult for "uninvolved" people to believe that, in our country, and at this time, human beings are being treated less humanly and under more deplorable conditions than are animals. A number of the "involved" citizenry—i.e., those who legislate and budget for institutions for the mentally retarded and those who administer them—were infuriated because the Senator reported only the worst of what he had seen, not mentioning the worthwhile programs that he undoubtedly was shown. Further, this latter group was severely critical of the Senator for taking "whirlwind" tours and, in the light of just a few hours of observation, damning entire institutions and philosophies.

During the time of these visits, I was a participant in a research project at The Seaside, a state of Connecticut regional center for the mentally retarded. The superintendent of The Seaside, Fred Finn, and I spent a considerable amount of time discussing, in particular, the debate between Senator Kennedy and New York Governor Nelson Rockefeller. We concluded the following: it does not require a scientific background or a great deal of observation to determine that one has entered the "land of the living dead"; it does not require too imaginative a mind or too sensitive a nose to realize that one has stumbled onto a dung hill, whether or not, as Cervantes wrote, it is covered with a piece of tapestry when a procession (of distinguished visitors) goes by; it is quite irrelevant how well the rest of an institution's program is being fulfilled if one is concerned with that part of it which is terrifying. No amount of rationalization can mitigate that which, to many of us, is cruel and inhuman treatment.

It is true that a short visit to the back wards (the hidden, publicly unvisited living quarters) of an institution for the mentally retarded will not provide, even for the most astute observer, any clear notion of the causes of the problems observed, the complexities of dealing with them, or ways to correct them. It is not difficult to believe that Senator Kennedy could not fully comprehend the subtleties, the tenuous relationships, the grossness of budgetary inequities, the long history of political machinations, the extraordinary difficulty in providing care for severely mentally retarded patients, the unavailability of highly trained professional leaders, and the near-impossibility in recruiting dedicated attendants and ward personnel. Further, I do not believe the conditions

Senator Kennedy claimed to have observed were due to evil people. As Seymour Sarason, Professor of Psychology at Yale University, wrote in the preface to our book (*Christmas in Purgatory: A Photographic Essay on Mental Retardation*), these conditions are ". . . not due to evil or incompetent or cruel people but rather to a conception of human potential and an attitude toward innovation which when applied to the mentally defective, result in a self-fulfilling prophecy. That is, if one thinks that defective children are almost beyond help, one acts toward them in ways which then confirm one's assumptions."

However, regardless of their antecedents, I believe, as well as do thousands of others who have been associated with institutions for the mentally retarded, that what Senator Kennedy reported to have seen he very likely did see. In fact, I know personally of few institutions for the mentally retarded in the United States that are completely free of dirt and filth, odors, naked patients groveling in their own feces, children in restraints and in locked cells, horribly crowded dormitories, and under-staffed and wrongly staffed facilities.

After a good deal of thought, I decided to follow through on what then seemed, and what eventually became, a bizarre venture. One of my friends, Fred Kaplan, is a professional photographer. On Thanks-giving Day, 1965, I presented the following plan to him. We were to arrange to meet with each of several key administrative persons in a variety of public institutions for the mentally retarded. If we gained an individual's cooperation, we would be taken on a "tour" of the back wards and those parts of the institution that he was *most* ashamed of. On the "tour" Fred Kaplan would take pictures of what we observed, utilizing a hidden camera attached to his belt.

Through the efforts of courageous and humanitarian colleagues, including two superintendents who put their reputations and profes-sional positions in jeopardy, we were able to visit the darkest corridors and vestibules that humanity provides for its journey to purgatory and, without being detected by ward personnel and professional staff, Fred Kaplan was able to take hundreds of photographs.

Our photographs were not always the clearest. On the other hand, in these conditions of secrecy it required a truly creative photographer to be able to take any pictures at all. Although these pictures cannot even begin to capture the total and overwhelming horror we saw, smelled, and felt, they represent a side of America that has rarely, if ever, been shown to the general public and is little understood by most of the rest of us.

I did not believe it was necessary to disclose the names of the institutions we visited. First, to reveal those names was, assuredly, an invitation to the dismissal of those who arranged for us to photograph their deepest and most embarrassing "secrets." However, involved was not only a matter of promises made to altruistic people but also an avoidance of the impression that the problems exposed were and are local rather than national ones. I was completely convinced that in numerous other institutions across America I could and would observe similar conditions—some, I am sure, even more frightening.

Had I known what I would actually be getting myself into and had I known what abnormal pressures would subsequently be exerted upon me as a result of this story and my efforts to bring it before the American people, I might have turned away from that first dormitory entrance as I was, finally, being admitted; and I might have fled to the shelter and protection of my academic "ivory tower" to ruminate on the injustices prevailing in society. As it was, I was in no way prepared for the degradation and despair I encountered.

As I entered this dormitory, housing severely mentally retarded adolescents and adults, I was still reminiscing about Senator Kennedy, Governor Rockefeller, and our fateful Thanksgiving dinner when an overwhelming stench enveloped me. It was the sickening, suffocating smell of feces and urine, decay, dirt and filth, of such strength as to hang in the air and, I thought then and am still not dissuaded, solid enough to be cut or shoveled away. But, as things turned out, the odors were among the gentlest assaults on our sensibilities. I was soon to learn about the decaying humanity that caused them. This story—my purgatory in black and white—which, ironically, was conceived of and written on the 700th anniversary of the birth of Dante, represents my composite impressions of what I consider to be the prevailing conditions of certain sectors of most institutions for the mentally retarded in this country. It is the hope of calling attention to the desperate needs of these institutions and, thereby, paving the way for upgrading all institutions for the mentally retarded in all dimensions of their responsibilities that this study was undertaken and this story written.

Several things strike a visitor to most institutions for the mentally retarded upon his arrival on the institution grounds. Sometimes there are fences, once in a while with barbed wire. Very frequently, the buildings impress him with their sheer massiveness and impenetrability. I have observed bars on windows and locks—many locks—on inside as well as outside doors. As I entered the dormitories and other buildings, I was impressed with the functional superiority of the new buildings but, on the other hand, the gross neglect in many of the older ones. I have observed gaping holes in ceilings of such vital areas as the main kitchen. In toilets, I frequently saw urinals ripped out, sinks broken, and the toilet bowls backed up. In every institution I visited—with the exception of The Seaside, which will be discussed later—I found incredible overcrowding. Beds are so arranged—side by side and head to head—that it is impossible, in some dormitories, to cross parts of the rooms without actually walking over beds. Oftentimes the beds are without pillows. I have seen mattresses so sagged by the weight of bodies that they were scraping the floor.

Before I go further, it would be well to point out a crucial factor giving rise to the overcrowdedness, the disrepair of older buildings, the excessive need for locks and heavy doors, and the enormity of buildings and the numbers of patients assigned to dormitories. In 1962, the President's Panel on Mental Retardation estimated that approximately 200,000 adults and children were cared for in residential institutions for the mentally retarded. States and localities spent, at that time, $300,-000,000 a year in capital and operating expenses for their care. At first glance, this appears to be a great deal of money and a cause for comfort, i.e. the mentally retarded have finally received their due. However, simple arithmetic tells us that $300,000,000 divided by 200,000 amounts to $1500 a year per person, or less than $30 a week, part of which is for capital development, *not only clothing, food, care, and treatment.* Nationally, the average per capita cost in institutions for the retarded was, in 1962, less than $5.00 per day, less than one-sixth the amount spent for general hospital care. Six states spent less than $2.50 a day per patient, while only seven states spent over $5.50 per day. In some checking that I have done recently, I learned that in our better zoos the larger animals require a much higher per capita expenditure. The average per capita daily cost for maintaining a retarded resident in each of the four institutions I first describe was at that time less than $7.00 and, in one state school, less than $5.00. In contrast, The Seaside, a regional center for the retarded sponsored by the Connecticut Department of Health spent $12.00 daily for care and treatment of each resident. Although, it may be true that money corrupts, it may be equally true that its absence is similarly corrupting.

> *Inasmuch as ye have done it unto one of the least*
> *of these my brethren, ye have*
> *done it unto me*
> **Matthew XXV, 40**

All of the doors in institutional buildings visited that are used as living quarters for young children, and moderately and severely retarded residents of any age, have locks. These locks are on all outside doors as well as all inside doors. Many of the doors are made of heavy gauge metal or thick wood. It is routine, second nature, for attendants to pass from room to room with a key chain in hand unlocking and locking doors as they pass.

Many dormitories for the severely and moderately retarded ambulatory residents have solitary confinement cells or, what is officially referred to and is jokingly called by many attendants, "therapeutic isolation." "Therapeutic isolation" means solitary confinement—in its most punitive and inhumane form. These cells are usually located on an upper floor, off to the side and away from the casual or official visitor's scrutiny. (Coincidentally, a United States senator had visited a dormitory at a state institution three days prior to one of my visits there. In discussing this with him weeks later, I showed him pictures taken of solitary confinement cells in that dormitory. As one might expect, he had not been shown these cells during his tour and I believe he was not absolutely sure that I had not concocted this coincidence to impress upon him the urgency of my mission.) Isolation cells are generally tiny rooms, approximately 7' × 7'. Some cells have mattresses, others blankets, still others bare floors. None that I had seen (and I found these cells in each institution visited) had either a bed, a wash stand, or a toilet. What I did find in one cell was a 13- or 14-year-old boy, nude, in a corner of a starkly bare room, lying on his own urine and feces. The boy had been in solitary confinement for several days for committing an institutional infraction (as I recall, it was directing abusive language to an attendant). Another child, in another institution, had been in solitary confinement for approximately five days for breaking windows. Another had been in isolation, through a long holiday weekend, because he had struck an attendant. Ironically, in the dormitory where this boy was being incarcerated, I saw another young man who had been "sent to bed early" because he had *bitten off* the ear of a patient several hours previously. Apparently, it is infinitely more serious to strike an attendant (and it should not be misunderstood that I condone this) than to bite off the ear of another resident.

In one institution I saw a young man who was glaring at me through the screen of the door in the solitary cell, feces splattered around this opening. He, too, was being punished for breaking an institutional regulation. In this particular dormitory, I had a good opportunity to interview the attendant in charge. I asked him what he needed most in order to better supervise the residents and provide them with a more adequate program. The attendant's major request was for the addition of two more solitary confinement cells, to be built adjacent to the existing two cells that, I was told, were always occupied, around the clock, day in and day out. Unfortunately, I have recent confirmation of the constant use of the solitary cells. Seven months after the above incident I revisited this dormitory. Both solitary confinement cells were occupied and there was a waiting list for other youngsters who were to receive this punishment.

I often saw restraints used with children. I observed many children whose hands were tied, legs bound, or waists secured. After discussion with a number of attendants and supervisors in the four institutions, I was convinced that one of the major reasons for the frequent use of solitary confinement and physical restraints was the extraordinary shortage of staff in practically all of these dormitories. The attendant who requested the construction of two additional solitary confinement cells was, with one assistant, responsible for the supervision of an old multi-level dormitory, housing over 100 severely retarded ambulatory residents. Almost in desperation he asked me, "What can one do with those patients who do not conform? We must lock them up, or restrain them, or sedate them, or put fear into them." At that point, I did not feel I had a response that would satisfy either him or me. I suffered in silence in much the same way, I imagine, men of conscience suffered upon reading Reil's description in 1803 of institutional problems that were astonishingly similar to those I encountered. He said then, "We lock these unfortunate creatures in lunatic cells, as if they were criminals. We keep them in chains in forlorn jails . . . where no sympathetic human being can ever bestow them a friendly glance, and we let them rot in their own filth. Their fetters scrape the flesh from their bones, and their wan, hollow faces search for the grave that their wailing and our ignominy conceals from them." My thoughts also went back to that anonymous writer who, in 1795, said, "A humanitarian is bound to shudder when he discovers the plight of the unfortunate victims of this dreadful affliction; many of them grovel in their own filth on unclean straw that is seldom changed, often stark naked and in chains, in dark, damp dungeons where no breath of fresh air can enter. Under such terrifying conditions, it would be easier for the most rational person to become insane than for a mad man to regain his sanity."

*I sometimes hold it half a sin to put
in words the grief I feel*
Alfred, Lord Tennyson

In each of the dormitories for severely retarded residents, there is what is called, euphemistically, the day room or recreation room. The odor in each of these rooms is overpowering, to the degree that after a visit to a day room I had to send my clothes to the dry cleaners in order to have the stench removed. The physical facilities often contributed to the visual horror as well as to the odor. Floors are sometimes made of wood and, as a result, excretions are rubbed into the cracks, thus providing a permanent aroma. Most day rooms have a series of bleacher-like benches on which sit denuded residents, jammed together, without purposeful activity or communication or any kind of interaction. In each day room is an attendant or two, whose main function seems to be to "stand around" and, on occasion, hose down the floor, "driving" excretions into a sewer conveniently located in the center of the room.

I was invited into female as well as male day rooms, in spite of the supervisor's knowledge that I, a male visitor, would be observing denuded females. In one such dormitory, with an overwhelming odor, I noticed feces on the wooden ceilings, and on the patients as well as the floors.

Early in the evening, sometimes at 5:00 p.m., patients are put to bed. This is to equalize the work load among the different shifts. During the day, I saw many patients lying on their beds, apparently for long periods of time. This was their activity. During these observations, I thought a good deal about the perennial cry for attendants and volunteer workers who are more sympathetic and understanding of institutionalized retarded residents. One of the things I realized was that attendants might be sympathetic, might interact more with patients, if institutional administrators made deliberate attempts to make patients cosmetically more appealing. For example, adult male residents should shave—or be shaven—more than once or twice a week. Dentures should be provided for any patient who needs them. It seems plausible to believe that it is much more possible to make residents more attractive and, therefore, more interesting to attendants than it is to attempt to convince attendants that they should enjoy the spectacle of unwashed, unkempt, odoriferous, toothless old men and women.

My friends forsake me like a memory lost
John Clare

The living quarters for older men and women were, for the most part, gloomy and sterile. There were rows and rows of benches on which sat countless human beings, in silent rooms, waiting for dinner call or bedtime. I saw resident after resident in "institutional garb." Sometimes, the women wore shrouds—inside out. I heard a good deal of laughter but saw little cheer. Even the television sets, in several of the day rooms, appeared to be co-conspirators in a crusade for gloom. These sets were not in working order, although, ironically, the residents continued to sit on their benches, in neat rows, looking at the blank tubes. I observed adult residents during recreation, playing "ring-around-the-rosy." Others, in the *vocational training center,* were playing "jacks." These were not always severely retarded patients. However, one very quickly got the feeling that this is the way they were being forced to behave. Or, as Hungerford said, ". . . in an institution there is always tomorrow so that he who starts out a student ends up, by default, an inmate." Lastly, I viewed old women and very young girls in the same dormitories and old men and young boys as comrades in

the day room. In the "normal" world, there is something appealing—
even touching—about such friendships. In the institution there is
something opportunistic, sinister, and ludicrous.

Suffer the little children . . .

The children's dormitories depressed me the most. Here, cribs were
placed—as in the other dormitories—side by side and head to head.
Very young children, one and two years of age, were lying in cribs
without contact with any adult, without playthings, without apparent
stimulation. In one dormitory that had over 100 infants and was connected to nine other dormitories that totalled 1,000 infants, I experienced my deepest sadness. As I entered, I heard a muffled sound
emanating from the "blind" side of a doorway. A young child was
calling, "Come, come play with me. Touch me." I walked to the door.
On the other side were 40 or more unkempt infants crawling around a
bare floor in a bare room. One of the children had managed to squeeze
his hand under the doorway and push his face through the side of the
latched door, crying for attention. His moan begged me for some kind
of human interaction.

In other day rooms, I saw groups of 20 and 30 very young children
lying, rocking, sleeping, sitting—alone. Each of these rooms was
without doors or adult human contact, although each had desperate
looking adult attendants "standing by."

During my visit to the above institution, I was told about the development of a new research center on the institutional grounds. The
assistant superintendent mentioned to me that the "material" for the
research center would come from the institution and this center would
require the addition of approximately 30 or 40 "items." I was quite
confused by this statement and, as a result of some verbal fumbling and
embarrassment, I finally did understand what was being said to me. At
that institution, and apparently at others in that state, patients are
called "material" and personnel are called "items." It was so difficult to
believe that this assistant superintendent was not either "pulling my
leg" or using some idiosyncratic jargon that, during my subsequent
visits to dormitories in that institution, I asked the attending physicians,
"how many 'items' do you have in this building? How much 'material'
do you have?" To my amazement, they knew exactly what I was asking
for and gave me the numbers immediately.

In another dormitory, I was taken on a tour by the chief physician
who was anxious to show me a child who had a very rare medical
condition. The doctor explained to me that, aside from the child's
dwarfism and misshapen body, one of the primary methods for diagnos-

ing this condition is the deep guttural voice. In order to demonstrate this, he pinched the child. The child did not make any sound. He pinched her again, and again—harder, and still harder. Finally, he insured her response with a pinch that turned into a gouge and caused the child to scream in obvious pain.

In some of the children's dormitories I observed "nursery programs." What surprised me most was their scarcity and also the primitiveness of those in operation. Therefore, I was not unprepared to see several children with severe head lacerations. I was told these were the "head bangers." Head banging is another condition that some people think is inevitable when confronted with young severely mentally retarded children. I challenge this. I have reason to believe that head banging can be drastically reduced in an environment where children have other things to do. Alice Metzner once said, "There are only two things wrong with most special education for the mentally handicapped, it isn't special, and it isn't education." From my observations of the "nursery programs" conducted at the state schools visited, I would have to agree only with the second part of Miss Metzner's complaint. The special education I observed at the state schools bore no resemblance to what I would consider to be "education." But, it was special. It was a collection of the most especially depressing "learning" environments I have ever had the misfortune to witness.

One may find his religion in the clinical setting
Albert T. Murphy

I have learned a great deal during my visits to these institutions about the treatment of the severely mentally retarded and of young children who are institutionalized. But, essentially, and possibly most importantly, I have learned something about the dominating factor that influences Man in his treatment of other human, beings. And this is a concept that is worth striving to understand. No doubt, the reader of this piece has asked himself several times, "Why do attendants and supervisors treat mentally retarded patients in the way this author describes?" It is probably almost impossible for you to believe that such conditions are allowed to exist. Because of my years in observing these affairs, I may have been a little further along the way in rationalizing and, to my shame, accepting them. That is to say, I knew with certainty that these conditions existed. However, I was about as puzzled as anyone else in explaining why we permit them to continue. Now, I may have a glimmer of enlightenment that I want to share with you.

It has always intrigued me to think about why anti-vivisectionists are so passionate in their beliefs concerning the use of animals for scientific experimentation. To me, animals have always been creatures to enjoy, to act kindly toward, and not to inflict any unnecessary punishment on. I believe this is the way most thoughtful human beings view the animal kingdom. I think of myself as a reasonable man. I have no interest—in fact I have revulsion—in inflicting unnecessary pain on any creature. However, I would be less than candid if I did not admit that stories about carefully controlled, and apparently necessary, animal experimentation never offend me. Further, I have never really lost any sleep or had any sustained grief in hearing about or observing cruelty to animals. I do not enjoy such spectacles; on the other hand, I have never been motivated enough to intervene directly to prevent them. However, there are people, some of our closest friends, who cry real tears and display deep emotions when confronted with cruelty to animals. During this study, I began to understand, finally, why anti-vivisectionists are the way they are and why I am so different. Further, I began to understand how human beings can be treated so dispassionately and cruelly in institutions. Anti-vivisectionists must conceive of animals in ways other people conceive of human beings. If you look at the anti-vivisectionists in this light, it is not difficult to understand their anguish in observing inhuman behavior to animals. On the other hand, certain human beings have been taught or trained—or this is part of their nature—to conceive of other human beings in ways that most of us think of animals. If this is so, it is not difficult to understand why, and how, institutional attendants and their supervisors can treat the mentally retarded in the ways they do. It isn't that these attendants are cruel or incompetent people—although, all too often, they are—but they have come to believe, for various reasons, that those in their charge are not really human. The words that are used in institutions describing certain mentally retarded residents give substance to my notion. When one views a group of human beings in an official kind of way as "material," an increased per capita expenditure for resident care and additional staff are not sufficient alone to bring about the massive changes in institutional treatment that are necessary. The use of such terms as "basket case," "vegetable," and others too offensive to record here indicate that the basic problem to be surmounted before state institutions for the mentally retarded will change substantially lies in the realm of our conception about human behavior and its amenability to change or, as Sarason has said, ". . . When one looks over the history of Man the most distinguishing characteristic of his development is the degree to which Man has underestimated the potentialities of men." Whatever ways we implement a program to reconstruct the philosophy and practices of institutions for the mentally retarded, our most forceful thrust must be in our attempts to reconceptualize our understanding of the nature and prerogatives of Man. More important than the desperately needed increased per capita expenditure for institutional care, more important than the obvious necessity of reducing the size of institutions, more important than the alleviation of their crowdedness, is the necessity for infusing a fundamental belief among all who work with the mentally retarded that each of these individuals is equally human—not equally intellectually able, not equally physically appealing, but equally human beings. Carl Sandburg stated this much more eloquently than I could: "There is only one man in the world; And his name is ALL MEN."

> *The Promised Land always lies on the other side*
> *of a wilderness*
> **Havelock Ellis**

I have just returned from a four day visit to The Seaside Regional Center, a small state institution of approximately 250 residents and somewhat over 100 staff, located in Waterford, Connecticut. This was one of many trips I had made to The Seaside during the past four years. However, this visit was somewhat different. I had returned for a specific purpose. I wanted to understand, for myself, why this residential center for the mentally retarded is so different from others described in this chapter and others I have seen throughout the country. On each of my visits to The Seaside, I could always anticipate something new and exciting. On this occasion I was not disappointed. However, I wanted something more—much more. I wanted some reason for the uniqueness of The Seaside, a reason other than the obvious. I knew that The Seaside expends approximately two times the per capita costs for its residents as compared with other institutions discussed in this chapter. Further, I knew a great deal about the sincerity, the zeal and hard work, of its staff and administration. All of those factors contribute to an institution that does not deal with "material" and "items," that does not deal in "human warehouses." All of those conditions contribute to the development of an extraordinarily dedicated and involved staff, in a setting small enough to allow every child care worker—as well as every teacher, nurse, and administrator—to know every child in the institution, and vice versa. But, at The Seaside, there is something more and I believe I now know a little of what that is.

A recent book by Kurt Vonnegut, Jr., developed what I believe is a profound insight, "We are what we pretend to be, so we must be careful about what we pretend to be." Reality is what we do, not how we wish things to be. Whether or not the staff at The Seaside feel deep compassion and tenderness toward residents—although I want to believe they do—is quite immaterial, for they behave in ways that can only lead to good for the children and others there. Whether the staff at The Seaside are better people—as people—or are wiser or more sensitive than other institutional staffs is not particularly important, for they behave as if they are. I am fatigued, exasperated, with professional and attendant staff who offer multitudes of excuses, rationalizations, and explanations for their behavior in institutions for the mentally retarded. Although I am not entirely unsympathetic to their plight (insofar as inadequate budgets, undermanned staffs and overcrowded dormitories may lead to the concessions they make and the kinds of programs they conduct), their behavior speaks volumes more about their character than does the "good will" which supposedly lies behind their compromises. For myself, I now prefer the man with the "black heart" who behaves decently for reasons neither he nor others know than the man of sterling mien who, because of unavoidable circumstances, behaves in ways which depress and compromise him.

I imagine I am saying that mental retardation can bring out the best in some people—as well as the worst. At The Seaside, I have found that it brings out the best in a lot of different adults who are involved professionally, interpersonally, and tangentially, with the residents. The Seaside has more people who demonstrate interest, show kindness, have feelings toward the residents and other staff, than do other places for the mentally retarded—notwithstanding the fact that every institution, large as well as small and those discussed earlier in this chapter as well as at The Seaside, has superb and dedicated attendants and professional staff as well as its quota of mediocre and poor staff. In my opinion, The Seaside has more superior personnel and fewer of the inefficient and uninterested. In the above, I believe, is the major difference between The Seaside and other institutions for the mentally retarded. But these warm-feeling and acting human beings are not indigenous to one small state institution. They are found everywhere and there would be many more if a higher value was placed on uncovering them, encouraging them, and nurturing their natural talents for helping other people.

About ten years ago, I made several trips to a large state institution for the mentally retarded, one not visited during this study. I became interested in and, for several days, visited a dormitory housing severely retarded ambulatory adults—one that was very similar in population to those living quarters discussed earlier in this article. However, this dormitory was, in a very important way, different. What made this dormitory different can best be illustrated with the following story.

On the occasion of one such visit, I was hailed by one of the attendants and asked to come into the day room. Upon entrance, the attendant called over a 35- or 40-year-old, partly denuded, incontinent male and said, "Dr. Blatt, you remember Charlie. Charlie has learned how to say 'hello' since your last visit. Charlie, say 'hello' to Dr. Blatt." Charlie grunted and the attendant, literally, went into a kind of ecstasy that is rarely shown by adults and, when it is, radiates warmth enough for anyone lucky enough to be touched by it. It should not be misunderstood that Charlie's grunt resembled anything like a "hello," or any other human utterance. In a way, this attendant's reaction to Charlie might have been considered as a kind of psychopathology of its own. However, I have a different understanding of it.

What type of man was this attendant? In 1938 he walked, literally off the streets, into that institution—an alcoholic, without a home of his own, purposeless and without a future—and asked for a job. He wasn't then, and isn't particularly now, an educated man. For 28 years he has served as an attendant in a dormitory for severely retarded patients. He knows every "boy" there and actually thinks of them as his children and they of him as their father.

Sometimes, in despair and helplessness, I ask myself why were these severely retarded human beings born. When one observes an attendant of the kind just described, it is possible to find at least a semblance of an answer. If not for the mentally retarded, this attendant might have been a drifter, an alcoholic, much less of a person than what he actually is. Would it be unfair to say that this attendant *needed* mental retardation in order to fulfill his own destiny and obtain the greatest good he could render to society?

Maybe the mentally retarded will enjoy the care and education they deserve when institutions cause those who minister to their needs to become better people, rather than more insensitive ones. During my last trip to The Seaside, I had the opportunity to see their magnificent day camp, which enrolled 100 community children in addition to the residents. I also took the time to visit all the living quarters, the workshop, and the vocational activity areas. Lastly, I reviewed case folders of children who particularly interested me. The following are excerpts of letters sent, unsolicited, to The Seaside from parents of children in residence there.

Mr. and Mrs. Richard LaCourse, of Groton, Connecticut, wrote:

> We are the parents of a seven year old retarded daughter who is at Seaside Regional Center. When she first went there she was not toilet trained, couldn't dress or undress herself. Her temper tantrums were quite often and severe. We certainly had no idea she'd be able to learn so much in such a short time, as she is a microcephalic. Today she goes to school, is toilet trained, can dress and undress herself, and she can talk a little more clearly than before. She has very few temper tantrums and gets along well with the other children and staff at Seaside.
>
> The way Seaside is conducted, we are able to have Debbie home quite often. We appreciate this very much. Since it is our wish, as well as Seaside's, to have her remain a part of the family.

Mr. and Mrs. Charles R. Watson, also of Groton, Connecticut, reported:

As our son was fortunate enough to be one of the first to go to Seaside Regional Center, we can honestly say that a year has done him a world of good and it almost seems like his rebirth. Formerly at _____ he was unable to walk or speak, having suffered from a paralysis, coupled with a brain injury and epilepsy. Today he is the picture of health and walking and running with the other children. He is also attempting to regain some speech.

From Mrs. Evelyn Mirable, of Manchester, Connecticut, Superintendent Fred Finn of Seaside received the following letter:

I am afraid that if I had not visited your Center I would have been forever devoid of hope for all residential retardates, inasmuch as my visit to _____ was such a shock. I am still going to endeavor in my efforts to get David admitted to your Center, or to a comparable setting, and I have made a firm vow that when and if he is so situated, I will turn as much concentrated effort as I can to helping those poor lost children that I saw at _____. I still can't get them out of my thoughts.

Mrs. Viola Hance, of Uncasville, Connecticut, wrote the following to Mr. Bert W. Schmickel, Deputy Commissioner of Health, in charge of the Connecticut Office of Mental Retardation:

At the time Gloria (her daughter) was admitted to _____ she was five years old and could walk as well as any child of that age. In the past three years, however, she had stopped walking almost altogether. She didn't know me and looked so bad that I expected a call any time that she had left us. In the eleven months that she has been at Seaside, she has gained weight, is walking better again, and always knows me when I visit her.

I could easily reproduce a dozen or two case histories of children and adults who have changed dramatically since reassignment to Seaside from other state institutions. However, the following, excerpted from a statement by Mrs. Sally Hughes Carr, who has a daughter at The Seaside, tells a great deal more about The Seaside environment:

We knew that by the time Betsy was one year old she would require institutional care, as her retardation was not mild. In spite of most of the medical advice we received which was in favor of placing her as soon as possible since it was obvious she would have to go eventually, we decided to keep her at home until she was about five if possible. It has proved to be a rewarding experience for all of us. Her father, her brothers and sister and I have all had the job and satisfaction of seeing her slow but steady development and have the opportunity to get to know the quiet, withdrawn but sweet and loving soul within her. Once one accepts the fact and degree of retardation of the child then every new accomplishment, however small, is exciting. This last year she has been attending a local day school for retarded children and the progress she has shown since she started is remarkable. Two months ago, just shortly after her fifth birthday, we had the fun and joy of seeing her start walking all on her own. She is soon to enter Seaside, a marvelous state training school for retarded children in Waterford, Connecticut.

I can truthfully say that while we are all going to miss her dreadfully when she starts up there, we are much better prepared for the change now than we would have been even a year ago and I would hate to think of having missed the last five years with our sweet silent little Peter Pan. We now know her, and have had a chance to give her something of our love and receive hers in return. There are heartaches and frustrating moments with a retarded child at home, but the benefits just in terms of the increased patience, understanding, and tolerance of the other members of the family far outweigh the problems. At least that has been the case for us.

A year has passed since I wrote the above, and I would now like to add a postscript.

Betsy entered Seaside Regional Center for Retarded Children in Waterford, Connecticut, a year ago last August. There has been much newspaper publicity lately about the terrible conditions in some state institutions for the mentally retarded. Seaside is the living proof that it doesn't *have* to be this way.

My husband and I drove up to look the school over for the first time with a considerable amount of apprehension. I must confess that my mental picture of a state school for the mentally retarded was very close to my picture of a penal institution. I was afraid that once Betsy entered the doors we would have lost her forever. I knew she'd get three meals a day but I wasn't at all sure she'd get the love I felt she needed. Would she get any exercise, or only sit tied to a chair to keep her out of trouble?

It was a very different couple who drove back after our day's tour of the school. We had expected to be shocked by the many children we would see who would be more severely and grotesquely retarded than our Betsy. Oddly enough, we saw these children, many of them, and yet we found to our amazement that instead of shock and sadness, the strongest emotion in our hearts on our drive back was a feeling of joy. We had been shown everything from the kitchen to the nursery. While the cleanliness and order were immediately apparent, what impressed us most was the overwhelming feeling of love and happiness, a wonderful cheerful warmth greeted us at every turn, from the children who ran out of their classroom to give us a hug and a kiss to the patient smile of an attendant crooning a nursery rhyme to an infant as she changed her diapers. This was no prison, but a big loving home. And so it has proved to be.

There are no restrictions on visiting or taking Betsy home. She comes home about once a month for a weekend, and, of course, for all the holidays, and it's always a pleasure to go up to get her or bring her back. She is no number at her school but a very special person. The director insists that the children each have their own lockers with their own clothes in them, for although this necessitates infinitely more sorting and separating of laundry, he feels very strongly that the children must keep their own individual identities and not become "institutionalized." The playground is literally teeming with fascinating swings in the shape of animals, merry-go-rounds, and what not. Many of them have been constructed by neighbors who not only have not resented the fact that they have a school for mentally retarded in their midst, but have given of their time and money to make the lives of the children as happy and full as possible.

I guess if I were able to talk to parents who have just learned that they have a retarded child I would tell them two things. First, don't be afraid to love and to get to know your child no matter who advises you to the contrary. And second, don't be afraid to investigate your state institutions. You may be pleasantly surprised as we were, and if you aren't, join those who are trying to do something about it. It can be done.

Life is a struggle, but not a warfare
John Burroughs

The Seaside is people! It is small! It is expensive to operate! But, it isn't as expensive as one might imagine. The Seaside appropriates approximately twice the amount, per patient, that other institutions for the retarded appropriate. However, in contrast with per capita costs in penal institutions, The Seaside has a very modest expenditure. In terms of human suffering—and the potential for human growth—places like The Seaside are among the few, really economical, government-sponsored facilities that I know of.

At The Seaside there is time, time for teaching a young child to use a spoon or fork, time for helping a child learn to use a zipper, time to heal a wound—either of the body or the soul. But, at The Seaside, there is no time for tomorrow. There is a fight against inertia. Children must be helped today for in too few tomorrows children become adults and residents become inmates.

At The Seaside, there is schooling. Some children attend school at the institution. The older and more capable youngsters attend school in the community—public school—with other children who are living at home. At The Seaside, it is not difficult to tell that this is an environment designed for children. The lawns are filled with swings and jungle gyms and bicycle paths. During Christmas time, each room is decorated welcoming Santa Claus and the spirit of Christmas. Rooms are clean and orderly. Furniture that children use is designed for children. Furniture that adults use is designed for adults.

There are adult residents at The Seaside. However, they are not in the same dormitories, or programs, with the children. Adults have other needs and the following may illustrate how some of these are met.

One of our difficulties in photographing activities at The Seaside was in our inability to take very many pictures of adult residents. There is a very good explanation for this. Most of the adults at The Seaside are working during the day—they are on institutional jobs or out in the community. Some, who could not be returned to their own homes, live in a work training unit. Here, they are together with friends and co-workers, under the careful supervision of cottage counselors. During the day they are on placement—working in the community—and in the evening they return to their "home" where they can receive special help and guidance in their successful attempts to integrate into normal communities and become contributing and useful members of society.

At The Seaside there is love, and love is believing in the fulfillment of another human being.

Afterthoughts and Recommendations

It is many months since I have visited the institutions described here. During that time, I have shown and discussed this story with a formidable, very heterogeneous but selected, number of individuals. Their backgrounds range from those in very high public office to undergraduate college students preparing as special class teachers. The sentiments of the aforementioned individuals, and others too numerous to mention, convinced me that this story must be brought to the American people as speedily as possible. In discussing this work with my colleagues, I have been able to resolve some of my anxieties insofar as the possible adverse consequences of publication. Further, I have been able to conceptualize a plan that might correct those antecedent conditions that led to the horror I observed.

The major questions that dictated caution and painful deliberation concerned themselves with whether or not this work represented an invasion of privacy of certain individuals, on the one hand, and whether the general public has a right to be protected from the knowledge of degradation, on the other. Insofar as invasion of privacy is concerned, I must question some types of privacy on moral grounds. I believe that the so-called privacy of the back wards of these institutions contributes to suffering, for outsiders do not know the conditions within these buildings and, therefore, do little or nothing to promote improvements. When privacy contributes to suffering, it loses its significance as a cherished privilege. For those who could so reason, I do not believe that there would be many in the institutions who would object to my exposure of these frightening conditions if such exposure offered some possibility for a better life and chance for the residents. Lastly, as I discussed this issue with a number of people, I began to wonder whose privacies were being protected, institutionalized residents' or ours?

This leads to the second consideration. Do people have a right to know, whether they request this knowledge or not, the unvarnished nature of human activity? In order to avoid hysterical reactions to this study, I have deliberately shied away from comparisons of what I have seen with what took place in another country, with other kinds of human beings, toward the solution of other problems. I do not want to, in any way, leave the impression that what goes on in American state institutions for the mentally retarded is, by administrative design, barbaric, inhuman, or callous. However, I see certain obvious major problems, not the least being the general public's unawareness of conditions in our back wards.

The American people have the *right to know.* In spite of what we wish to know, in spite of the pain that knowing may bring to us, we have the right to be informed about any serious conditions that affect the human condition. There is a maturity that comes to a people when it no longer needs the protection of ignorance and, thus, of ignoring what needs to be attended to. Only very young children, with their fantasies, or sick adults, with theirs, believe that ignoring a problem can make it go away.

My recommendations derive from many sources: my experiences prior to this story, what I observed during the study, the reactions of many astute individuals to this study, and the advice of students and colleagues. In addition to the emergency need for at least doubling per capita expenditures in state institutions and for reducing the sizes of institutional populations wherever and however possible, my study of this problem leads to an additional set of recommendations that may contribute to an improvement of institutional programs and facilities:

1. In each state, a board of institutional visitors should be appointed by the governor or other constituted authority. This board would be responsible for reporting directly to the highest state officials. Appointments to this board should be made irrespective of political party affiliation and these appointments should be contingent on both knowledge of the broad field of human welfare and demonstrated public service. Members of this board of visitors would not be, concurrently, members of any particular institution's staff or board of trustees.
2. Within each state institution for the mentally retarded, each department (e.g., medical, psychological, educational, nursing, cottage life) should have a board of advisors. This board of advisors, through periodic visits and consultations, would know the institution and its problems intimately and thus be in positions to advise and assist in the resolution of difficulties. In essence, the advisory board would be organized for direct consultation and assistance to the institutional staff. As this board would not be responsible for rating institutional personnel or recommending their salary increments or promotions, it is possible that members of this board would become involved with the most pressing and severe problems of the institution—without "endangering" the positions of the staff that trusts them. In this way, it would be possible for problems currently secreted from the outside world to be given the exposure and ventilation needed for satisfactory solutions to them.
3. Can one any longer ignore the needed relationship between the state institution for the mentally retarded and the state university? In each state, a state university should be given responsibility and resources to provide comprehensive in-service training and consultation for all institutional employees, from the chief administrative officer to the rawest attendant recruit.
4. In each state, at least one state institution for the mentally retarded should be designated as a center for the in-service training of *all* personnel to be employed for state service in institutions and clinics for the mentally re-

tarded. As a condition for employment as institutional superintendent, psychologist, teacher, nurse, or attendant the candidate would have to spend a specified period of time at the training center. His preparation program would range from a few weeks to one calendar year, depending upon his background and experiences and the nature of the position he intends to assume. During this training program, the candidate would be involved in clinical experiences that relate directly to this future employment, would participate in seminars, colloquia, and other instructional experiences designed to prepare him for the sensitive and demanding activities of work with the mentally retarded. At the end of the candidate's training program, the director of this facility and his staff would rate the candidate and recommend him, or not recommend him, for employment. To the degree that this program is workable with currently employed staff, every inducement and encouragement should be provided to permit them to complete this preparation.

There is a shame in America. Countless human beings are suffering—needlessly. Countless more families of these unfortunate victims of society's irresponsibility are in anguish for they know, or suspect, the truth. Unwittingly, or unwillingly, they have been forced to institutionalize their loved ones into a life of degradation and horror.

I challenge every institution in America to look at itself, now! I challenge each institution to examine its program, its standards, its admission policies, its personnel, its budget, its philosophy, its objectives. I challenge every institution—and every governor and every legislator—to justify its personnel and their practices, its size and development, and its budget.

My experiences during Christmas 1965 require me to call for a national examination of every institution for the mentally retarded in America—an examination that will inspect the deepest recesses of the most obscure back ward in the least progressive state. I call for a national examination of state budgets for the care and treatment of the retarded. I hold responsible each superintendent, each commissioner of mental health, each governor, each thoughtful citizen for the care and treatment of individuals committed for institutionalization in their state.

To some degree, all of us talk and behave as if we will not change. Yet, it is absolutely certain that we will change; what we profess now, in one way or another, we regret later. By the above I mean that the most difficult truth each of us has to learn and live with is the knowledge that we aren't perfect. It was my intent in this article to point out some of the more serious imperfections of state institutional programs for the mentally retarded in this country. It is my belief that, now that our most indefensible practices have been laid bare for public scrutiny, men of good will from all walks of life and all professions will sit down at the planning table and seek solutions to the plight of our brethren.

Postscript

It is not necessary here to discuss the flood of extraordinarily encouraging mail and calls I have received in response to the first edition of *Christmas in Purgatory*. It may be instructive to mention some of the negative, or otherwise puzzling, comments and hectoring that came to me.

One well-intentioned clergyman believes that I exhibited bad taste in reproducing photographs of nude men and women. An acquaintance in our field thinks our use of a concealed camera immoral and he believes our work to be a fake, comparing the atypical worst I had seen with "posed pictures" theatrically staged at The Seaside. A wise and beloved Commissioner of Mental Health asked me if these conditions exist in his state's institutions (How can I tell him about something he, as the principal responsible officer, should be aware of—and doing something about?). In another state that I have deep feeling for, a legislator who has championed mental health legislation circulated copies of *Christmas in Purgatory* in the vain hope that it would help in the passage of social welfare legislation. He received scant support from his own party who did not want the "opposition governor" to gain stature through such legislation in, this, an election year. The bill appeared doomed for many weeks, but subsequently passed, due, I have been informed, in some part to the influence of our book.

Albert Camus wrote, "Again and again there comes a time in history when the man who dares to say that two and two make four is punished with death." I have written the truth, as plainly and as simply as I see it—not for power or fame, for there has been precious little of either connected with this assignment and there has been a good deal of grief. I would be surprised if this work changes radically the nature of institutions. My current depression will not permit such grand thoughts. On the other hand, Camus wrote further, "Perhaps we can't stop the world from being one in which children are tortured but we can reduce the number of tortured children."

In spite of those who protest this presentation, there will be no turning back; the truth can no longer be concealed. Some good must come from all this pain and anguish to so many institutionalized residents and their families. Once seeds are sown, one only has to wait for the crop to harvest. It has also been said that, when the bellman is dead, the wind will toll the bell.

So hurry wind! Or revive yourselves noble bellringers.

chapter 3

MEMORIAL TO THE LEGISLATURE OF MASSACHUSETTS[1]

(1843)

Dorothea L. Dix

Gentlemen,—I respectfully ask to present this Memorial, believing that the *cause,* which actuates to and sanctions so unusual a movement, presents no equivocal claim to public consideration and sympathy. Surrendering to calm and deep convictions of duty my habitual views of what is womanly and becoming, I proceed briefly to explain what has conducted me before you unsolicited and unsustained, trusting, while I do so, that the memorialist will be speedily forgotten in the memorial.

About two years since leisure afforded opportunity and duty prompted me to visit several prisons and almshouses in the vicinity of this metropolis. I found, near Boston, in the jails and asylums for the poor, a numerous class brought into unsuitable connection with criminals and the general mass of paupers. I refer to idiots and insane persons, dwelling in circumstances not only adverse to their own physical and moral improvement, but productive of extreme disadvantages to all other persons brought into association with them. I applied myself diligently to trace the causes of these evils, and sought to supply remedies. As one obstacle was surmounted, fresh difficulties appeared. Every new investigation has given depth to the conviction that it is only by decided, prompt, and vigorous legislation the evils to which I refer, and which I shall proceed more fully to illustrate, can be remedied. I shall be obliged to speak with great plainness, and to reveal many things revolting to the taste, and from which my woman's

1 The author commends, and is deeply grateful to, Roche Laboratories of Nutley, New Jersey, and the Medical Library of the W. E. Fernald State School, Waverley, Massachusetts, for making reprints of this classic and timeless address available to the mental health–mental retardation community.

nature shrinks with peculiar sensitiveness. But truth is the highest consideration. *I tell what I have seen*—painful and shocking as the details often are—that from them you may feel more deeply the imperative obligation which lies upon you to prevent the possibility of a repetition or continuance of such outrages upon humanity. If I inflict pain upon you, and move you to horror, it is to acquaint you with sufferings which you have the power to alleviate, and make you hasten to the relief of the victims of legalized barbarity.

I come to present the strong claims of suffering humanity. I come to place before the Legislature of Massachusetts the condition of the miserable, the desolate, the outcast. I come as the advocate of helpless, forgotten, insane, and idiotic men and women; of beings sunk to a condition from which the most unconcerned would start with real horror; of beings wretched in our prisons, and more wretched in our almshouses. And I cannot suppose it needful to employ earnest persuasion, or stubborn argument, in order to arrest and fix attention upon a subject only the more strongly pressing in its claims because it is revolting and disgusting in its details.

I must confine myself to few examples, but am ready to furnish other and more complete details, if required. If my pictures are displeasing, coarse, and severe, my subjects, it must be recollected, offer no tranquil, refined, or composing features. The condition of human beings, reduced to the extremest states of degradation and misery, cannot be exhibited in softened language, or adorn a polished page.

I proceed, gentlemen, briefly to call your attention to the *present* state of insane persons confined within this Commonwealth, in *cages, closets, cellars, stalls, pens! Chained, naked, beaten with rods,* and *lashed* into obedience.

As I state cold, severe *facts,* I feel obliged to refer to persons, and definitely to indicate localities. But it is upon my subject, not upon localities or individuals, I desire to fix attention; and I would speak as kindly as possible of all wardens, keepers, and other responsible officers, believing that *most* of these have erred not through hardness of heart and wilful cruelty so much as want of skill and knowledge, and want of consideration. Familiarity with suffering, it is said, blunts the sensibilities, and where neglect once finds a footing other injuries are multiplied. This is not all, for it may justly and strongly be added that, from the deficiency of adequate means to meet the wants of these cases, it has been an absolute impossibility to do justice in this matter. Prisons are not constructed in view of being converted into county hospitals, and almshouses are not founded as receptacles for the insane. And yet, in the face of justice and common sense, wardens are by law compelled to receive, and the masters of almshouses not to refuse, insane and idiotic subjects in all stages of mental disease and privation.

It is the Commonwealth, not its integral parts, that is accountable for most of the abuses which have lately and do still exist. I repeat it, it is defective legislation which perpetuates and multiplies these abuses. In illustration of my subject, I offer the following extracts from my Note-book and Journal:—

Springfield. In the jail, one lunatic woman, furiously mad, a State pauper, improperly situated, both in regard to the prisoners, the keepers, and herself. It is a case of extreme self-forgetfulness and oblivion to all the decencies of life, to describe which would be to repeat only the grossest scenes. She is much worse since leaving Worcester. In the almshouse of the same town is a woman apparently only needing judicious care, and some well-chosen employment, to make it unnecessary to confine her in solitude, in a dreary unfurnished room. Her appeals for employment and companionship are most touching, but the mistress replied "she had no time to attend to her."

Northampton. In the jail, quite lately, was a young man violently mad, who had not, as I was informed at the prison, come under medical care, and not been returned from any hospital. In the almshouse the cases of insanity are now unmarked by abuse, and afford evidence of judicious care by the keepers.

Williamsburg. The almshouse has several insane, not under suitable treatment. No apparent intentional abuse.

Rutland. Appearance and report of the insane in the almshouse not satisfactory.

Sterling. A terrible case; manageable in a hospital; at present as well controlled perhaps as circumstances in a case so extreme allow. An almshouse, but wholly wrong in relation to the poor crazy woman, to the paupers generally, and to her keepers.

Burlington. A woman, declared to be very insane; decent room and bed; but not allowed to rise oftener, the mistress said, "than every other day; it is too much trouble."

Concord. A woman from the hospital in a cage in the almshouse. In the jail several, decently cared for in general, but not properly placed in a prison. Violent, noisy, unmanageable most of the time.

Lincoln. A woman in a cage. *Medford.* One idiotic subject chained, and one in a close stall for seventeen years. *Pepperell.* One often doubly chained, hand and foot; another violent; several peaceable now. *Brookfield.* One man caged, comfortable. *Granville.* One often closely confined; now losing the use of his limbs from want of exercise. *Charlemont.* One man caged. *Savoy.* One man caged. *Lenox.* Two in the jail, against whose unfit condition there the jailer protests.

Dedham. The insane disadvantageously placed in the jail. In the almshouse, two females in stalls, situated in the main building; lie in wooden bunks filled with straw; always shut up. One of these subjects is supposed curable. The overseers of the poor have declined giving her a trial at the hospital, as I was informed, on account of expense.

Franklin. One man chained; decent. *Taunton.* One woman caged. *Plymouth.* One man stall-caged, from Worcester Hospital. *Scituate.* One man and one woman stall-caged. *West Bridgewater.* Three idiots. Never removed from one room. *Barnstable.* Four females in pens and stalls. Two chained certainly. I think all. Jail, one idiot. *Wellfleet.* Three insane. One man and one woman chained, the latter in a bad condition. *Brewster.* One woman violently mad, solitary. Could not see her, the master and mistress being absent, and the paupers in charge having strict orders to admit no one. *Rochester.* Seven insane; at present none caged. *Milford.* Two insane, not now caged. *Cohasset.* One idiot, one insane; most miserable condition. *Plympton.* One insane, three idiots; condition wretched.

Besides the above, I have seen many who, part of the year, are chained or caged. The use of cages all but universal. Hardly a town but can refer to some not distant period of using them; chains are less common; negligences frequent; wilful abuse less frequent than sufferings proceeding from ignorance, or want of consideration. I encountered during the last three months many poor creatures wandering reckless and unprotected through the country. Innumerable accounts have been sent me of persons who had roved away unwatched and unsearched after; and I have heard that responsible persons, controlling the almshouses, have not thought themselves culpable in sending away from their shelter, to cast upon the chances of remote relief, insane men and women. These, left on the highways, unfriended and incompetent to control or direct their own movements, sometimes have found refuge in the hospital, and others have not been traced. But I cannot particularize. In traversing the State, I have found hundreds of insane persons in every variety of circumstance and condition, many whose situation could not and need not be improved; a less number, but that very large, whose lives are the saddest pictures of human suffering and degradation. I give a few illustrations; but description fades before reality.

Danvers. November. Visited the almshouse. A large building, much out of repair. Understand a new one is in contemplation. Here are from fifty-six to sixty inmates, one idiotic, three insane; one of the latter in close confinement at all times.

Long before reaching the house, wild shouts, snatches of rude songs, imprecations and obscene language, fell upon the ear, proceeding from the occupant of a low building, rather remote from the principal building to which my course was directed. Found the mistress, and was conducted to the place which was called *"the home"* of the *forlorn* maniac, a young woman, exhibiting a condition of neglect and misery blotting out the faintest idea of comfort, and outraging every sentiment of decency. She had been, I learnt, "a respectable person, industrious and worthy. Disappointments and trials shook her mind, and, finally, laid prostrate reason and self-control. She became a maniac for life. She had been at Worcester Hospital for a considerable time, and had been returned as incurable." The mistress told me she understood that, "while there, she was comfortable and decent." Alas, what a change was here exhibited! She had passed from one degree of violence to another, in swift progress. There she stood, clinging to or beating upon the bars of her caged apartment, the contracted size of which afforded space only for increasing accumulations of filth, a *foul* spectacle. There she stood with naked arms and dishevelled hair, the unwashed frame invested with fragments of unclean garments, the air so extremely offensive, though ventilation was afforded on all sides save one, that it was not possible to remain beyond a few moments without retreating for recovery to the outward air. Irritation of body, produced by utter filth and exposure, incited her to the horrid process of tearing off her skin by inches. Her face, neck, and person were thus disfigured to hideousness. She held up a fragment just rent off. To my exclamation of horror, the mistress replied: "Oh, we can't help it. Half the skin is off sometimes. We can do nothing with her; and it makes no difference what she eats, for she consumes her own filth as readily as the food which is brought her."

It is now January. A fortnight since two visitors reported that most wretched outcast as "wallowing in dirty straw, in a place yet more dirty, and without clothing, without fire. Worse cared for than the brutes, and wholly lost to consciousness of decency." Is the whole story told? What was seen is: what is reported is not. These gross exposures are not for the pained sight of one alone. All, all, coarse, brutal men, wondering, neglected children, old and young, each and all, witness this lowest, foulest state of miserable humanity. And who protects her, that worse than Pariah outcast, from other wrongs and blacker outrages? I do not *know* that such *have been.* I do know that they're are to be dreaded, and that they are not guarded against.

Some may say these things cannot be remedied, these furious maniacs are not to be raised from these base conditions. I *know* they are. Could give *many* examples. Let *one* suffice. A young woman, a pauper, in a distant town, Sandisfield, was for years a raging maniac. A cage, chains, and *the whip* were the agents for controlling her, united with harsh tones and profane language. Annually, with others (the town's poor), she was put up at auction, and bid off at the lowest price which was declared for her. One year, not long past, an old man came forward in the number of applicants for the poor wretch. He was taunted and ridiculed. "What would he and his old wife do with such a mere beast?" "My wife says yes," replied he, "and I shall take her." She was given to his charge. He conveyed her home. She was washed, neatly dressed, and placed in a decent bedroom, furnished for comfort and opening into the kitchen. How altered her condition! As yet *the chains* were not off. The first week she was somewhat restless, at times violent, but the quiet, kind ways of the old people wrought a change. She received her food decently, forsook acts of violence, and no longer uttered blasphemies or indecent language. After a week the chain was lengthened, and she was received as a companion into the kitchen. Soon she engaged in trivial employments. "After a fortnight," said the old man, "I knocked off the chains and made her a free woman." She is at times excited, but not violently. They are careful of her diet. They keep her very clean. She calls them "father" and "mother." Go there now, and you will find her "clothed," and, though not perfectly in her "right mind," so far restored as to be a safe and comfortable inmate.

Newburyport. Visited the almshouse in June last. Eighty inmates. Seven insane, one idiotic. Commodious and neat house. Several of the partially insane apparently very comfortable. Two very improperly situated; namely, an insane man, not considered incurable, in an out-building, whose room opened upon what was called "the dead room," affording, in lieu of companionship with the living, a contemplation of corpses. The other subject was a woman in a *cellar.* I desired to see her. Much reluctance was shown. I pressed the request. The master of the house stated that she was *in the cellar;* that she was *dangerous to be approached;* that she had lately attacked his wife, and *was often naked.* I persisted, "If you will not go with me, give me the keys and I will go alone." Thus importuned, the outer doors were opened. I descended the stairs from within. A strange, unnatural noise seemed to proceed from beneath our feet. At the moment I did not much regard it. My conductor proceeded to remove a padlock, while my eye explored the wide space in quest of the poor woman. All for a moment was still. But judge my horror and amazement, when a door to a closet *beneath* the *staircase* was opened, revealing in the imperfect light a female apparently wasted to a skeleton, partially wrapped in blankets, fur-nished for the narrow bed on which she was sitting. Her countenance furrowed, not by age, but suffering, was the image of distress. In that contracted space, unlighted, unventilated, she poured forth the wailings of despair. Mournfully she extended her arms and appealed to me: "Why am I consigned to hell? dark—dark—I used to pray, I used to read the Bible—I have done no crime in my heart. I had friends. Why have all forsaken me!—my God, my God, why hast *thou* forsaken me!" Those groans, those wailings, come up daily, mingling with how many others, a perpetual and sad memorial. When the good Lord shall require an account of our stewardship, what shall all and each answer?

Perhaps it will be inquired how long, how many days or hours, was she imprisoned in these confined limits? *For years!* In another part of the cellar were other small closets, only better, because higher through the entire length, into one of which she by turns was transferred, so as to afford opportunity for fresh whitewashing, etc.

Saugus. December 24. Thermometer below zero; drove to the poorhouse; was conducted to the master's family-room by himself; walls garnished with handcuffs and chains, not less than five pairs of the former; did not inquire how or on whom applied; thirteen pauper inmates; one insane man; one woman insane; one idiotic man; asked to see them; the two men were shortly led in; appeared pretty decent and comfortable. Requested to see the other insane subject; was denied decidedly; urged the request, and finally secured a reluctant assent. Was led through an outer passage into a lower room, occupied by the paupers; crowded; not neat; ascended a rather low flight of stairs upon an open entry, through the floor of which was introduced a stove-pipe, carried along a *few feet,* about six inches above the floor, through which it was reconveyed below. From this entry opens a room of moderate size, having a sashed window; floor, I think, painted; apartment *entirely* unfurnished; no chair, table, nor bed; neither, what is seldom missing, a bundle of straw or lock of hay; cold, very cold; the first movement of my conductor was to throw open a window, a measure imperatively necessary for those who entered. *On the floor* sat a woman, her limbs immovably contracted, so that the knees were brought upward to the chin; the face was concealed; the head rested on the folded arms. For clothing she appeared to have been furnished with *fragments* of many discharged garments. These were folded about her, yet they little benefited her, if one might judge by the constant shuddering which almost convulsed her poor crippled frame. Woeful was this scene. Language is feeble to record the misery she was suffering and had suffered. In reply to my inquiry if she could not change her position, I was answered by the master in the negative, and told that the contraction of limbs was occasioned by "neglect and exposure in former years," but *since she had been crazy,* and before she fell under the charge, as I inferred, of her present *guardians.* Poor wretch! she, like many others, was an example of what humanity becomes when the temple of reason falls in ruins, leaving the mortal part to injury and neglect, and showing how much can be endured of privation, exposure, and disease without extinguishing the lamp of life.

Passing out, the man pointed to a something, revealed to more than one sense, which he called "her bed; and we throw some blankets over her at night." Possibly this is done; others, like myself, might be pardoned a doubt if they could have seen all I saw and heard abroad all I heard. The *bed,* so called, was about *three* feet long, and from a half to three-quarters of a yard wide; of old ticking or tow cloth was the case; the contents might have been a *full handful* of hay or straw. My attendant's exclamations on my leaving the house were emphatic, and can hardly be repeated.

The above case recalls another of equal neglect or abuse. Asking my way to the almshouse in Berkeley, which had been repeatedly spoken of as greatly neglected, I was answered as to the direction, and informed that there were "plenty of insane people and idiots there." "Well taken care of?" "Oh, well enough for such sort of creatures!" "Any violently insane?" "Yes, my sister's son is there,—a real tiger. I kept him here at my house awhile, but it was too much trouble to go on: so I carried him there." "Is he comfortably provided for?" "Well enough." "Has he decent clothes?" "Good enough; wouldn't wear them if he had more." "Food?" "Good enough; good enough for him." "One more question,—has he the comfort of a fire?" "Fire! fire, indeed! what does a crazy man need of fire? Red-hot iron wants fire as much as he!" And such are sincerely the ideas of not a few persons in regard to the actual wants of the insane. Less regarded than the lowest brutes. No wonder they sink even lower.

Ipswich. Have visited the prison there several times; visited the almshouse once. In the latter are several cases of insanity; three especially distressing, situated in a miserable out-building, detached from the family-house, and confined in stalls or pens; three individuals, one of whom is apparently very insensible to the deplorable circumstances which surround him, and perhaps not likely to comprehend privations or benefits. Not so the person directly opposite to him, who looks up wildly, anxiously by turns, through those strong bars. Cheerless sight! strange companionship for the mind flitting and coming by turns to some perception of persons and things. He, too, is one of the returned incurables. His history is a sad one. I have not had all the particulars, but it shows distinctly what the most prosperous and affluent may come to be. I understand his connections are excellent and respectable; his natural abilities in youth were superior. He removed from Essex County to Albany, and was established there as the editor of a popular newspaper. In course of time he was chosen a senator for that section of the State, and of course was [?] a judge in the Court of Errors.

Vicissitudes followed, and insanity closed the scene. He was conveyed to Worcester, after a considerable period, either to give place to some new patient or because the county objected to the continued expense, he, being declared incurable, was removed to Salem jail, thence to Ipswich jail; associated with the prisoners there, partaking the same food, and clad in like apparel. After a time the town complained of the expense of keeping him in jail. It was cheaper in the almshouse. To the almshouse he was conveyed, and there perhaps must abide. How sad a fate! I found him in a quiet state, though at times was told that he is greatly excited. What wonder, with such a companion before him, such cruel scenes within! I perceived in him some little confusion as I paused before the stall against the bars of which he was leaning. He was not so lost to propriety but that a little disorder of the bed-clothes, etc., embarrassed him. I passed on, but he asked, in a moment, earnestly, "Is the lady gone—gone quite away?" I returned. He gazed a moment without answering my inquiry if he wished to see me. "And have you, too, lost all your dear friends?" Perhaps my mourning apparel excited his inquiry. "Not all." "Have you any dear father and mother to love you?" and then he sighed and then laughed and traversed the limited stall. Immediately adjacent to this stall was one occupied by a *simple* girl, who was "put there to be out of harm's way." A cruel lot for this privation of a sound mind. A madman on the one hand, not so much separated as to secure decency; another almost opposite, and no screen. I do not know how it is argued that mad persons and idiots may be dealt with as if no spark of recollection ever lights up the mind. The observation and experience of those who have had charge of hospitals show opposite conclusions.

Violence and severity do but exasperate the insane: the only availing influence is kindness and firmness. It is amazing what these will produce. How many examples might illustrate this position! I refer to one recently exhibited in Barre. The town paupers are disposed of annually to some family who, for a stipulated sum, agree to take charge of them. One of them, a young woman, was shown to me well clothed, neat, quiet, and employed at needlework. Is it possible that this is the same being who, but last year, was a raving mad woman, exhibiting every degree of violence in action and speech; a very tigress wrought to fury; caged, chained, beaten, loaded with injuries, and exhibiting the passions which an iron rule might be expected to stimulate and sustain. It is the same person. Another family hold her in charge who better understand human nature and human influences. She is no longer chained, caged, and beaten; but, if excited, a pair of mittens drawn over the hands secures from mischief. Where will she be next year after the annual sale?

It is not the insane subject alone who illustrates the power of the all-prevailing law of kindness. A poor idiotic young man, a year or two since, used to follow me at times through the prison as I was distributing books and papers. At first he appeared totally stupid, but cheerful expressions, a smile, a trifling gift, seemed gradually to light up the void temple of the intellect, and by slow degrees some faint images of thought passed before the mental vision. He would ask for books, though he could not read. I indulged his fancy, and he would appear to experience delight in examining them, and kept them with a singular care. If I read the Bible, he was reverently, wonderingly attentive; if I talked, he listened with a half-conscious aspect. One morning I passed more hurriedly than usual, and did not speak particularly to him. "Me, me, me a book." I returned. "Good morning, Jemmy: so you will have a book to-day? Well, keep it carefully." Suddenly turning aside, he took the bread brought for his breakfast, and, passing it with a hurried earnestness through the bars of his iron door, "Here's bread, ain't you hungry?" Never may I forget the tone and grateful affectionate aspect of that poor idiot. How much might we do to bring back or restore the mind if we but knew how to touch the instrument with a skilful hand!

My first visit to Ipswich prison was in March, 1842. The day was cold and stormy. The turnkey very obligingly conducted me through the various departments. Pausing before the iron door of a room in the jail, he said: "We have here a crazy man whose case seems hard; for he has sense enough to know he is in a prison and associated with prisoners. He was a physician in this county, and was educated at Cambridge, I believe. It was there or at one of the New England colleges. Should you like to see him?" I objected that it might be unwelcome to the sufferer, but, urged, went in. The apartment was very much out of order, neglected, and unclean. There was no fire. It had been forgotten amidst the press of other duties. A man, a prisoner waiting trial, was sitting near a bed where the insane man lay, rolled in dirty blankets. The turnkey told him my name; and he broke forth into a most touching appeal that I would procure his liberation by prompt application to the highest State authorities. I soon retired, but communicated his condition to an official person before leaving the town, in the hope he might be rendered more comfortable. Shortly I received from this insane person, through my esteemed friend, Dr. Bell, several letters, from which I venture to make a few extracts. They are written from Ipswich, where is the general county receptacle for insane persons. I may remark that he has at different times been under skilful treatment, both at Charlestown and Worcester; but being, long since, pronounced incurable, and his property being expended, he became chargeable to the town or county, and was removed, first to Salem jail, thence to that at Ipswich by the desire of the high sheriff, who requested the commissioners to remove him to Ipswich as a more retired spot, where he would be less likely to cause disturbance. In his paroxysms of violence, his shouts and turbulence disturb a whole neighborhood. These still occur. I give the extracts literally: "Respected lady, since your heavenly visit my time has passed in perfect quietude, and for the last week I have been entirely alone. The room has been cleansed and whitewashed, and is now quite decent. I have read your books and papers with pleasure and profit, and retain them subject to your order. You say, in your note, others shall be sent if desired, and if any particular subject has interest it shall be procured. Your kindness is felt and highly appreciated," etc. In another letter he writes, "You express confidence that I have self-control and self-respect. I have, and, were I free and in good circumstances, could command as much as any man." In a third he says, "Your kind note, with more books and papers, were received on the 8th, and I immediately addressed to you letter superscribed to Dr. Bell; but, having discovered the letters on your seal, I suppose them the initials of your name, and now address you directly," etc.

The original letters may be seen. I have produced these extracts, and stated facts of personal history, in order that a judgment may be formed from few of many examples as to the justness of incarcerating lunatics in all and every stage of insanity, for an indefinite period or for life, in dreary prisons, and in connection with every class of criminals who may be lodged successively under the same roof, and in the same apartments. I have shown, from two examples, to what condition men may be brought, not through crime, but misfortune, and that misfortune embracing the heaviest calamity to which human nature is exposed. In the touching language of Scripture may these captives cry out: "Have pity upon me! Have pity upon me! for the hand of the Lord hath smitten me." "My kinsfolk have failed, and my own familiar friend hath forgotten me."

The last visit to the Ipswich prison was the third week in December. Twenty-two insane persons and idiots: general condition gradually improved within the last year. All suffer for want of air and exercise. The turnkey, while disposed to discharge kindly the duties of his office, is so crowded with business as to be positively unable to give any but the most general attention to the insane department. Some of the subjects are invariably confined in small dreary cells, insufficiently warmed and ventilated. Here one sees them traversing the narrow dens with ceaseless rapidity, or dashing from side to side like caged tigers, perfectly furious, through the invariable condition of unalleviated confinement. The case of one *simple* boy is peculiarly hard. Dec. 6, 1841, he was committed to the house of correction, East Cambridge, from Charlestown, as an *insane* or *idiotic* boy. He was unoffending, and competent to perform a variety of light labors under direction, and was often allowed a good deal of freedom in the open air. Sept. 6, 1842, he was directed to pull some weeds (which indulgence his harmless disposition permitted) without the prison walls, merely, I believe, for the sake of giving him a little employment. He escaped, it was thought, rather through sudden waywardness than any distinct purpose. From that time nothing was heard of him till in the latter part of December, while at Ipswich, in the common room, occupied by a portion of the lunatics not furiously mad, I heard some one say, "I know her, I know her," and with a joyous laugh John hastened toward me. "I'm so glad to see you, so glad to see you! I can't stay here long: I want to go out," etc. It seems he had wandered to Salem, and was committed as an insane or *idiot* boy. I cannot but assert that most of the idiotic subjects in the prisons in Massachusetts are unjustly committed, being wholly incapable of doing harm, and none manifesting any disposition either to injure others or to exercise mischievous propensities. I ask an investigation into this subject for the sake of many whose association with prisoners and criminals, and also with persons in almost every stage of insanity, is as useless and unnecessary as it is cruel and ill-judged. If it were proper, I might place in your hands a volume, rather than give a page, illustrating these premises.

Sudbury. First week in September last I directed my way to the poor-farm there. Approaching, as I supposed, that place, all uncertainty vanished as to which, of several dwellings in view, the course should be directed. The terrible screams and imprecations, impure language and amazing blasphemies, of a maniac, now, as often heretofore, indicated the place sought after. I know not how to proceed. The English language affords no combinations fit for describing the condition of the unhappy wretch there confined. In a stall, built under a woodshed on the road, was a naked man, defiled with filth, furiously tossing through the bars and about the cage portions of straw (the only furnishing of his prison) already trampled to chaff. The mass of filth within diffused wide abroad the most noisome stench. I have never witnessed paroxysms of madness so appalling: it seemed as if the ancient doctrine of the possession of demons was here illustrated. I hastened to the house overwhelmed with horror. The mistress informed me that ten days since he had been brought from Worcester Hospital, where the town did not choose any longer to meet the expenses of maintaining him; that he had been "dreadful noisy and dangerous to go near" ever since. It was hard work to give him food at any rate; for what was not immediately dashed at those who carried it was cast down upon the festering mass within. "He's a dreadful care; worse than all the people and work on the farm beside." "Have you any other insane persons?" "Yes: this man's sister has been crazy here for several years. She does nothing but take on about him; and maybe she'll grow as bad as he." I went into the adjoining room to see this unhappy creature. In a low chair, wearing an air of deepest despondence, sat a female no longer young; her hair fell uncombed upon her shoulders; her whole air revealed woe, unmitigated woe. She regarded me coldly and uneasily. I spoke a few words of sympathy and kindness. She fixed her gaze for a few moments steadily upon me, then grasping my hand, and bursting into a passionate flood of tears, repeatedly kissed it, exclaiming in a voice broken by sobs: "Oh, my poor brother, my poor brother. Hark, hear him, hear him!" then, relapsing into apathetic calmness, she neither spoke nor moved; but the tears again flowed fast as I went away. I avoided passing the maniac's cage; but there, with strange curiosity and eager exclamations, were gathered, at a safe distance, the children of the establishment, little boys and girls, receiving their early lessons in hardness of heart and vice; but the demoralizing influences were not confined to children.

The same day revealed two scenes of extreme exposure and unjustifiable neglect, such as I could not have supposed the whole New England States could furnish.

Wayland. Visited the almshouse. There, as in Sudbury, caged in a woodshed, and also *fully exposed* upon the *public* road, was seen a man at that time less violent, but equally debased by exposure and irritation. He then wore a portion of clothing, though the mistress remarked that he was "more likely to be naked than not"; and added that he was "less noisy than usual." I spoke to him, but received no answer. A wild, strange gaze, and impatient movement of the hand, motioned us away. He refused to speak, rejected food, and wrapped over his head a torn coverlet. Want of accommodations for the imperative calls of nature had converted the cage into a place of utter offence. "My husband cleans him out once a week or so; but it's a hard matter to master him sometimes. He does better since the last time he was broken in." I learnt that the confinement and cold together had so affected his limbs that he was often powerless to rise. "You see him," said my conductress, "in his best state." *His best state!* What, then, was the *worst?*

Westford. Not many miles from Wayland is a sad spectacle; was told by the family who kept the poorhouse that they had twenty-six paupers, one idiot, one simple, and one insane, an incurable case from Worcester Hospital. I requested to see her, but was answered that she "wasn't fit to be seen. She was naked, and made so much trouble they did not know how to get along." I hesitated but a moment. I must see her, I said. I cannot adopt descriptions of the condition of the insane secondarily. What I assert for fact, I must see for myself. On this I was conducted above stairs into an apartment of decent size, pleasant aspect from abroad, and tolerably comfortable in its general appearance; but the inmates—grant I may never look upon another such scene! A young woman, whose person was partially covered with portions of a blanket, sat upon the floor; her hair dishevelled; her naked arms crossed languidly over the breast; a distracted, unsteady eye and low, murmuring voice betraying both mental and physical disquiet. *About the waist was a chain,* the extremity of which was fastened into the wall of the house. As I entered, she raised her eyes, blushed, moved uneasily, endeavoring at the same time to draw about her the insufficient fragments of the blanket. I knelt beside her and asked if she did not wish to be dressed. "Yes, I want some clothes." "But you'll tear 'em all up, you know you will," interposed her attendant. "No, I won't, I won't tear them off"; and she tried to rise, but the waist-encircling chain threw her back, and she did not renew the effort, but, bursting into a wild, shrill laugh, pointed to it, exclaiming, "See there, see there, nice clothes!" Hot tears might not dissolve that iron bondage, imposed, to all appearance, most needlessly. As I left the room, the poor creature said, "I want my gown." The response from the attendant might have roused to indignation one not dispossessed of reason and owning self-control.

Groton. A few rods removed from the poorhouse is a wooden building upon the roadside, constructed of heavy board and plank. It contains one room, unfurnished, except so far as a bundle of straw constitutes furnishing. There is no window, save an opening half the size of a sash, and closed by a board shutter. In one corner is some brick-work surrounding an iron stove, which in cold weather serves for warming the room. The occupant of this dreary abode is a young man, who has been declared incurably insane. He can move a measured distance in his prison; that is, so far as a strong, heavy chain, depending from an *iron collar which invests his neck* permits. In fine weather—and it was pleasant when I was there in June last—the door is thrown open, at once giving admission to light and air, and affording some little variety to the solitary in watching the passers-by. But that portion of the year which allows of open doors is not the chiefest part; and it may be conceived, without drafting much on the imagination, what is the condition of one who for days and weeks and months sits in darkness and alone, without employment, without object. It may be supposed that paroxysms of frenzy are often exhibited, and that the tranquil state is rare in comparison with that which incites to violence. This, I was told, is the fact.

I may here remark that severe measures, in enforcing rule, have in many places been openly revealed. I have not seen chastisement administered by stripes, and in but few instances have I seen the *rods* and *whips,* but I have seen blows inflicted, both passionately and repeatedly.

I have been asked if I have investigated the causes of insanity. I have not; but I have been told that this most calamitous overthrow of reason often is the result of a life of sin: it is sometimes, but rarely, added, they must take the consequences; they deserve no better care. Shall man be more just than God, he who causes his sun and refreshing rains and life-giving influence to fall alike on the good and the evil? Is not the total wreck of reason, a state of distraction, and the loss of all that makes life cherished a retribution sufficiently heavy, without adding to consequences so appalling every indignity that can bring still lower the wretched sufferer? Have pity upon those who, while they were supposed to lie hid in secret sins, "have been scattered under a *dark veil of forgetfulness,* over whom is spread a heavy night, and who unto themselves are more grievous than the darkness."

Fitchburg. In November visited the almshouse: inquired the number of insane. Was answered, several, but two in close confinement, one idiotic subject. Saw an insane woman in a dreary, neglected apartment, unemployed and alone. Idleness and solitude weaken, it is said, the sane mind; much more must it hasten the downfall of that which is already trembling at the foundations. From this apartment I was conducted to an out-building, a portion of which was enclosed, so as to unite shelter, confinement, and solitude. The first space was a sort of entry, in which was a window; beyond, a close partition with doors indicated where was the insane man I had wished to see. He had been returned from the hospital as incurable. I asked if he was violent or dangerous. "No." "Is he clothed?" "Yes." "Why keep him shut in this close confinement?" "Oh, my husband is afraid he'll run away; then the overseers won't like it. He'll get to Worcester, and then the town will have money to pay." "He must come out; I wish to see him." The opened door disclosed a squalid place, dark, and *furnished* with straw. The crazy man raised himself slowly from the floor upon which he was couched, and with unsteady steps came toward me. His look was feeble and sad, but calm and gentle.

"Give me those books, oh, give me those books," and with trembling eagerness he reached for some books I had carried in my hand. "Do give them to me, I want them," said he with kindling earnestness. "You could not use them, friend; you cannot see them." "Oh, give them to me, do"; and he raised his hand and bent a little forward, lowering his voice, *"I'll pick a little hole in the plank and let in some of God's light."*

The master came round. "Why cannot you take this man abroad to work on the farm? He is harmless. Air and exercise will help to recover him." The answer was in substance the same as that first given; but he added, "I've been talking with our overseers, and I proposed getting from the blacksmith an iron collar and chain, then I can have him out by the house." An iron collar and chain! "Yes, I had a cousin up in Vermont, crazy as a wildcat, and I got a collar made for him, *and he liked it.*" "Like it! how did he manifest his pleasure?" "Why, he left off trying to run away. I kept the almshouse at Groton. There was a man there from the hospital. I built an out-house for him, and the blacksmith made him an iron collar and chain, so we had him fast, and the overseers approved it, and"—I here interrupted him. "I have seen that poor creature at Groton in his doubly iron bondage, and you must allow me to say that, as I understand you remain but one year in the same place, and you may find insane subjects in all, I am confident, if overseers permit such a multiplication of collars and chains, the public will not long sanction such barbarities; but, if you had at Groton any argument for this measure in the violent state of the unfortunate subject, how can you justify such treatment of a person quiet and not dangerous, as is this poor man? I beg you to forbear the chains, and treat him as you yourself would like to be treated in like fallen circumstances."

Bolton. Late in December, 1842; thermometer 4° above zero; visited the almshouse; neat and comfortable establishment; two insane women, one in the house associated with the family, the other *"out of doors."* The day following was expected a young man from Worcester

Hospital, incurably insane. Fears were expressed of finding him "dreadful hard to manage." I asked to see the subject who was "out of doors"; and, following the mistress of the house through the deep snow, shuddering and benumbed by the piercing cold, several hundred yards, we came in rear of the barn to a small building, which might have afforded a degree of comfortable shelter, but it did not. About two-thirds of the interior was filled with wood and peat. The other third was divided into two parts; one about six feet square contained a cylinder stove, in which was no fire, the rusty pipe seeming to threaten, in its decay, either suffocation by smoke, which by and by we nearly realized, or conflagration of the building, together with destruction of its poor crazy inmate. My companion uttered an exclamation at finding no fire, and busied herself to light one; while I explored, as the deficient light permitted, the cage which occupied the undescribed portion of the building. "Oh, I'm so cold, so cold," was uttered in plaintive tones by a woman within the cage; "oh, so cold, so cold!" And well might she be cold. The stout, hardy driver of the sleigh had declared 'twas too hard for a man to stand the wind and snow that day, yet here was a woman caged and imprisoned without fire or clothes, not naked, indeed, for one thin cotton garment partly covered her, and part of a blanket was gathered about the shoulders. There she stood, shivering in that dreary place; the gray locks falling in disorder about the face gave a wild expression to the pallid features. Untended and comfortless, she might call aloud, none could hear. She might die, and there be none to close the eye. But death would have been a blessing here. "Well, you shall have a fire, Axey. I've been so busy getting ready for the funeral!" One of the paupers lay dead. "Oh, I want some clothes," rejoined the lunatic; "I'm so cold." "Well, Axey, you shall have some as soon as the children come from school; I've had so much to do." "I want to go out, do let me out!" "Yes, as soon as I get time," answered the respondent. "Why do you keep her here?" I asked. "She appears harmless and quiet." "Well, I mean to take her up to the house pretty soon. The people that used to have care here kept her shut up all the year; but it *is* cold here, and we take her to the house in hard weather. The only danger is her running away. I've been meaning to this good while." The poor creature listened eagerly: "Oh, I won't run away. Do take me out!" "Well, I will in a few days." Now the smoke from the kindling fire became so dense that a new anxiety struck the captive. "Oh, I shall smother, I'm afraid. Don't fill that up, I'm afraid." Pretty soon I moved to go away. "Stop, did you walk?" "No." "Did you ride?" "Yes." "Do take me with you, do, I'm so cold. Do you know my sisters? They live in this town. I want to see them so much. Do let me go"; and, shivering with eagerness to get out, as with the biting cold, she rapidly tried the bars of the cage.

The mistress seemed a kind person. Her tones and manner to the lunatic were kind; but how difficult to unite all the cares of her household, and neglect none! Here was not wilful abuse, but great, very great suffering through undesigned negligence. We need an asylum for this class, the incurable, where conflicting duties shall not admit of such examples of privations and misery.

One is continually amazed at the tenacity of life in these persons. In conditions that wring the heart to behold, it is hard to comprehend that days rather than years should not conclude the measure of their griefs and miseries. Picture her condition! Place yourselves in that dreary cage, remote from the inhabited dwelling, alone by day and by night, without fire, without clothes, *except when remembered;* without object or employment; weeks and months passing on in drear succession, not a blank, but with keen life to suffering; with kindred, but deserted by them; and you shall not lose the memory of that time when they loved you, and you in turn loved them, but now no act or voice of kindness makes sunshine in the heart. Has fancy realized this to you? It *may* be the state of some of those you cherish! Who shall be sure his own hearthstone shall not be so desolate? Nay, who shall say his own mountain stands strong, his lamp of reason shall not go out in darkness! To how many has this become a heart-rending reality. If for selfish ends only, should not effectual legislation here interpose?

Shelburne. November last. I found no poorhouse, and but few paupers. These were distributed in private families. I had heard, before visiting this place, of the bad condition of a lunatic pauper. The case seemed to be pretty well known throughout the county. Receiving a direction by which I might find him, I reached a house of most respectable appearance, everything without and within indicating abundance and prosperity. Concluding I must have mistaken my way, I prudently inquired where the insane person might be found. I was readily answered, "Here." I desired to see him; and, after some difficulties raised and set aside, I was conducted into the yard, where was a small building of rough boards imperfectly joined. Through these crevices was admitted what portion of heaven's light and air was allowed by man to his fellow-man. This shanty or shell enclosing a cage might have been eight or ten feet square. I think it did not exceed. A narrow passage within allowed to pass in front of the cage. It was very cold. The air within was burdened with the most noisome vapors, and desolation with misery seemed here to have settled their abode. All was still, save now and then a low groan. The person who conducted me tried, with a stick, to rouse the inmate. I entreated her to desist, the twilight of the place making it difficult to discern anything within the cage. There at last I saw a human being, partially extended, cast upon his back, amidst a mass of filth, the sole furnishing, whether for comfort or necessity, which the place afforded. There he lay, ghastly, with upturned, glazed eyes and fixed gaze, heavy breathings, interrupted only by faint groans, which seemed symptomatic of an approaching termination of his sufferings. Not so thought the mistress. "He has all sorts of ways. He'll soon rouse up and be noisy enough. He'll scream and beat about the place like any wild beast half the time." "And cannot you make him more comfortable? Can he not have some clean, dry place and a fire?" "As for clean, it will do no good. He's cleaned out now and then; but what's the use for such a creature? His own brother tried him once, but got sick enough of the bargain." "But a fire: there is space even here for a small box stove." "If he had a fire, he'd only pull off his clothes, so it's no use." "But you say your husband takes care of him, and he is shut in here in almost total darkness, so that seems a less evil than that he should lie there to perish in that horrible condition." I made no impression. It was plain that to keep him securely confined from escape was the chief object. "How do you give him his food? I see no means for introducing anything here." "Oh," pointing to the floor, "one of the bars is cut shorter there: we push it through there." "There? Impossible! You cannot do that. You would not treat your lowest dumb animals with that disregard *to decency!*" "As for what he eats or where he eats, it makes no difference to him. He'd as soon swallow one thing as another."

Newton. It was a cold morning in October last that I visited the almshouse. The building itself is ill-adapted for the purposes to which it is appropriated. The town, I understand, have in consideration a more advantageous location, and propose to erect more commodious dwellings. The mistress of the house informed me that they had several insane inmates, some of them very bad. In reply to my request to see them she objected "that they were not fit; they were not cleaned; that they were very crazy," etc. Urging my request more decidedly, she said they should be got ready if I would wait. Still no order was given which would hasten my object. I resumed the subject, when, with manifest unwillingness, she called to a colored man, a cripple, who, with several others of the poor, was employed in the yard, to go and get a woman up, naming her. I waited some time at the kitchen door to see what all this was to produce. The man slowly proceeded to the remote part of the wood-shed where, part being divided from the open space, were two small rooms, in the outer of which he slept and lived, as I understood. There was his furniture, and there his charge. Opening into this room only was the second, which was occupied by a woman, not old, and furiously mad. It contained a wooden bunk filled with filthy straw, the room itself a counterpart to the lodging-place. Inexpressibly disgusting and loathsome was all; but the inmate herself was even more horribly repelling. She rushed out, as far as the chains would allow, almost in a state of nudity, exposed to a dozen persons, and vociferating at the top of her voice, pouring forth such a flood of indecent language as might corrupt even Newgate. I entreated the man, who was still there, to go out and close the door. He refused. That was *his place!* Sick, horror-struck, and almost incapable of retreating, I gained the outer air, and hastened to see the other subject, to remove from a scene so outraging all decency and humanity. In the apartment over the last described was a crazy man, I was told. I ascended stairs in the woodshed, and, passing through a small room, stood at the entrance of the one occupied,—occupied with what? The furniture was a wooden box or bunk containing straw, and something I was told was a man,—I could not tell, as likely it might have been a wild animal,— half-buried in the offensive mass that made his bed, his countenance concealed by long, tangled hair and unshorn beard. He lay sleeping. Filth, neglect, and misery reigned there. I begged he might not be roused. If sleep could visit a wretch so forlorn, how merciless to break the slumber! Protruding from the foot of the box was—nay, it could not be the feet; yet from these stumps, these maimed members, were swinging chains, fastened to the side of the building. I descended. The master of the house briefly stated the history of these two victims of wretchedness. The old man had been crazy about twenty years. As, till within a late period, the town had owned no farm for the poor, this man, with others, had been annually put up at auction. I hope there is nothing offensive in the idea of these *annual sales* of old men and women,— the sick, the infirm, and the helpless, the middle-aged, and children. Why should we not *sell* people as well as otherwise blot out human rights: it is only being *consistent,* surely not worse than chaining and caging naked lunatics upon public roads or burying them in closets and cellars! But, as I was saying, the crazy man was annually sold to some new master; and a few winters since, being kept in an out-house, the people within, being warmed and clothed, "did not reckon how cold it was"; and so his feet froze. Were chains now the more necessary? He cannot run. But he might *crawl* forth, and in his transports of frenzy "do some damage."

That young woman,—her lot is most appalling. Who shall dare describe it? Who shall have courage or hardihood to write her history? That young woman was the child of respectable, hard-working parents. The girl became insane. The father, a farmer, with small means from a narrow income had placed her at the State Hospital. There, said my informer, she remained as long as he could by any means pay her expenses. Then, then only, he resigned her to the care of the town, to those who are, in the eye of the law, the guardians of the poor and needy. She was placed with the other town paupers, and given in charge to a man. I assert boldly, as truly, that I have given but a *faint representation* of what she was, and what was her condition as I saw her last autumn. Written language is weak to declare it.

Could we in fancy place ourselves in the situation of some of these poor wretches, bereft of reason, deserted of friends, hopeless, troubles without, and more dreary troubles within, overwhelming the wreck of the mind as "a wide breaking in of the waters,"—how should we, as the terrible illusion was cast off, not only offer the thank-offering of prayer, that so mighty a destruction had not overwhelmed our mental nature, but as an offering more acceptable devote ourselves to alleviate that state from which we are so mercifully spared?

It may not appear much more credible than the fact above stated, that a few months since a young woman in a state of complete insanity was confined entirely naked in a pen or stall in a barn. There, unfurnished with clothes, without bed and without fire, she was left—but not alone. Profligate men and idle boys had access to the den, whenever curiosity or vulgarity prompted. She is now removed into the house with other paupers; and for this humanizing benefit she was indebted to the remonstrances, in the first instance, *of an insane man.*

Another town now owns a poorhouse, which I visited, and am glad to testify to the present comfortable state of the inmates; but there the only provision the house affords for an insane person, should one, as is not improbable, be conveyed there, is a closet in the cellar, formed by the arch upon which the chimney rests. This has a close door, not only securing the prisoners, but excluding what of light and pure air might else find admission.

Abuses assuredly cannot always or altogether be guarded against; but, if in the civil and social relations all shall have "done what they could," no ampler justification will be demanded at the great tribunal.

Of the dangers and mischiefs sometimes following the location of insane persons in our almshouses, I will record but one more example. In Worcester has for several years resided a young woman, a lunatic pauper of decent life and respectable family. I have seen her as she usually appeared, listless and silent, almost or quite sunk into a state of dementia, sitting one amidst the family, "but not of them." A few weeks since, revisiting that almshouse, judge my horror and amazement to see her negligently bearing in her arms a young infant, of which I was told she was the unconscious parent. Who was the father, none could or would declare. Disqualified for the performance of maternal cares and duties, regarding the helpless little creature with a perplexed or indifferent gaze, she sat a silent, but, oh, how eloquent, a pleader for the protection of others of her neglected and outraged sex! Details of that black story would not strengthen the cause. Needs it a mightier plea than the sight of that forlorn creature and her wailing infant? Poor little child, more than orphan from birth, in this unfriendly world! A demented mother, a father on whom the sun might blush or refuse to shine!

Men of Massachusetts, I beg, I implore, I demand pity and protection for these of my suffering, outraged sex. Fathers, husbands, brothers, I would supplicate you for this boon; but what do I say? I dishonor you, divest you at once of Christianity and humanity, does this appeal imply distrust. If it comes burdened with a doubt of your righteousness in this legislation, then blot it out; while I declare confidence in your honor, not less than your humanity. Here you will put away the cold, calculating spirit of selfishness and self-seeking; lay off the armor of local strife and political opposition; here and now, for once, forgetful of the earthly and perishable, come up to these halls and consecrate them with one heart and one mind to works of righteousness and just judgment. Become the benefactors of your race, the just guardians of the solemn rights you hold in trust. Raise up the fallen, succor the desolate, restore the outcast, defend the helpless, and for your eternal and great reward receive the benediction, "Well done, good and faithful servants, become rulers over many things!"

But, gentlemen, I do not come to quicken your sensibilities into short-lived action, to pour forth passionate exclamation, nor yet to move your indignation against those whose misfortune, not fault, it surely is to hold in charge these poor demented creatures, and whose whole of domestic economy or prison discipline is absolutely overthrown by such proximity of conflicting circumstances and opposite conditions of mind and character. Allow me to illustrate this position by a few examples: it were easy to produce hundreds.

The master of one of the best-regulated almshouses, namely, that of Plymouth, where every arrangement shows that the comfort of the sick, the aged, and the infirm, is suitably cared for, and the amendment of the unworthy is studied and advanced, said, as we stood opposite a latticed stall where was confined a madman, that the hours of the day were few when the whole household was not distracted from employment by screams and turbulent stampings, and every form of violence which the voice or muscular force could produce. This unfortunate being was one of the "returned incurables," since whose last admission to the almshouse they were no longer secure of peace for the aged or decency for the young. It was morally impossible to do justice to the sane and insane in such improper vicinity to each other. The conviction is continually deepened that hospitals are the only places where insane persons can be at once humanely and properly controlled. Poorhouses converted into madhouses cease to effect the purposes for which they were established, and instead of being asylums for the aged, the homeless, and the friendless, and places of refuge for orphaned or neglected childhood, are transformed into perpetual bedlams.

This crying evil and abuse of institutions is not confined to our almshouses. The warden of a populous prison near this metropolis, populous not with criminals only, but with the insane in almost every stage of insanity, and the idiotic in descending states from silly and simple, to helpless and speechless, has declared that, since their admission under the Revised Statutes of 1835, page 382, "the prison has

often more resembled the infernal regions than any place on earth!"
And, what with the excitement inevitably produced by the crowded
state of the prisons and multiplying causes, not subject to much modification, there has been neither peace nor order one hour of the twenty-
four. If ten were quiet, the residue were probably raving. Almost without
interval might, and *must,* these be heard, blaspheming and furious, and
to the last degree impure and indecent, uttering language from which
the base and the profligate have turned shuddering aside and the
abandoned have shrunk abashed. I myself, with many beside, can bear
sad witness to these things.

Such cases of transcendent madness have not been few in this
prison. Admission for a portion of them, not already having been discharged as incurable from the State Hospital, has been sought with
importunity and pressed with obstinate perseverance, often without
success or advantage; and it has not been till application has followed
application, and petition succeeded petition, that the judge of the
probate, absolutely wearied by the "continual coming," has sometimes
granted warrants for removal. It cannot be overlooked that in this delay
or refusal was more of just deliberation than hardness; for it is well
known that, in the present crowded state of the hospital, every new
patient displaces one who has for a longer or a shorter time received
the benefit of that noble institution.

A few months since, through exceeding effort, an inmate of this
prison, whose contaminating influence for two years had been the
dread and curse of all persons who came within her sphere, whether
incidentally or compelled by imprisonment, or by daily duty, was removed to Worcester. She had set at defiance all efforts for controlling
the contaminating violence of her excited passions; every variety of
blasphemous expression, every form of polluting phraseology, was
poured forth in torrents, sweeping away every decent thought, and giving reality to that blackness of darkness which, it is said, might convert
a heaven into a hell. There, day after day, month after month, were the
warden and his own immediate household; the subordinate officials,
and casual visitors; young women detained as witnesses; men,
women, and children, waiting trial or under sentence; debtors and
criminals; the neighborhood, and almost the whole town, subjected to
this monstrous offence—*and no help!* the *law* permitted her there, and
there she remained till July last, when, after an application to the judge
so determined that all refusal was refused, a warrant was granted for
her transfer to the State Hospital. I saw her there two weeks since.
What a change! Decent, orderly, neatly dressed, capable of light employment, partaking with others her daily meals. Decorously, and without any manifestation of passion, moving about, not a rational woman
by any means, but no longer a nuisance, rending off her garments and

tainting the moral atmosphere with every pollution, she exhibited how much could be done for the most unsettled and apparently the most hopeless cases by being placed in a situation adapted to the wants and necessities of her condition. Transformed from a very Tisiphone, she is now a controllable woman. But this most wonderful change may not be lasting. She is liable to be returned to the prison, as have been others, and then no question but in a short time like scenes will distract and torment all in a vicinity so much to be dreaded.

Already has been transferred from Worcester to Concord a furious man, last July conveyed to the hospital from Cambridge, whose violence is second only to that of the subject above described. While our *Revised Statutes* permit the incarceration of madmen and madwomen, epileptics and idiots, in prisons, all responsible officers should, in ordinary justice, be exonerated from obligation to maintain prison discipline. And the fact is conclusive, if the injustice to prison officers is great, it is equally great toward prisoners; an additional penalty to a legal sentence pronounced in a court of justice, which might, we should think, in all the prisons we have visited, serve as a sound plea for false imprisonment. If reform is intended to be united with punishment, there never was a greater absurdity than to look for moral restoration under such circumstances; and, if that is left out of view, we know no rendering of the law which sanctions such a cruel and oppressive aggravation of the circumstances of imprisonment as to expose these prisoners day and night to the indescribable horrors of such association.

The greatest evils in regard to the insane and idiots in the prisons of this Commonwealth are found at Ipswich and Cambridge, and distinguish these places only, as I believe, because the numbers are larger, being more than twenty in each. Ipswich has the advantage over Cambridge in having fewer furious subjects, and in the construction of the buildings, though these are so bad as to have afforded cause for presentment by the grand jury some time since. It is said that the new County House, in progress of building, will meet the exigencies of the case. If it is meant that the wing in the new prison, to be appropriated to the insane, will provide accommodation for all the insane and idiotic paupers in the county, I can only say that it could receive no more than can be gathered in the three towns of Salem, Newburyport, and Ipswich, supposing these are to be removed, there being in Ipswich twenty-two in the prison and eight in the almshouse; in Salem almshouse, seventeen uniformly crazy, and two part of the time deranged; and in that of Newburyport eleven, including idiots. Here at once are sixty. The returns of 1842 exhibit an aggregate of one hundred and thirty-five. Provision is made in the new prison for fifty-seven of this class, leaving seventy-eight unprovided for, except in the almshouses.

From such a fate, so far as Danvers, Saugus, East Bradford, and some other towns in the county reveal conditions of insane subjects, we pray they may be exempt.

I have the verbal and written testimony of many officers of this Commonwealth, who are respectable alike for their integrity and the fidelity with which they discharge their official duties, and whose opinions, based on experience, are entitled to consideration, that the occupation of prisons for the detention of lunatics and of idiots is, under all circumstances, an evil, subversive alike of good order, strict discipline, and good morals. I transcribe a few passages which will place this mischief in its true light. The sheriff of Plymouth County writes as follows:

> I am decidedly of the opinion that the county jail is a very improper place for lunatics and idiots. The last summer its bad effects were fully realized here, not only by the prisoners in jail, but the disturbance extended to the inhabitants dwelling in the neighborhood. A foreigner was sentenced by a justice of the peace to thirty days' confinement in the house of correction. He was to all appearance a lunatic or madman. He destroyed every article in his room, even to his wearing apparel, his noise and disturbance was incessant for hours, day and night. I consider prisons places for the safe keeping of prisoners, and all these are equally entitled to humane treatment from their keepers, without regard to the cause of commitment. We have in jails no convenience to make the situation of lunatics and idiots much more decent than would be necessary for the brute creation, and impossible to prevent the disturbance of the inmates under the same roof.

In relation to the confinement of the insane in prisons the sheriff of Hampshire County writes as follows:—

> I concur fully in the sentiments entertained by you in relation to this unwise, not to say inhuman, provision of our law (see Rev. Stat. 382) authorizing the commitment of lunatics to our jails and houses of correction. Our jails preclude occupation, and our houses of correction cannot admit of that variety of pursuit, and its requisite supervision, so indispensable to these unfortunates. Indeed, this feature of our law seems to me a relic of that ancient barbarism which regarded misfortune as a crime, and those bereft of all sensibility, as having forfeited not only all title to compassion, but to *humanity,* and consigned them without a tear of sympathy, or twinge of remorse, or even a suspicion of injustice, to the companionship of the vicious, the custody of the coarse and ignorant, and the horrors of the hopeless dungeon. I cannot persuade myself that anything more than a motion by any member of our Legislature is necessary to effect an immediate repeal of this odious provision.

The sheriff of Berkshire says, conclusively, that "jails and houses of correction *cannot* be so managed as to render them suitable places of confinement for that unfortunate class of persons who are the subjects of your inquiries, and who, never having violated the law, should not be ranked with felons or confined within the same walls with them. Jailers and overseers of houses of correction, whenever well qualified for the management of criminals, do not usually possess those peculiar qualifications required in those to whom should be intrusted the care of lunatics."

A letter from the surgeon and physician of the Prison Hospital at Cambridge, whose observation and experience have laid the foundation of his opinions, and who hence has a title to speak with authority, affords the following views:

> On this subject, it seems to me, there can be but one opinion. No one can be more impressed than I am with the great injustice done to the insane by confining them in jails and houses of correction. It must be revolting to the better feelings of every one to see the innocent and unfortunate insane occupying apartments with or consigned to those occupied by the criminal. Some of the insane are conscious of the circumstances in which they are placed, and feel the degradation. They exclaim sometimes in their ravings, and sometimes in their lucid intervals, "What have *I* done that I must be shut up in jail?" and "Why do you not let me out?" This state of things unquestionably retards the recovery of the few who do recover their reason under such circumstances, and may render those permanently insane who under other circumstances might have been restored to their right mind. There is also in our jails very little opportunity for the classification of the insane. The quiet and orderly must in many cases occupy the same rooms with the restless and noisy,—another great hindrance to recovery.
>
> *Injustice* is also done to the *convicts:* it is certainly very wrong that they should be doomed day after day and night after night to listen to the ravings of madmen and madwomen. This is a kind of punishment that is not recognized by our statutes, and is what they ought not to be called upon to undergo. The confinement of the criminal and of the insane in the same building is subversive of that good order and discipline which should be observed in every well-regulated prison. I do most sincerely hope that more permanent provision will be made for the pauper insane by the State, either to restore Worcester Insane Asylum to what it was originally designed to be or else make some just appropriation for the benefit of this very unfortunate class of our "fellow-beings!"

From the efficient sheriff of Middlesex County I have a letter upon this subject, from which I make such extracts as my limits permit:

> I do not consider it right, just, or humane, to hold for safe keeping, in the county jails and houses of correction, persons classing as lunatics or idiots. Our prisons are not constructed with a view to the proper accommodation of this class of persons. Their interior arrangements are such as to render it very difficult, if not impossible, to extend to such persons that care and constant oversight which their peculiarly unfortunate condition absolutely demands; and, besides, the occupation of prisons for lunatics is unquestionably subversive of discipline, comfort, and good order. Prisoners are thereby subjected to unjust aggravation of necessary confinement by being exposed to an almost constant disquiet from the restless or raving lunatic. You inquire whether "it may not justly be said that the qualifications for wardenship, or for the offices of overseer, do

not usually embrace qualifications for the management of lunatics, whether regarded as curable or incurably lost to reason," and also whether "the government of jails and houses of correction for the detention or punishment of offenders and criminals can suitably be united with the government and discipline fitted for the most unfortunate and friendless of the human race; namely, pauper lunatics and idiots, a class not condemned by the laws, and I must add not mercifully protected by them." The first of the preceding questions I answer in the *affirmative,* the last *negatively.* [Here follow similar testimonies from the warden of the Cambridge prison, the sheriff of Dukes County, the warden of the prison at South Boston, and the master of the Plymouth almshouse.]

It is not few, but many, it is not a part, but the whole, who bear unqualified testimony to this evil. A voice strong and deep comes up from every almshouse and prison in Massachusetts where the insane are or have been protesting against such evils as have been illustrated in the preceding pages.

Gentlemen, I commit to you this sacred cause. Your action upon this subject will affect the present and future condition of hundreds and of thousands.

In this legislation, as in all things, may you exercise that "wisdom which is the breath of the power of God."

Respectfully submitted,

D. L. Dix

85 Mt. Vernon Street, Boston
January, 1843

chapter 4

TEAR DOWN THE WALLS OF HELL![1]

George W. Albee

The text of this sermon is from the Gospel according to St. Matthew, Chapter 25, verse 40:

> *Inasmuch as ye have done it unto one of the least of these my brethren, ye have done it unto me.*

Titicut was what the Indians used to call the area around Bridgewater, Massachusetts, where there is now a state hospital for the criminally insane. (There are lots *worse* places than Bridgewater, but all of them are also state hospitals!)

The Titicut Follies is a movie produced and directed by Frederick Wiseman. Mr. Wiseman is a lawyer who keeps asking embarrassing questions about the way society treats its victims—its criminals, its insane—and also its other victims who live in ghettos almost as confining as the walls of the hospital you have just seen. His earlier movie, called *The Cool World,* a film of the book by Warner Miller, was a great critical success but a financial failure. The present movie is also in trouble!

The state of Massachusetts is violently angry with Mr. Wiseman. Especially angry are the politicians of the state, who claim that by making this film he invaded the privacy of the inmates without first

[1] Professor Albee of Case Western Reserve University was invited to discuss the film *Titicut Follies* at a colloquium there in the spring of 1968. After previewing the film, he wrote this paper. A copy of it reached Brian O'Connell, Executive Director of the National Association for Mental Health, who had it reproduced and sent to NAMH state and local chapters throughout the country. Many of these Associations reproduced it for Boards. It appears here in print for the first time.

obtaining their permission. The politicians say that the inmates will be embarrassed if they ever recover and learn that they have been thus exposed to the public. Mr. Wiseman, on the other hand, says that the public's right to know is most important. He claims that photos in a mental hospital are no more of an invasion of privacy than photos of an auto accident. Maybe they are no worse than photos of a bombed and burned group of children in a Viet village. The courts will decide.

Some cynics say that the politicians in Massachusetts are more worried about their own embarrassment at letting the world see the kind of horror that some Massachusetts citizens are experiencing. The film has won prizes in New York and in Europe, but if Massachusetts has its way it will be banned from further showings anywhere. There is a kind of magical thinking here. Maybe if no one knows about them these places will not quite exist.

You have just *seen* Hell. You may feel a sense of shock. But you haven't *smelled* Hell yet. Every citizen, especially every Legislator, and particularly every Governor, should be forced to spend time each year on a back ward. The sights are bad enough. But the smells are worse.

They say that Governor Rhodes vomited during his first visit to a state institution. But his reaction has not resulted in any improvement in our state system. Next time he should spend a week and vomit every day.

Ohio is 49th among the 50 states in per capita state expenditures. We are, therefore, below the national average on every one of the 15 indices of good care published biennially by the Joint Information Service.

Last year the *Plain Dealer* did a brilliant exposé of one of our local state hospitals. For 1,700 patients (inmates) there were 2 psychiatrists, both of whom were administrators and who, therefore, were not regularly available. Twelve of the remaining 15 physicians were unlicensed foreign doctors, not especially interested in psychiatry, who could be expected to leave after getting a license. Because there were 13 nurses for the 1,700 inmates, untrained attendants dispensed the medicines, including narcotics. There is a 100% turnover of attendants each year!

Governor, we should all vomit!

One of the first things you notice about a state hospital is its characteristic odor. It hits you at the front door and gets worse as you approach certain wards, which In-Group sophisticates usually refer to as "Rose Gardens." There is no language to describe this institutional smell. By mid-winter it is almost overpowering. Most state hospitals have antiquated heating systems, without thermostats. There is one choice regarding heat—full blast or none. Often the heat in these ancient buildings is overwhelming, and the low humidity in combination with the heat is reminiscent, appropriately enough, of Death Valley.

Part of the identification equipment of the hospital employee is a tangle of keys hanging on the right groin. The constant scraping sound of locking and unlocking doors to wards, and the jangle of keys in time to the footsteps of the jailers, are part of the cacophonous music of the institution.

The inmates come as a shock. They always seem older, more lumpy, and bedraggled than people outside. Actually it is the absence of clothes, makeup, and, often, teeth. You people wouldn't look so hot in gunny sacks either!

With respect to the inmates, one is aware of the importance of restraining devices and methods. Burton Blatt and Fred Kaplan, visiting a number of institutions for the retarded in preparing their book, *Christmas in Purgatory,* reported that: "We saw children with hands tied and legs bound" (p. 13). Attendants devise ingenious restraints out of twisted sheets in the absence of other devices. Often, in these scientific days, chemical restraints replace physical restraints. Although there are many, many worse hospitals than Bellevue, the following description will give you the flavor of the "treatment" environment:

> Bellevue is so dirty that the health of its patients is endangered. The toilets are filthy, there are not enough for the number of patients who use them, and they have no seats—the patients must sit on the bare porcelain. There is a chronic shortage of clean linen and pajamas. The beds are filthy, and, more often than not, their mattresses are soiled and urine-stained. The wards are drab, monotonous, poorly lit, and poorly furnished —as well as being infested with roaches and mice. (Leonard, 1966)

Frank Leonard points out that Bellevue is seriously understaffed, to the extent that it is dangerous either to work or be an inmate there. Staffing is worse elsewhere. Bellevue has 25 nurses for 19 wards. A local state hospital, by contrast, has 8 nurses for nearly 2,000 inmates. The thing that Leonard found hardest to take was the brutality. He points out that "the worst of it is directed at the patients who are the sickest, because they are hardest to control.' They are also the least likely to make complaints, and the least likely to be believed if they should complain. A mental patient's testimony is easy to discredit just because he is a mental patient."

A recent careful investigation of another (anonymous) state hospital by two social scientists (Kantor and Gelineau, *International Journal of Social Psychiatry,* Autumn 1965) found that many attendants, out of malice combined with sheer boredom, teased and insulted the inmates for sport. They assigned them tasks which they could not possibly complete and then punished them for not completing them. Attendants often prevented the inmates for whom they had a dislike from seeing their doctors, or even from having visits from members of their own families, by deliberately manipulating visiting hours. Attendants might also punish an inmate by writing his name "accidentally" on the list scheduled for electric-shock convulsions.

But surely these are the *worst* places—the exceptional ones! Aren't most hospitals pretty well run? Here is what Blatt and Kaplan reported:

> We know personally of few institutions for the mentally retarded in the United States that are completely free of dirt and filth, odors, naked patients grovelling in their own feces, children in locked cells, horribly crowded dormitories, and understaffed and wrongly staffed facilities. (Introduction, 1966)

The Joint Commission felt that state hospitals were so hopeless that no more should be built and that no more cases should be added to those with more than 1,000 beds.

Many of our "hospitals" are horribly overcrowded still, despite the higher discharge rate since the massive use of chemical treatment. The *admission* rate continues to climb, and the *survival* rate continues to *increase.*

As Seymour Sarason has pointed out (in his Preface to *Christmas in Purgatory*), we are employing a self-fulfilling prophecy in our conceptual approach to psychopathology. We regard the mentally retarded person or the schizophrenic as incapable of improvement; then we treat them in ways which prevent any possibility of their improvement, thereby validating our original prognosis. As Sarason says: "That most of these patients did not improve did not reflect the validity of the diagnosis but the dishearteningly effective way in which state hospitals unwittingly went about confirming their diagnoses."

Another disheartening fact is that despite the modest reduction in total population in our state mental institutions, achieved largely through massive use of drugs for the past ten years, there has been a frightening increase in the number of children hospitalized. The rise of serious mental disorders in children is alarming to everyone and the practice of integrating these disturbed children with adult patients on the wards of state mental hospitals is cause for even further alarm. Yet separate intensive treatment facilities rarely exist and we are hospitalizing our children, often for life sentences, in these adult horror houses.

In some institutions for the retarded there *are* separate facilities for children. Listen:

> In one dormitory, that had over 100 infants and was connected to nine other dormitories that totaled 1,000 infants, we experienced a heartbreaking encounter. As we entered, we heard a muffled sound emanating from a "blind side" of a doorway. A young child seemed to be calling. "Come. Come play with me. Touch me." We walked to the door. On the other side were 40 or more unkempt infants crawling around a bare floor in a bare room. One of the children managed to squeeze his hand under the doorway and push his face through the side of the latched door. His

moan was the clearest representation we have ever heard of the classical lonely, hopeless man. (Blatt & Kaplan, 1966, p. 34)

What is to be done? Most angry reformers who expose the terrible conditions in the state hospitals suggest that the answer is to hire more doctors and nurses, more highly trained professionals who will be available to treat the inmates. Karl Menninger catches our attention and imagination when he says we can cure people in a barn if we have the trained personnel.

When the reformer learns that it is impossible to recruit professionals because there are not nearly enough to go around, he pushes the solution back a step and suggests that more professional people must be trained. This, for years, has been the strategy of the National Institute of Mental Health. Its Director makes speeches around the country pointing to the encouraging growth in the total number of mental health professionals as a result of NIMH support of training programs.

But somehow this solution does not withstand careful scrutiny. There are fewer psychiatrists—members of the American Psychiatric Association—working in state hospitals today than there were twenty years ago when the membership of the Association was only one quarter its present size! In other words, there has been a fourfold increase in the number of qualified psychiatrists in this country in two decades, but fewer psychiatrists are working now in state hospitals than then!

Where *do* psychiatrists work? Eighty percent of psychiatric practice is private—in their own private offices or in general hospitals.

Here is another paradox. The more highly-trained the professional, the milder the problems of his patients! The highest trained professional of them all—the psychoanalyst—usually restricts his caseload to selected affluent neurotics with relatively definable and treatable problems. On the other hand, the most disturbed schizophrenic receives most of his "treatment" in a state hospital from a "psychiatric aide" who is paid wages that qualify him for poverty level classification.

The most common private psychiatric patient today is an upper middle class, white, non-Catholic female between the ages of thirty and forty. She is usually a college graduate and she is often in one of the professions.

Training more psychiatrists obviously is not the answer to staffing the state hospitals. Of all the psychiatrists whose training has been funded by the National Institute of Mental Health over the past twenty years, only one percent is now working full-time in public health, education or welfare agencies!

There is still a *further* mismatch between the cultural forces operating in American medicine and the demands for care by the kind of people you have seen in this film. The American Medical Association opposes the practice of having doctors work for salaries. The preferred system—the American Medical Association way—is for the patient to pay his doctor directly. This assures, of course, the "freedom to choose one's own doctor" (which is just about the *most* important freedom there is, at least according to the AMA!). But the people in our state hospitals are too poor to pay fees for service. They are in state hospitals because they do *not* have hospitalization insurance that takes care of the rest of us in general hospital psychiatric units where a bed costs $60 a day! It is the *poor* who become the inmates. Suggesting that they choose their own doctors makes as much sense as suggesting that they choose their own diamond-cutters or silversmiths.

Many serious mental conditions require intensive care and intervention over a long period. The cost of psychiatric intervention of this kind is so prohibitive as to be beyond the reach of any but the most affluent. How can a poor family afford private care for a mentally disturbed relative? The answer, of course, is that it cannot. (Sixty percent of the children of poor families have never even been once to a dentist, and an even higher percentage of Negro children generally have never been to a dentist.) Anyway, where is a poor person to find a psychiatrist? They do not spend much time in the central city, except as agency consultants.

But there are further problems. California, Illinois, Pennsylvania, New York, and Massachusetts—five states—claim the services of more than half of all psychiatrists in the country. Massachusetts, and particularly Boston, is exceedingly well-endowed. There are more psychiatrists in greater Boston than in nine Appalachian states.

Boston is Psychiatry Land. At the beginning of this decade the Joint Commission on Mental Illness and Health, after an exhaustive study of the nation's needs and resources in the mental health field, recommended that each state strive to reach the impossibly high goal of one mental health clinic for every 50,000 of its citizens. Recognizing the impossibility of reaching this goal, it was still held out as an ideal worth striving for. Boston, it turns out, *exceeds by thirty percent this idealized goal.* Yet a recent survey by William Ryan uncovered the startling fact that five large groups of Bostonians with serious emotional problems are receiving practically no help at all: disturbed children, adolescents, multi-problem families, aged people, and discharged state hospital victims are barely served by psychiatry. Clergymen have more Bostonians in treatment than do psychiatrists! Settlement houses are doing more intervention with emotionally disturbed children than child psychiatry clinics!

Obviously the solution is *not* to train more professionals, *nor* to open more clinics and hospitals.

Yet this solution is the only one our "leaders" can dream up.

Recently I read the report of a conference on the mental health problems of Appalachia, sponsored by the National Institute of Mental Health. The experts conferred and discussed, analyzed and examined. It turns out that there are five identifiable groups in Appalachia with serious emotional problems for whom no help is available. These five groups include: seriously disturbed children, adolescents, multi-problem families, the aged people, and discharged state mental hospital victims! Shades of Boston!

What solution did the experts come up with? The establishment of some traveling mental health clinics! If Boston, with a cheap and efficient public transportation system, and visible, fixed, long-established psychiatric clinics, is not reaching any of these same groups, how can circuit-riding clinics moving from hollow to hollow in Appalachia provide any real intervention?

No, there is only one solution. *The state hospitals must be torn down—taken apart piece by piece and stone by stone,* and then like Carthage, be plowed under.

But what will we do for the poor people whom we now commit to the state hospitals? Could *any* solution be worse than the one we have been using all these years?

Who are these victims, anyway?

Who are the people we commit to our state mental hospitals? Surprisingly, they are *not* predominantly a group of psychotics! Some fifty percent are not psychotic at all! They are diagnosed as various kinds of "personality disturbances" (often a polite way of labeling a chronic alcoholic), or they are psycho-neurotics, or "transient situational personality disturbances," and many of them receive the diagnosis of "without mental disorder." (Two thousand people last year were hospitalized in the U.S. with this latter "diagnosis." Most puzzling.)

Of the fifty percent who *are* psychotic, half of *these* are elderly people with so-called *chronic brain syndromes.* Now a parenthetical interruption. (It is hard to decide which group in the state hospital is most pathetic, but probably an honest poll would award this dubious distinction to the elderly.) Last year the *Washington Post* published an article about the horrors of Virginia State Hospitals, and particularly about the desolation on the senile wards. Although the first mental hospital in this country was established in Williamsburg, Virginia, there is little else about its mental hospital system of which the Old Dominion can be proud. According to *Post* writer Helen Dewar, whose article is illustrated by Harold Isen's drawings, which could have been labeled "Scenes from Dachau or Buchenwald," it is hard to know how to react to the senile wards:

> The atmosphere in the old-age wards is chilling. Walking off an elevator at Western State, you are stunned by the sight of scores of old women, seemingly not seeing, not understanding, just being. Some sit around a

row of cafeteria tables, staring. They wear only the simplest of smocks. Some mumble to themselves, some talk quite loudly to themselves.

Behind them were other old women—slouching, not sitting—in chairs around a blurring television set. Nobody seemed to be aware of the T.V. set.

In the huge sleeping wards off to the side were women too feeble even to be dressed and put in front of the T.V. or at the cafeteria tables.

One tiny woman wasn't strong enough to walk, yet she balanced on the small of her back and held her legs in the air for hours, rotating them as if riding a bicycle.

From one bed in a huge ward, a vein-sculptured hand stretched out from under the covers, the hand clutching a doll.

"She's the only friend I have," muttered the old woman.

(Dewar, 1967, pp. E1–E2)

The aged don't belong in these places. Nor do the alcoholics and the sociopaths. We can do better in designing institutions. The Danes could teach us, if we weren't too smug to think we have something to learn.

Only twenty-five percent of first admissions to our state hospitals are functionally psychotic. Yet the state hospital allegedly exists to protect society from dangerous individuals! But it is only from *this* group, not from the other seventy-five percent coming in, that we will find our dangerous ones. How many of these functionally psychotic individuals are really dangerous? Thomas J. Scheff reports on research which indicates that nearly two-thirds of the people we commit involuntarily to our public mental hospitals are neither dangerous nor helpless, usually the most cited reasons for first commitment. Most functionally psychotic people are more terrified than dangerous. Research data reveal that only a relatively few active mental cases are dangerous to others. (There is a slightly higher than average suicide rate in this group but it is not very much higher than average either.) Former mental patients actually commit fewer crimes than non-patients from their own social class.

If it is really the protection of society that interests us we probably should commit drunken drivers rather than mental cases!

So why keep the state hospitals going? Why?

The Joint Commission on Mental Illness and Health recognized the failures of the state mental hospitals. It insisted that "No money will be spent to build mental hospitals of more than 1,000 beds, or to add a single patient to mental hospitals presently [1961] having 1,000 or more patients."

Another Joint Commission recommendation suggested that state institutions be divided into those "intended primarily as intensive treatment centers (i.e., true hospitals)" and other "facilities for humane and progressive care of various classes of the chronically ill or disabled, among them the aged" (1961).

The recommendations are widely ignored.

Maybe a movement to close these damned concentration camps would call attention to them and to the problems they hide!

Let's tear them down!

My proposal is neither new, nor the choleric view of a psychologist. Back in 1958, in his Presidential Address to the American Psychiatric Association, Harry C. Solomon said:

> The large mental hospital is antiquated, outmoded, and rapidly becoming obsolete. We can still build them but we cannot staff them; and therefore we cannot make true hospitals of them. After 114 years of effort, in this year 1958, rarely has a state hospital an adequate staff as measured against the minimum standards set by our Association, and these standards represent a compromise between what was thought to be adequate and what was thought had some possibility of being realized. . . . I do not see how any reasonably objective view of our mental hospitals today can fail to conclude they are bankrupt beyond remedy. I believe therefore that our large mental hospitals should be liquidated as rapidly as can be done in an orderly and progressive fashion.

In July 1965, another leader in American psychiatry, Daniel Blain, in his own Presidential Address said: ". . . the dedication to excellence, the creativity, the sense of renewal—does not lie in continuing in the old way to build more mental hospital beds, hiring more people to do the same kind of work they have always done. The buildings and the beds may be shiny and new, but the instrumentality is obsolete" (1965, p.11).

Who *cares enough* to want to destroy these monuments to man's inhumanity?

Most of us get over our shock and pass on to other things.

Who is responsible? The Germans said they didn't know the camps were there. We do not even have this escape.

We *know* they are there. Are *we,* therefore, responsible?

It is exceedingly difficult philosophically to unravel questions of responsibility for the institutionalized conditions resulting in the damage and disruption to human existence so common among hospitalized psychotics.

The Kerner Commission's Report on the riots (1968) assigns blame to white society for the existence of slums and for the conditions which led to violence. But defenders of the white middle-class have criticized this conclusion, taking a position that says, in effect, "I haven't done anything to them; why should I be blamed?" One answer to this question would hold that those who allow discrimination to exist without raising their voices in protest, those who recognize and accept the principle of restrictive covenants by living silently in restricted neighborhoods, those who belong to social clubs which are known to have strict standards concerning the racial and religious qualifications for membership—all such persons participate actively in the conspiracy to deprive others of their freedom and their self-respect. Similarly, those who know about the conditions that prevail in most state hospitals and do not scream to heaven for massive change are as guilty as any sadist attendant on the wards.

This argument holds that inaction, condonement, non-participation, and detachment are as reprehensible as active opposition to justice, freedom and equality.

Nearly half a century ago sociologist E. A. Ross wrote a book called *Sin and Society*. It was concerned with the inadequacy of our American system of ethics, largely derived from an individualistic rural culture and inappropriate for our rapidly expanding industrializing and urbanizing society. Professor Ross said:

> Unlike the oldtime villain, the latterday malefactor does not wear a slouch hat and a comforter, breathe forth curses and an odor of gin, go about his nefarious work with clenched teeth and an evil scowl. In the supreme moment his lineaments are not distorted with rage, or lust, or malevolence. . . . Among our criminals of greed, one begins to meet the 'grandstyle' of the great criminals of ambition, Macbeth or Richard III. The modern high-power dealer of woe wears immaculate linen, carries a silk hat and a lighted cigar, sins with a calm countenance and a serene soul, leagues and months from the evil he causes. Upon this gentlemanly presence the eventual blood and tears do not obtrude themselves . . . Among the chiefest sinners are now enrolled men who are pure and kindhearted, loving in their families, faithful to their friends, and generous to the needy. . . . (quoted in Cohen, p. 91–92)

Lenny Bruce once said he did not trust a clergyman who owned more than one suit. Is there anyone here he could trust?

References

Blain, Daniel. Presidential Address to the American Psychiatric Association. *American Journal of Psychiatry,* July, 1965, p. 11.

Blatt, Burton & Kaplan, Fred. *Christmas in Purgatory* (Boston: Allyn & Bacon, 1966).

Cohen, Nathan. *Social Work in the American Tradition* (New York: Dryden Press, 1958, pp. 91–92.

Dewar, Helen. *Washington Post,* Thursday, August 17, 1967, pp. E1–E2.

Joint Commission on Mental Illness and Health. *Action for Mental Health,* 1961.

Kanter and Gelineau. *International Journal of Social Psychiatry,* Autumn, 1965.

Leonard, Frank. And an attendant's view. *Fact,* May–June, 1966, pp. 29–35.

Lettvin, Jerome. *The New Yorker,* March 23, 1968, pp. 28–29.

chapter 5

SPOILED HUMANITY

On January 4, 1968, I had a nightmare. I awoke terrified, not being able to forget the ghoulish textures and sounds of that experience. We were in the jungle, fighting—who?

One of our men was hit very hard. His head was almost gone and parts of his body were torn away. He wouldn't die. He continued to talk, to ask for water, to hope he wasn't causing us too much trouble. And my reaction? During the nightmare, or after I had returned to the real illusion—wakefulness—I kept saying, over and over again, "Die, die you louse!" The nightmare was not in his dying but in his living. I would tolerate death but not life that does not resemble life, that is disguised as death but is too obstinate to die. I was embittered with this man who was beginning to smell, with this offensive spoiled piece of humanity, who had not the decency, character, and good judgment to die without the agonizing fuss he perpetrated on us.

Which parts of the above were in the nightmare and which were the aftermath meanderings of a disturbing experience is impossible to judge. However, as I drove that morning to the ———— state school for a meeting with its superintendant, Dr. ————, I could not erase from my thoughts the inhuman wish I had for the death of another human being.

Say it is fate, coincidence, retribution, or immanent justice for moral transgressions of the night before. For whatever the reason, the nightmare continued at ————. That afternoon, I learned or reconfirmed several things I now believe:

1. The realities of life can be as terrifying as our subconscious ghost swirling through the blackness of those pits we construct in our brains between midnight and dawn.

2. Over a period of time, being forced to contend with "spoiled humanity" de-humanizes us.
3. We cannot tell people to act as human beings and expect that they will heed our advice or command. Under certain conditions, people will behave as we suppose humans should behave; under other conditions, they will not.

On that afternoon at ———, I asked to see ——— building, their domicile for male severely retarded ambulatory adults. Accompanied by the institutional steward and John Callahan and Phil Dick of our central office, I revisited purgatory for the first time since those eventful days of late 1965 and early 1966. Goading John and Phil to enter that foul-smelling, evil-sounding den of disaster—they preferring to go directly to lunch, not wanting to risk Herculean tests of their appetites—I pushed the three of us into the rancid kitchen as we entered from the sweet smelling outdoors, surrounded by towering pines, picturesque snow-covered glades, meadows, and country walks.

Stumbling amidst those buried lives, the indelicate care, the blatant—and subtle—pandemonium, were shapeless forms who milled about mumbling incoherently, incognitant, incognizant, inert. One hundred and forty-eight grinning, frowning, shrieking, silent, wasted, and forsaken brothers greeted us. Their welcome made me suck in my breath, clench my teeth, resolute in my purpose to expiate for some debt or abnormal obligation, to once again tremble through this bitter experience, see every room, every cell, every defiled body, and ask the same warped questions:

> How many patients do you have?
> How many attendants are on duty here?
> Where are the solitary cells?
> Why does it stink here?
> God! How can you work here? YOU appear to be human.

We were taken first to the dormitory, where beds were lined—row upon row, sides and heads abutting—beds without pillows, without a sign that this one's yours or that one's mine, beds arranged and covered "by the numbers" assigned to men who long ago ceased to exist as men, who were now on the cruelest of journeys nearing road's-end in ——— Building.

On several of these beds we saw huge mounds of tattered, colorless clothing, waiting to be sorted and stored. In attendants' areas, closets, and even in one solitary confinement cell, we noticed piles and piles of garments—unrecognizable, faded and shapeless (clothes for unrecognizable, misshapen people)—assigned randomly to building residents and collected periodically on washday for eventual countless reassignments. I have read descriptions of the beauty and loftiness of communal life. Possibly, devotees of such systems have some valid argument. However, I am irrevocably persuaded that there is nothing implicitly uplifting or ennobling in communal underwear, and I feel certain that no political or welfare manifesto can convince me otherwise.

From the dormitory, we proceeded to the day room. A day room is that place in the residential facility intended to resemble most the family or living room. This is the area for group interaction and fellowship or, possibly, for television, quiet games or parties. The ———— Building day room is quite large, I should guess 40' x 50', contained by peeling walls and ceiling, and a cement floor—the center of which has a circular sewer of about one foot diameter.

Entering the day room, we observed 50 to 60 adults in varying degrees of nakedness—most of them completely bare, others with a shirt, underwear, a sock. Some were standing, others lying on the cement floor, and a group were sitting or sprawling along benches that circled much of the room. In the center stood the matron (I always believed this term was reserved for women attendants in institutions; in our state institutions, all charge attendants are officially matrons). Mr. ————, the matron, is a young athletic-looking man. He was wielding a slop broom seemingly trying to push the recently accumulated debris, feces, and urine into the floor sewer—conveniently installed for such purposes by our efficient engineering service. He was facing away from the entrance and, as the moans and other noises of the room were quite vigorous, we now accidentally became undetected observers.

I am not certain how many minutes we remained unnoticed. I do know that I walked to the left of the day room, having been told that an isolation room was located off that section. Further, I remember peering into that confinement window and observing a teenage boy wrapped in a blanket, lying on the bare floor of the cubicle—no bed, no toilet, just the hopeless, unremitting and inevitable program toward the destruction of a man. I further remember that, as I turned to rejoin our group, I stumbled over one young man lying on the floor adjacent to the isolation room and that that clumsiness, in turn, caused me to trip onto another one, lying nearby. Possibly, all of the aforementioned lasted no more than 60 or 80 seconds for, as I returned to the day room entrance, Mr. ———— was still engaged in his sweeping chores. Why didn't I call out to him to announce our presence? I prefer to think—yes, I truly believe—our failure to make our visit known, to either shout out or stride out across the room, resulted from our hesitation to interrupt him while he was performing his work and our unwillingness to negotiate a walk through that horrible, surrealistic, irrational arrangement of life. It may be that John Callahan and I huddled together, unwilling to retreat from the reassurance of our togetherness, and the comfort of swift escape, if need be, through the exit an arm's length away. Of this I am certain, there was no mendacity to our behavior, if, for no other reason than the fact—consciously obvious even to us—that we were overwhelmed by the situation and incapable of then planning anything so cunning as a secret observation.

We stared, gazing rigidly in fear and wonderment, for possibly a minute, no more. In an instant or two the setting changed totally. Mr. —————— shouted some command at one of the denuded men who was seated on a bench. I didn't hear his words but it seemed that he was issuing some instructions or orders. Apparently unsatisfied with the man's reaction to his message, before our horror-struck eyes he lifted that filthy slop broom and, over and over and over again, beat it down upon the naked cowering body, a steady stream of curses spewing from his enraged tongue.

As with all nightmares—at least those I have—this one lasted no more than two or three minutes. As with all nightmares, it is the preoccupation with the morbidity of our reactions that has lasting and telling effects on our personality and behavior. One may ponder why these fleeting seconds so profoundly disturb me and, on the other hand, why those responsible for the System and who perpetrated and were participant to the specific misdeed toss off with incredulous disdain my indictment that evil inhumanity permeates that environment. I believe that any discomfort the Superintendent and Mr. —————— derived from the incident obtained not from the fact that a staff member acted cruelly, but from the embarrassment and threat of my accusation which was made forcefully and officially.

The question I ask is: What was so offensive to me but not to them? Rhetorical and essentially unresolvable questions usually expect no answer. However, I have an answer, albeit metaphysical and introspective. I cannot tolerate spoiled organic matter, especially spoiled humanity. I gag at the sight and smell of piled garbage and decay, with its swarming maggots and oozing slime that pulsates in its primitive living cellular and animal parasitic kingdom. Neither, I suspect, can Superintendent —————— tolerate spoiled garbage, for didn't he include in his newest building a specially built walk-in refrigerator for *Garbage*—so it wouldn't spoil between the time of its storage and removal to the institutional dump?

I cannot tolerate human garbage and that is what these patients have been turned into, and that is how I believe they are now viewed at —————— Building.

It is always fruitless—more, a denial of rational life—to attempt to convince someone that supercrescence, filth, slime, all things scatalogical, and all things uretic are natural and, consequently, completely acceptable facets of our human eminence. Yet, there are those among us who, rather than conceive of and develop programs for people that are ideational counterparts to refrigeration and sanitary engineering, delude themselves and others into accepting and perpetrating environments nurturing human garbage. Their ministry is not education or social welfare. Their mission is not rehabilitation and a return to human dignity and participation. Their ministry is delusion and deception and hypocrisy—to accept for their brothers that which they would not tolerate in a barrel of garbage. They have traded their brothers' birthright for a stainless steel walk-in cooler and have been able to accept and justify the coexistence of fresh unspoiled garbage and humanity turned sour and rotten. In so doing, they have traded their own birthright and humanism. Words cannot describe how deeply all of this offends me.

chapter 6

RESTRAINT, SECLUSION, AND PUNISHMENT

Woe to the misbegotten, the senile, and the legally incarcerated! Woe to anyone we think subhuman, for the becoming is in the thinking and the being is not what is but the apprehension of what will be. Pity those who believe that God is dead or that death is God. Beware of the Gods who live, who deign to judge the humanity of a man as well as his spirit, worth, and utilitarian competency. Beware of he who will forsake a human for the cause of humanity. Look carefully at philosophies and institutions that explain and justify to human beings and at systems that brutalize both the offender and the offended.

For some time, I have been studying first-hand the various forms in which brutality is permitted to be expressed in our state schools for the mentally retarded. Some of man's inhumanity is legal; some is quasi-legal; some, if detected, would result in dismissal or, possibly, criminal proceedings. It is hoped that studies of these types of behaviors may lead to some notions concerning the foundations of human abuse, notions that may give rise, eventually, to universal practices divested of the cruelty, brutality, and human divisiveness that we, in our generations, are noted for and accept as natural conditions of civilization.

At one state school, in the dormitory housing the most severely retarded ambulatory women, four solitary confinement cells are continuously filled, and a waiting list exists for their use. During a recent visit, I found two young women in one cell, lying nude in the corner, their feces smeared on the walls, ceiling, and floor—two bodies huddled in the darkness, on a bare terrazzo floor, without competency or understanding of the wrongs they have committed and with no hope that those on the other side of the cell will ever comprehend this unholy incarceration. On the next floor was a girl who has been in a solitary cell for five years, never leaving—not for food or toileting or sleep. This cell—this concrete and tile cubicle—without furniture or mattress or blanket or washstand, is one human being's total universe. Across the hall, on the other side of the day room, is another cell where paces a sixteen- or seventeen-year-old girl, nude and assaultive, incontinent and non-verbal. One day each month her parents call for her. She is washed and dressed and they take her home or for a ride in the country or, possibly, to a restaurant. One day each month her clothes remain on her, she communicates, she is a human being.

At the above institution, an attendant in another dormitory was found kicking a patient who was in the throes of an epileptic seizure. The attendant was dismissed by the superintendent. Many employees became angered by this and a "work slowdown" erupted, with a genuine strike imminent. During one tense moment, while negotiations and recriminations were exchanged between labor and management, an employee told the superintendent that management had committed the one unpardonable sin, placing the welfare of patients above that of employees.

Recently, a retarded boy was accepted to a state school for the mentally retarded. During the admission interview with a school physician, the child's mother was told that her son would be placed in the "worst building" with 140 residents, most substantially older than he with no more than three attendants on duty during any one shift. She was told that she could not see her son until three months after his admission. The physician added that after six months, if the family should want to take their son home for a visit, a state school social worker would conduct an investigation to determine if the family was suitable for such an arrangement. The mother said that as she had adequately cared for the child since birth such an investigation seemed somewhat out of place. The mother was also told that most of the residents in the dormitory were nude and many were abusive in their behavior. She learned that there were no chairs in the dormitory because the "State" did not provide them. In answer to the question, "Do the residents have anything to do?", the admitting physician replied, "No." This parent decided, on admission day, to withdraw her application for placement, despite the family doctor's warning that she was in poor health and physically unable to care for the child any longer.

Recently, a patient at a state school hospital became critically ill with high fever, shock, and coma. The staff physician diagnosed a "severe virus infection" and prescribed penicillin. At postmortem, the patient was diagnosed as having had acute purulent meningitis, due to pneumococcus infection. The case was presented at a clinical-pathological conference, attended by an outside consultant, resident physicians, and three of the twelve school staff doctors, one of whom was the physician attending the case. The consultant, in presenting the post-mortem finding, concentrated on the birth injury which had caused the patient's retardation and, undoubtedly to avoid embarrassment for the staff, only briefly mentioned, without further comment, the existence of the acute and fatal meningitis. It is general medical practice that in a case such as this, the diagnosis of an acute viral illness is made only after all treatable bacterial infections have been ruled out; lumbar puncture, to exclude meningitis, is mandatory under such circumstances. Penicillin was given for this presumed "viral infection," yet it should be general knowledge that penicillin is ineffective against viral infections. Penicillin, improperly prescribed, happened to be the correct treatment, but to have been successful it would have required a larger dosage administered intravenously. Since neither the superintendent nor assistant superintendent attends the clinical-pathological conferences, they probably do not know of this medical error. Neither do the nine staff doctors who failed to attend this conference nor, most disturbingly, do those who did—including the physician involved—since in an attempt to spare feelings, the error was not discussed.

Recently, in a state school, a senior physician recommended that a resident have seven healthy teeth extracted in order to prevent her from eating the threads of the day-room rug.

At another institution, a child was found to be in severe diabetic ketoacidosis on a Friday, after a Thursday holiday (a "skeleton duty" day). The emergency request for blood sugar measurement was begun by the laboratory technician more than five hours after the initial request. Other key laboratory tests were unavailable. This medical emergency requires expert nursing, frequent and immediate monitoring of blood and urine tests, and even then, has a significant mortality. The physician recommended immediate transfer to a community hospital, where these facilities were available. The assistant superintendent flatly refused this transfer because of a shortage of funds for this purpose, and considered the matter closed. The staff physician, through personal contacts, was able to arrange transfer to a research ward at a large city hospital at no charge to the state. That research unit is not supposed to provide this type of emergency service. The physician in charge of the research unit, however, admitted the patient since he recognized that without this subterfuge, the patient would have died.

Recently, in a state school, a severely retarded child choked to death when an attendant fed her a whole hard-boiled egg. There was no subsequent postmortem, inquiry or investigation, or even a staff conference to determine the possibility of any negligence or other unusual circumstances surrounding this unfortunate incident.

Within twenty-four hours, during a hepatitis epidemic at a state school, twenty-seven of seventy-one patients in one building were diagnosed as having this dread disease. A request was made by the physician in charge of the building to the director of nursing for extra personnel, since only three staff members were on duty at that time. The director promised to send help several times, but left suddenly for a three day vacation without assigning additional help or someone to succeed him in his absence.

At one state school, a seven-year-old was tied—hands and feet—to the four corners of her dormitory crib. The physician explained that this restraint was necessary because the child had tied an elastic band around her finger until it became gangrenous, and subsequently attempted to eat the finger. When mittens were put on, she began eating a toe. Now she is restrained in bed to prevent her from biting herself.

At another state school, George is described by the dormitory physician as a "monster." He is in seclusion twenty-four hours a day because, the physician explains, when permitted freedom he bites and kicks the other children. The physician, describing George as one who "Frankenstein's monster would be afraid of," pointed out a victim of George's behavior who now has only half an ear lobe.

I was once visited by a member of the Parent's Association of one of our state schools. She wanted me to know, just as she knew, of certain conditions existing in a particular building at the school. She was especially concerned with that building since she was its representative to the Parent's Association and her own son is a resident there. The building she described is very old and was meant to house approximately 75 people. Now it must serve 117. About 20 of these soil frequently and cannot feed themselves. Twelve of the residents are aggressive and violent. On the other hand, 70 of the residents can dress and care for themselves and 17 have attained the status of "worker boys." These are residents who are able to help the attendant with chores around their dormitory, primarily with feeding others.

All of these residents, with the exception of the "worker boys," are crowded each morning into the incredibly drab day room, many of them naked and all without shoes. Under these conditions, even the more capable ones regress when placed with the profoundly retarded and the violent. This visitor also described extraordinarily inadequate bathing and showering facilities. The residents aren't even soaped and, with so many being untidy, permanent odors remain on their bodies. At 4:30 p.m., everyone is brought into the dining room for supper, the majority of them naked. She has never seen pajamas or nightgowns on any residents, yet she claims parents often supply these. She said that each person has only one threadbare blanket to use for cover, this being inadequate on cold winter nights. When new blankets come to the building, they "disappear fast." Sleeping arrangements are so crowded that beds are touching, end to end and side to side. The doors of the sleeping wards are locked. When my visitor inquired about the fire hazard, she was told it was necessary to lock the wards so that attendants may take turns having their evening meal. During the night (11:00 p.m. to 7:00 a.m.) there is only one attendant on duty for the entire building. Should there be a fire, it would result in a catastrophe, especially during the winter when piles of snow block the fire escape doors. This visitor, whom I regard as an intelligent and sensitive person, feels insulted, degraded, and humiliated by a state which forces her son to live under such circumstances. These conditions are unfit to be called humane or decent, and ironically, the family is charged $7.70 each day for such care.

In 1911, Dr. L. Vernon Briggs framed for Massachusetts the first state law on the use of restraint. Our pioneering, illustrious history does not exclude us from the perpetration of abuses, couched in the legal terminology of "restraint" and "seclusion." During a recent month, at one of our state schools, there were 11 seclusion orders and 103 restraint orders issued. At another school, during the same month, there were no seclusion or restraint orders issued.

How is it possible for one state school to conduct its affairs without the necessity to restrain or seclude its residents while another state school—with ostensibly the same kinds of patients with the same kinds of problems—must resort frequently to the restraining jacket and the solitary cell? Where is the influence of our illustrious predecessors, those great humanists who conceived of and built residential centers for the care and humane treatment of those afflicted with amentia? What are the causes of brutality, callousness, insensitivity toward another human being, professional malpractice and incompetence, unreasonable or excessive or unnecessary restraint or seclusion? Is it only the budget that is deficient? Or the overcrowded conditions of the state schools? Is it the understaffed and overworked employees? Surely, the aforementioned are very much related to the unforgivable conditions described in this chapter and elsewhere in this book. Surely, more funds, more appropriate staff, and less crowded conditions would have obviated a multitude of sins, some more horrible than even those reported here. However, funds and staff and physical conditions are only part of that total fabric, human abuse, which we must better understand some day.

I have developed two hypotheses concerning the conditions leading to human abuse and the consequences of such practices. Hopefully, these hypotheses will provide us with a way of studying an aspect of human behavior that, although unpleasant and frightening, may well be the cornerstone of an eventual theory of group behavior leading to an eventual society of civilized men.

It is hypothesized that human beings conceived of as animals, or not as human beings, are treated as animals, or not as human beings. Secondly, animals conceived of as other than animals are not treated as animals. The following is, with the exception of two word changes, a direct quote from the *Boston Globe,* June 5, 1968:

> Each year the U.S. Food and Drug Administration condemns millions of children to death by poisoning. The FDA does this, it says, to test the safety of drugs.
> The test children suffer horribly. Their bodies shake with spasms, they stagger, they arch and roll in agony, their eyes bulge from their heads and discharge tears, and they go into convulsions. The more fortunate die in hours, but many suffer for weeks—or even months: The luckless survivors are re-used.

The above is unbelievable, horrifying, excruciatingly painful to the reader. Our civilization has not degenerated to the degree where such practices occur. I have substituted the word "children" for the word "animals" which appeared in the original advertisement sponsored by United Action for Animals. Why did I deliberately mislead you? As long as one believed that this report concerned with children was a news story, in a reputable newspaper, the horror of it all became an overwhelming burden. However, how often have we read such advertisements or newspaper stories concerning animals? This we can contend with and, in fact, most of us aren't even slightly affected or moved by such cruelties. The hypothesis, stated above, and discussed elsewhere in this book, is that it is almost impossible to deliberately torture another human being (unless the torturer has a rare pathology of his own) without agreeing and believing that the victim is not "really" human. Once that belief is inculcated, man can—and does—perpetrate the ultimate abuse and inhumane treatment. The problem before us is that of developing better ways of insuring that those dealing with people are given every opportunity and encouragement to develop conceptions that continuously confirm and reconfirm the basic worth of these human beings.

It is hypothesized that a society is judged most harshly by that of which it should be most ashamed, and that judgment is the most accurate reflection of the society's sickness. Further, from the multitude of conditions and situations which can bring shame to a society (that which demonstrates inhumane treatment of humans is the most shameful) that sickness has the power to flood out whatever good the society is accomplishing.

What are the consequences of the above hypotheses if, as you can agree for purposes of discussion, their repeated testing would not cause us to disown them? We may come to understand that our most difficult task ahead in a national program to reform residential and community settings for the mentally retarded will not be how to raise sufficient funds, or build better facilities, or pass more appropriate legislation. Our most formidable hurdle will be to engage the support and involvement of people whose conceptions of human potential are optimistic and whose views of humanity do not exclude any one segment from membership in the human family. Our task will be not only to enjoin those with such conceptions to enlist in the movement, but to find ways of helping people without such convictions to deal more effectively with their prejudices and biases concerning the possibilities that all human beings are valuable and changeable. Society's judgment of the progress that has been made on behalf of the mentally retarded will continue to be harsh and, in its own way, prejudiced, until such time as the most severely retarded and the most severely neglected receive the treatment due them as human beings.

Earlier this year, I received a telephone call from the assistant superintendent of one of our state schools who, during the superintendent's vacation, was acting as chief officer. This assistant superintendent has been at the school for many years, the same institution described earlier in reference to a budding insurrection resulting from the dismissal of an employee for kicking a child. He has had the reputation of being a kindly man, although one not noted for relishing "head-on" encounters with employees, a mild person with distaste for controversy or disagreement. He called for advice, or rather, reaction. A chief nurse reported to him that an attendant kicked at a child and, although only grazing her, severe disciplinary action was indicated. The assistant superintendent told me that after a lengthy hearing, and in consideration of the ten-year employment record of the attendant, he placed her on three-week suspension without pay. Yesterday, I received a carbon of a letter he sent to this attendant, informing her of his action and his displeasure with her behavior. Although I find it difficult to be happy receiving news of anyone's suspension or discharge, I felt a sense of progress and timeliness and hope when I received that suspension notice. Maybe, at least at that state school, the corner has been turned and the reformation has begun. Maybe, it is a portent of things to come when a conservative administrator has the conviction and courage to suspend a permanent employee for what, heretofore, has been a common and unnoted occurrence. I will keep that carbon, and, someday long after my tenure as commissioner is completed, I may well frame it. It is truly a symbol of what we have been and what lies ahead for all of us.

chapter 7

LIMBUS: MAN'S
SUBTLE CATASTROPHE

A child, Debbie, who is in treatment at our University Psycho-Educational Clinic, wrote a poem:

> *Snow is very white,*
> *Snow is oh so very white,*
> *But it will get dirty.*
>
> *Ants are so small,*
> *Ants are interesting,*
> *But they will die off.*
>
> *Winter is a season,*
> *It is very pretty,*
> *But it will leave us.*
>
> *Bees buzz all the time,*
> *It seems that they never stop,*
> *But they do.*

Debbie has expressed for me, better than I ever could, the feeling of hopelessness and helplessness that permeates the minds and souls of those in our institutions and those others of us who visit there. For the ordinary condition in our institutions is not one involving violence or brutality or illegal treatment—although these are much more ordinary in institutions than they are in the community. The ordinary condition is boredom more than brutality, legal abuse more than illegal assault, and a subtle degradation rather than a blatant holocaust. However, this genteel catastrophe is deadening, it's overwhelming, for it floods out whatever opportunities residents and staff have to rise together in some common attempt for personal dignity and mutual human concern. This subtle catastrophe is the mortar filling in the cracks and anchoring the devastation and permanence manufactured by the heavy hand of the System. The subtle catastrophe is the belief most have that everything—anything—will either get dirty, die off, or leave us. Nothing can escape the plague, everyone and everything is doomed eventually to ignoble demise or perpetual anonymity, dying as we all must but never having lived. The subtle catastrophe is knowing that all is forsaken, that not only is God dead but He never was and neither are we. One cries, not because he is in pain but because he does not know what pain is or what love is. To be in pain, one must be alive. The previous chapter illustrates examples of restraint, seclusion, and punishment. This chapter will deal with legal abuse, sanctioned mendacity, and chaos as a reflection not of a deliberate program but of the consequence of a hopeless System.

About a month ago, I visited one of the state schools, having been invited to meet with and address a group of attendants who were working on a project designed to habilitate our so-called "back ward" residents. By prearrangement, I went directly to the Administration Building for a brief meeting and informal discussion with one of the institutional administrators, concerning a couple of then current problems. He was in a highly agitated state. During the previous night, in the building housing the most severely retarded ambulatory male patients, a forty-year-old resident was stabbed in the testicles by an unknown assailant. The attendant on duty bandaged the wound as best she could and wrapped it in a diaper. She noted on her building chart that the man should be seen by the building physician in the morning. The patient was returned to bed and remained there, alone, throughout the night, without any medical attention, other than the treatment of a night attendant. By morning, the physician's examination disclosed that the man required immediate surgery and hospitalization.

Until recently, in many of our institutions, a major responsibility of the institutional dentist was to extract teeth of those who bit themselves or other people or ate "inedible" matter. I have seen and spoken with innumerable girls and boys—ten, fifteen, twenty years old—with hardly any teeth in their mouths, because teeth have been removed in years past for committing such "offenses." Today, in one institution, the dentist may not extract teeth without the authorization of a staff physician who will rule on the medical need for such treatment. In another institution, finally, appliances are used for those who bite themselves or others. These appliances—although not very comfortable-appearing to the observer—discourage enthusiasm for extracting healthy teeth.

In another institution, as one enters the main Administration Building, he reads a prominently displayed sign, stating: NO VISITORS ARE PERMITTED ON LEGAL HOLIDAYS. As institutions attempt to get along with skeleton staffs on legal holidays, thus permitting personnel to enjoy these days with their own families, the decision had been made that it would be inconvenient to permit visitors on such days. At times, I found it difficult to convince—really convince, so that programatic changes were implemented—colleagues and certain institutional staff that it is morally wrong to base administrative policy on whether it is or isn't convenient for the staff. This is not to say that staff needs and conveniences should receive no consideration. The staff are entitled to as much consideration as possible, *as long as the needs of residents are the first priority,* rather than the last. To this day, I am not able to convince the institutional superintendent who made the ruling about no holiday visiting that it is an insensitive disregard of the needs of his residents and their families.

In one state school, children in a particular dormitory go to bed each night wearing dungarees instead of pajamas, on mattresses without sheets or pillows. In that dormitory each child is given a pair of socks, a shirt, dungarees (usually not underwear) each day. There is no "ownership" to these garments, only temporary usage until the next batch of laundry comes in and the child receives another pair of socks, another shirt, another pair of dungarees. At this same institution, in another dormitory for children of approximately the same age and level of ability, each child has pajamas. Each bed has a clean sheet. There is order to the building and sufficient supplies and equipment to maintain basic health and care. The matron in the first building is new at the job, doesn't know her "way around" too well, and doesn't know how to get all the things she needs for the children in her building. The second matron has been at the institution many years, is friendly with the steward and the treasurer, has a good deal of personal prestige and power. Her children are well cared for. In one of the infirm buildings of this institution, inhabited by sixty children—most of whom are in cribs much of the day—two attendants are on duty during feeding time. In one hour, these two attendants are required to spoon feed sixty children. Averaging two minutes per child, they complete this arduous task with an incredible degree of good humor, warmth, and good will—this, in spite of the inescapable conclusion that some of those children require, at least, one half hour for feeding. When one understands that "feeding time" may well be the only human contact of any durable length (two minutes!) that some of these children have, the viciousness of this practice becomes excruciatingly clear. As a minimum essential, and incredible as this may sound to a State Bureau of Personnel, the proper feeding of such children requires twenty to thirty matrons, attendants, and volunteers, if it is to be accomplished in a one hour period. Problems such as this, incidentally, require us to consider and reconsider the feasibility of unitizing a residential school along geographic lines rather than along etiological or competency lines. Such unitization—e.g. placing all children from a particular geographic home area in residence together, regardless of etiology or level of functioning—distributes through many residential facilities of the institution both difficult management problems as well as residents who might facilitate care and treatment programs. There are many problems to be found with such unitization, problems that we have not begun to understand—much less solve. However, the spectre of sixty young unable children being fed by two attendants in an hour's time, makes it clear that some change—some radical change—in the System is required. Lastly, it should not be necessary to give any further evidence to support the need for change. We must begin with this need as a "given." If we cannot agree on this, we are in desperately unimaginable difficulty.

Several months ago, I was presented with a critical problem concerning a twelve-year-old boy and the need for his placement in a residential facility for disturbed children. The child was evaluated by the one children's unit the Commonwealth maintains for the disturbed as "disturbed with primary mental retardation." Our state school Community Evaluation and Rehabilitation Center evaluated the child as "retarded with primary emotional disturbance." The children's facility for the disturbed did not feel competent to accept this youngster; nor did the state school for the mentally retarded. All the while, during this period of diagnosing and rediagnosing and classifying and reclassifying, the child was excluded from any community treatment or care facility. He was not in school, he was not in treatment, he was not in day care. He was creating incredible disorder and tension in the home. In order to ease the unbearable strain at home, he was placed, eventually, in a state hospital for the mentally ill. As the state hospital had no facilities for children and no patients younger than sixteen years, it was thought best to place him in a living unit with the youngest adult male patients. However, it was soon learned that this child could not possibly remain in this dormitory. He was physically and sexually abused by several aggressive patients and, literally, his well-being was imperiled as long as he remained in that situation. Consequently, he was transferred to a unit housing older and, oftentimes, senile patients. In this setting, the child became the aggressor and physically assaulted several of the older men. At the present time, this boy is in solitary seclusion at this institution, and has been in seclusion for several months. We have not succeeded in placing him in a more appropriate children's unit for the disturbed. We have not succeeded in interesting the state school for the retarded in accepting responsibility for him. Nor have we developed or planned to develop new special facilities for the disturbed retarded child. This child may well continue to remain in solitary seclusion until such time as he is old enough to fend for himself in an adult dormitory in the state hospital. I am pessimistic that facilities and programs will be made available quickly enough ever to benefit this child. Lastly, there are more than a few children with problems of a similar nature, children who "fall between the cracks," children who are neither eligible for one program or another, children who are excluded from school and exempted from the state facility, children who are called "retarded" by the adolescent unit of the state hospital and "disturbed" by the state school for the mentally retarded, children who are "encouraged" to leave school at the earliest possible age (sixteen) yet are declared "not feasible" for vocational rehabilitation, children who are—as a colleague once remarked to me—CLINICALLY HOMELESS.

Such a child is "David." David was born at full term, with a normal delivery, but mother reported delay in reaching infantile milestones. Further, she reported the onset of continuous rocking behavior commencing at ten months and David's failure, ever, to cry. Reputedly, the boy acquired a vocabulary of approximately twenty words by age two but, subsequently, discarded verbal communications and became increasingly egocentric and hyperactive. Mother, nevertheless, thought of David as bright, fully comprehending of his speech, and remarkable for his ability to demonstrate perfect musical pitch and rhythm, the latter skill acquired some time beyond the age of two. Father, now divorced from mother, was described by her as ineffectual, frustrated, and abusive. The marriage was dissolved in David's third year. Mother is described by clinic as alert, vivacious, and attractive, somewhat aggressive, and currently combating a mild overweight problem. At the present time, she is remarried and describes the situation as quite satisfactory. David has been evaluated at numerous hospitals, clinics, residential centers, and state schools. There has been more or less general agreement vis-à-vis the diagnosis, with most evaluations concluding with "Infantile Autism," "Schizoid Reaction, Childhood Type," or "Kanner's Syndrome." Under the provisions of our Commonwealth legislation for the emotionally disturbed, Chapter 750, David's parents succeeded in entering him in a first-rate residential center for disturbed children. However, because of his hyperactive and assaultive behavior, as well as the minimal progress he was making there, the school returned him to Massachusetts in February, 1968. Since that time, David has been evaluated at one state school and rejected as not eligible for admission due to the presence of "Kanner's Syndrome." At another state school, he was rejected because that facility's "present staffing pattern, groupings of children, open visiting and parent participation policies preclude a residential admission, at least at the present time." The children's unit of the state mental hospital will not accept the child and they evaluate him as "severe mental defective with behavioral reaction." After repeated case conferences, one could conclude that the Commonwealth had little to offer David or his family and that "diagnoses" are very valuable insofar as controlling who is admitted and who is excluded from a treatment facility. It appears ironic that, in spite of the vigorous build-up today of facilities and programs for disturbed and retarded children and adults, there continues to be greater and greater numbers of *clinically homeless people* —those neither wanted by any agency nor the clear-cut responsibility of any agency and, more often than not, those who present the most serious and urgent problems and needs.

We have a System whereby, if a clinical home is found for a child, we may deprive him of rights, privileges, and resources guaranteed to those "on the outside." "Sonny" was admitted to the state school at the age of one month. Now twelve years later, recent evaluations of Sonny indicate that his long-range outlook was reasonable enough to warrant efforts at rehabilitation. Sonny suffers from a rare disorder which limits severely the movement of his tongue, lips, and lower face. This causes people to undervalue his intelligence; for example, having a somewhat blank expression, he is thought to be less alert than he actually is. Even more damaging to his general development and his unfolding self-concept is the fact that he is increasingly unwilling to attempt to use speech or voice as a means of communication. An eminent reconstructive surgeon associated with a nearby large general hospital outlined a specific treatment program designed to increase the strength and usefulness of the chest musculature, to improve the pharyngeal and palatal musculature that he does possess and, eventually, to involve Sonny in an intensive speech therapy program. Further, certain operative procedures dealing with the restoration of speech components would be considered. Lastly, Sonny would be afforded a complete dental therapy program designed to bring the teeth in proper alignment so as to allow lip closure and formation of fricatives. The surgeon had agreed to arrange for the medical expenses for Sonny's treatment. However, the hospital expenses, which would be considerable, were an obligation that faced the state school if the child was to receive this chance for rehabilitation. The total budgeted allocation available to this institution for the hospital care of its residents is $4,000 a year. Sonny's hospitalization, alone, would exceed that amount. Essentially, the Commonwealth does not allocate funds for anything more than the most emergency and necessary outside hospital treatment. Because of these budgetary restrictions, so-called "elective surgery" is rarely viewed by the Commonwealth as its responsibility. Very intensive and dedicated investigation and follow-up by the institutional assistant superintendent revealed that an institutionalized child is not eligible for Medicaid even though the child's family meets the eligibility requirements for this program, which was the case in this situation. That is to say, had Sonny lived at home he would have been eligible for the surgery, therapy, and hospitalization under the provisions of Medicaid which his family was eligible for. However, because he is in the Commonwealth's custody, the Commonwealth is responsible for his health and welfare. However, the Commonwealth did not then—and does not now—allocate sufficient funds to discharge such responsibilities. Consequently, children such as Sonny do not receive the care and treatment that would have been guaranteed to them had they not been placed in a state facility that, one would suppose, should guarantee each such resident adequate care and treatment. Fortunately, in this particular case, the devotion of the aforementioned assistant superintendent to this child and his needs led him to a satisfactory solution to the problem and Sonny, eventually, received the treatment he needed through sponsorship of another Commonwealth agency.

Such cases as David's and Sonny's lead, almost inevitably, to angry confrontations, denials and denunciations, irreparable breaks in relationships, and lasting enmities—not only between and among families and professionals, but between one professional worker and another and between one "good" person and another "good" person. Too many times, our battles are virtuous but, unfortunately, so are our opponents' battles. Unfortunately, our opponents might well 'have been our friends and our causes often are forgotten before they are realized and long, long before we forgive our enemies their transgressions. We have not learned well enough that Institutions and Systems, much more than individuals, are responsible for the earth's good and evil. When we attempt to comprehend and cope with good or evil, we persist in studying individuals and individual actions. We hardly recognize Institutional and Group and System influence. We do not understand that the true and pervasive mendacity is the mendacity of the System. While I was in office, I had a rather thick file on the activities and correspondence concerning a Mrs. Baker. Mrs. Baker is a member of a church group, committed to provide volunteer service to one of our state schools. In the course of her involvement there she became very frustrated—enraged—at the conditions she observed at the school. An articulate and forceful, as well as humanitarian, woman, she goaded herself to, eventually, petition the governor for his support in changing the conditions she was forced to observe at the state school. After repeated attempts to communicate and receive support from the Administration, the Commissioner of Mental Health, my office, parent groups, newspapers, and numerous other individuals and organizations, she succeeded eventually in having the Board of Trustees of the state school hold a special meeting to consider her specific charges. I attended that meeting as did other members of our central office staff and the superintendent and key staff of the state school. Essentially, she called for a replacement of the superintendent, a reorganization of the state school administration, an increase in budgetary allocations to the school, more active involvement, inspection, and supervision of the facility by the central office, and legislation enabling the modification of certain practices and the development and enlargement of Commonwealth-supported care and treatment programs. She disclosed that there is ample documentation supporting the following conditions of neglect and mistreatment. I quote from her report:

1. We found not only the children nude, filthy, and bruised, but also sitting, sleeping and eating with moist and dried on feces covering them and their surroundings.
2. We found children heavily medicated and lying on filthy sheetless beds, uncovered and with flies crawling up and down, and in and out of their noses and mouths.
3. We found children playing in, and eating garbage.
4. We found cockroaches and other bugs infesting exposed foods and greasy dishes, and having the run of the building.
5. We found unlocked medical cabinets, and observed unsupervised and poor dispensing of medicines.
6. We found poor plumbing, locked bathroom doors, exposed electrical cords, poor ventilation, poor lighting, broken windows and screening, knobless and broken doors, drainless floors, filthy and chaotic laundry room conditions, broken and inadequate furnishings.
7. We found hopeless, apathetic, and frustrated patients and employees with no supervision, no evident instruction in procedures, and no schedule or program to follow; their plea to us was that there was continual lack of cooperation from the nursing office.

She reported that the minimum medical care and the minimum standards of fitness for human habitation were not available to children or employees, and that the conditions that existed at this state school were due directly to a lack of leadership, supervision, inspection, and training which should have been provided by both the central office and the superintendent of the state school and his administrative staff. Her petitions included reference to inefficient health, sanitation, and safety maintenance control and inefficient methods for recording pertinent data on resident and personnel status. She attempted to document a lack of qualitative purchasing, resulting in false economy. She alluded to misappropriation of funds and unjust distribution of funds as well as inefficient inventory control leading to a tolerated frequent pilferage. Mrs. Baker wrote letters of protest to the governor who sent them to us to prepare responses for his signature. She charged and accused and we justified and defended. Finally, at the Board of Trustees meeting, I found myself almost—but not quite—defending our policies and programs at the state school and denying the charges Mrs. Baker had been making. Obviously, there was a good deal more truth in her charges than falsification. Obviously, I—as well as many other individuals around that Trustees' table—was as anxious as Mrs. Baker to change the conditions she described. However, I—and perhaps others there too—realized that she (and all of us at one time or another) was attacking "evil people" rather than "an evil System." Certainly, some superintendents are more creative than others and some have more good will than others and some are more optimistic than others. However, to get at the root cause of the problems she so eloquently delineated and discussed, what is needed is a great deal more than just changing superintendents and certain staff. The subtleness of man's subtle catastrophe lies not only in what is around us but who—and, more likely what—caused what is around us.

> *Snow is very white,*
> *Snow is oh so very white,*
> *But it will get dirty.*

I hope that, some day, Debbie can write that there is always time for a new snowfall, for a second chance, for one more opportunity. There is always tomorrow.

chapter 8
THE FIRST DAY

For some time, I have thought that we will understand institutions better and begin to appreciate their complexities more than heretofore if we could but observe in institutions on a regular and sustained basis. Further, we have learned that there are times in the lives of institutionalized residents and employees that are much more critical periods than other times. Therefore, regular observations in institutions should account for both the ordinary and general kinds of activities and involvements people have and, secondly, should devote special emphasis to these so-called critical periods.

For several years, I had wanted to study carefully the first hours of a newly admitted resident. From general visitations to institutions and casual observations there, I became interested in such questions as:

1. What are the first words spoken to a family bringing their child to the institution for residential placement?
2. How are parents' questions and concerns dealt with?
3. How is the newly admitted resident separated from his family?
4. How is he introduced to other residents and staff?
5. What kinds of attempts are made to orient him to his new surroundings?
6. What are his minute-by-minute and hour-by-hour activities during these first several eventful hours?

These and other questions have intrigued me for a number of reasons. First, I was not—and am not now—able to locate such documentation, or even an expression of this interest, in the literature. Secondly, I believe that such observations can illuminate problems and provide insights concerning attitudes towards residents and their families that few comparable time segments of institutional activities can offer. For example, it is very revealing of the ethos of an institution to learn what happens to a child immediately after his parents leave him in his new residential dormitory. Does the attendant make an attempt to introduce him to another child or to another attendant? Does she ask him if he is hungry, if he would like a glass of milk and a cookie? Does she bring him into the day room, "deposit" him there, and leave? Eleanor Tessmer, one of my doctoral students and an instructor in our Department, and Lucy Juralewicz, another student, became interested in these kinds of questions. We met regularly and, eventually, decided to design an exploratory study that would permit the observation of newly admitted residents. An agreement was arranged with the state school; we were to be notified immediately when a decision had been made to admit a new resident, and we were to be given full entrée and opportunity to observe the first several hours and subsequent days of that newly admitted resident's life. Lastly, the resident's full record and all admission data were to be made available for our study and evaluation.

Eleanor Tessmer and Lucy Juralewicz were to be notified—night or day—when an individual was about to be placed in residence. Working as a team, the two young women went immediately to the state school to wait for the family and the new resident and to follow their first few hours on this critical day. Although these matters are very important—especially for those interested in such observation from a technical viewpoint—this chapter will not explore questions concerning the reliability of dual observers, the effects of participant-observation, utilization of recording devices, and the effects of the observer on the natural setting.

The remainder of this chapter will present, as faithfully as possible from the lengthy observational reports of the two young women, summaries of the first few hours of the first day of each of two newly admitted residents to the state school.

"Billy"

Billy was brought for admission to the state school in November. His age on admission was four years and seven months and he was presented with a diagnosis of severe mental retardation due to organic brain damage of undetermined etiology. He walked at eighteen months, had little or no speech, was not toilet trained, and was very noisy, very hyperactive, and exhibited many temper tantrums. The home evaluation reported that the father, a mechanic, and the mother, a housewife who at times works as a waitress, had been unable to obtain any help from community agencies and were literally at their wits' end before resorting to a request for admission to the state school. The parents reported that nothing seemed to keep Billy happy. They reported he was selfish, wanted to be the center of attention, pulled drapes down, tore scatter rugs, ripped sheets, didn't play with other children, had bitten many children but didn't any longer. Father and mother hit Billy very often. Father and mother reported that "sometimes I could kill him." Both parents were under great, overwhelming strain, with no help in sight, with no relief, and with little hope of ever attracting community support for care or treatment. Two weeks prior to admission, the following letter was sent by the state school superintendent to the parents:

> Dear Mr. and Mrs. _____:
> There is a vacancy in _____ Building. Enclosed are papers for commitment. Bring him here to the School on Mon., Nov. 1, between the hours of 9–11 A.M. or 1–3 P.M.
> Applicant should complete forms with date and sign the first or application section of commitment paper, being sure that Billy's name is written the same throughout, and that your own name and signature exactly agree.
> Line 12 refers to places lived and not the names of people. When the section is completed Billy should be taken to your family physician, or any registered physician in practice of medicine in _____ for 3 years, who will complete the medical certificate section.
> We require a copy of the Birth Certificate, Baptism Certificate, register number, and subscriber's name. We suggest you bring along whatever clothing you have on hand for Billy marked with his full name. You will be notified from time to time as to his need of clothing.
> Please be advised that there is a charge for the care and support of committed patients to the State Schools—maximum charge of $4.50 per day. Please see the last paragraph of the attached letter regarding the matter.
>
> Signed   Dr. _____
> Superintendent

On November 1, at 12:50 p.m., a young, well-dressed woman arrived at the information desk in the Administration Building, requesting admission for her son. She handed papers (admission forms) to the woman at the desk who proceeded to look them over. The woman, Mrs. _____, then went out to her car to get her son. Both parents returned with a screaming Billy. A second employee came to the information desk and asked the father to sign some papers. While father was signing papers, Billy ran down the hall, screaming and uncontrolled.

About ten minutes later, during which time the family was left alone, a well-dressed elderly woman from Social Service came to the information desk and introduced herself to the _____ family. She explained the admission procedures, "After you see the doctor, you will take Billy to _____ Building, and then you will come back here." Mrs. B, from Social Service, left, saying as she went, "We'll see you later."

About five minutes later, a third person came in with forms in her hand. She brought the family downstairs to the doctor's admissions office. She left the family there alone, all the while Billy running and screaming in the corridors and in and out of offices. About twenty minutes later a female doctor came by and went into the admissions office. She asked the father if the family was going to supply clothes for Billy. He answered, "Yes, they are in the car." The doctor then asked the name, address, and religion of family members. Billy, meanwhile, asked for water. He was very restless. He banged his head on the legs of the desk and then on the floor. He began to cry. The doctor looked up and said, "I have many forms to fill out. Why don't you take him for a walk." Father took Billy out of the office, trying to control him and amuse him.

Back in the doctor's admissions office, mother answered numerous questions concerning birth, illnesses, health histories, siblings, hospitalizations, and insurance. Mother asked no questions nor was she asked if she had any questions.

At about 1:45 p.m., mother was asked to get father and Billy because the doctor wanted to have Billy weighed. Billy would not stand on the scale. Therefore, the doctor weighed the father holding Billy and then the father alone. As father and mother were trying to put Billy's coat on him and receive directions to the Social Service area and, subsequently, to the dormitory where Billy is to be placed, the doctor said, "Good thing you don't have to do this every day." Then the doctor left. The parents went to Social Service to speak with Mrs. B. She told them to take Billy to _____ Building first and, then, return to her office. If they would wait outside, a nurse would show them the way to the dormitory. At about 1:55, a nurse drove up to the Administration Building, got out of the car, and approached the family, saying, from a distance, "You folks going down to _____ Building?" They answered in the affirmative, the mother asking, "Should we bring his clothes?" The nurse said, "Is he being admitted today?" Father took Billy in his car and nurse took the forms from the mother which the doctor had filled out previously. The family followed nurse to _____ Building. To this point, nurse had not spoken anything to Billy.

As both cars arrived at the Building, another nurse greeted them outside the entrance at the top of the stairs. All entered, with the father carrying three boxes labeled "Billy _____," containing the boy's clothes.

Inside the Building waiting room, father and son were left with two or three nurses while mother was taken to ward to be shown where Billy would sleep. A nurse supervisor tried to interact with Billy and he bit her. Later, the supervisor took father to day room and explained the kind of activities Billy would participate in, saying, "This is where Billy will play." Then, she showed father the ward where he would sleep and the exact bed he would have.

When all had returned to the waiting room, the supervisor took Billy's hand and, followed by mother and father and two observers, brought him to the day room. Another nurse was already in the day room with about twenty children. It was a large square room, divided by a three-quarter height cinder block wall, one side for the girls and the other for the boys. There were no toys, the children often playing with different articles of their own clothing such as shoes, socks, shoe-strings. On seeing Billy, the day room nurses interacted with Billy warmly, holding him, tickling him, trying to evoke a reaction. The parents watched from the hall doorway while Billy wandered about the day room. They left without saying goodbye. After the parents left, a nurse came out of the day room to prepare for Billy's bath. A second nurse remained in the day room with Billy while the nurse supervisor and two young girls, residents, went to the waiting room to get the three boxes of Billy's clothing.

At about 2:30, the nurse went to the day room to prepare Billy for his bath. He was brought to the wash room, his clothes removed, and showered. Then, he was carried to a table in the wash room where the nurse supervisor held him and another nurse dressed him. When he wasn't being held down, he attempted to bite one of the other children who was being diapered on an adjoining table. Finally, underwear was placed on him, his nails were clipped, and medication was applied on the large area of his lower back before securing a diaper on him. He was then carried to the nurse's toilet where he was weighed, with one of the nurses holding him, then returned to the wash room where his dressing was completed, and, at which time, he attempted to bite another boy.

At about 3:00, Billy was brought to the dormitory. The supervisor told the dormitory nurse, "This is Billy _____. He bites. He can eat by himself and he'll come to you when he wants to." During this time, Billy explored the dorm. He amused himself by picking up bits of cardboard from the floor. Eventually, he noticed that three children were in bed, apparently ill. He went to two people who came to visit one of the children in bed. They seemed to be complete strangers to Billy. However, he hugged them and then resumed his exploring, without making any noises and apparently quite content and happy.

At about 3:10, the nurse decided—hesitantly, because she was worried about his biting—to put Billy in the day room. She told the day room nurse, a young woman, about Billy, that he was a new boy, to watch him carefully, and that he bites. As soon as he entered the day room, Billy immediately went after three or four children and tried to bite them. The young nurse assigned herself to restrain him as a more or less full-time responsibility, in spite of the fact that she was responsible for other children in the room. After about five minutes of such restraint, Billy lay down on the floor, thumb in mouth. As other children approached him, he would lash out at them or try to bite. The young nurse would tell the other children to leave Billy alone. After about ten minutes of lying on the floor, he got up and ran around the room. He tried door handles, wandered from wall to wall, aimlessly moving about.

By 3:40, Billy was on his back, apparently asleep. Children, one by one or in pairs, came to him, touched his hair, or sat around him. He ignored them and continued to sleep. He may have slept longer but, by 3:55, one of the boys, who was playing, accidentally kicked him in the head. He rolled over and slowly sat up and started to cry. He hit a boy who was nearby. He recognized one of the two observers and went over to her, trying to talk to her. He ran around the room, met two boys who had previously showed him some attention. They hugged him, without any biting or screaming incidents.

At 4:00, Tommy rammed Billy's head against the far wall. He cried out, the nurse going over to help him. The other children came around, the nurse holding him close to comfort him. He stopped crying.

Little things happened. There was an elimination accident (not Billy involved) which Billy ignored, while some of the other children were attracted to the cleaning up process. An older child patted Billy on the head, quite affectionately. A boy took a string away from Billy. He went after it and retrieved it. There were these and several little incidents, each somewhat meaningless, yet altogether very meaningful.

By 4:35, children were lined up for supper at the door. Billy was on the floor again and Tom kicked him in the back. Children left for supper, a nurse taking Billy by the hand. The children were seated and, on his own, Billy went into the dining room and sat down at the table. This was not the proper procedure as he was supposed to wait his turn, with the other children, before being served. However, he screamed and wanted to eat. A nurse said, "Let him eat anyway." She placed him in a chair, dished out what looked like oatmeal, and Billy ate his supper alone.

His first day is soon to end for, after supper, it is back to the dormitory and preparation for bedtime. What terrors await him there and tomorrow?

"Andy"

On November 8, Andy was presented to the state school for admission. At that time, he was 57 years 11 months, mongoloid, and diagnosed as having early senile dementis, bilateral cataracts, and bilateral mild deafness. In recent years, he has indicated a decreasing interest in life, forgetfulness, stubbornness, and hallucinations. He is presented, now, for admission because his sister, who has cared for him for many years, is physically unable to manage him any longer.

During Andy's early life, he lived with his family. For the past twenty years, he has been living with his sister. Formerly, he had many friends, was very easy to get along with, played a good game of checkers, could be sent to the store shopping, and—although not independent—was little trouble and, in fact, a valued family member. During the past three to five years, however, there has been a gradual change in his character. He has become stubborn, forgetful, and seemed to lose interest in his surroundings. These personality changes, added to his physical limitations and the deteriorating heart condition of his sister, necessitated this request for admission.

About three weeks prior to admission, Andy's sister received the following letter from the state school superintendent:

> Dear Mrs. _____:
> We now have a vacancy in our Institution for the admission of your brother, Andy _____, and the necessary papers are enclosed for his commitment. The papers are in duplicate—one set is for the Court. We are asking that you bring Andy to the school where he will be cared for at our _____ Building on Mon., Nov. 8, between the hours of 9–11 A.M. or 1–3 P.M.
>
> You, as applicant, should complete, date and sign and have notarized the application section of both copies of the commitment paper, being sure that Andy's name is written the same throughout and that your own name and signature exactly agree. Please note that line 13 refers to places lived in and not to names of people. When this first section is completed Andy should be taken to your family physician, or any registered physician in the practice of medicine three years in Massachusetts, who will complete the medical certificate section. The next step is to take Andy, with the papers, to your nearest District Court, where the Judge will complete the Order of Commitment section. We enclose a letter for you to present to the court stating our willingness to admit Andy at this time.
>
> When the papers are in order Andy should be brought to the School on Mon., Nov. 8. We require a copy of the Birth Certificate, copy of Baptismal Certificate if baptized, and if he is covered by Blue Cross–Blue Shield protection we need to know the registration number and the subscriber's name. We suggest you bring along whatever clothing Andy has on hand, marked with his full name; you will be notified from time to time as to his need of clothing.
>
> Please be advised that there is a charge for the care and support of committed patients to State Schools. For your information, the maximum charge is $4.50 per day. Please see the last paragraph of the enclosed letter regarding this matter.
>
> Very truly yours,
>
> _____ _____
> Superintendent

On November 8, at 1:55 p.m., a man carrying a suitcase, with a woman and Andy wearing sunglasses, sneakers, khaki pants, a green jacket, checkered shirt, and cap, approached the information desk of the Administration Building at the state school. The woman at the desk began talking to Andy, apparently knowing him from previous visits there. "How are you, Andy?" His niece (sister's daughter) repeated the question to him in a louder voice. Andy replied, "Good." The woman at the information desk looked at the forms, which were handed to her by the niece, and said, "As soon as the other girl gets back, we'll take care of you."

At about 2:05, the other clerk returned and asked the family to follow her downstairs to the doctor's admission room, leaving them there to wait for the admitting physician. Various people came in and out of the room, saying hello, or peeking in.

At 2:50, the admitting doctor entered. She said, "Hi, I'm Dr. _____." The doctor began filling in the forms, asking questions concerning Andy. The niece answered all of the questions, nephew with Andy at the opposite wall. Doctor asked niece questions concerning religion, date of birth, medical history, medical diagnosis, disabilities, Andy's ability to drive a car, pistol license, mental illness in the family, age of walking and talking, social security, disabilities pensions, baptism, communion, knowledge of right from wrong, legal guardianship, who should be called in case of emergency, etc., etc., etc. The niece mentioned that Andy had never been institutionalized before and this was a very difficult choice for the family to make. The physician proceeded to say, "What a nice place _____ (the building where Andy is to be assigned) is, lots of men, clean and airy, good staff, in the spring he will be able to work in the garden." The niece was handed a form concerning visitations. The doctor asked if they would supply his clothes. Then the niece spoke about a concern of hers. Andy had been getting tired lately and the niece was worried that this day might be too grueling for him. The doctor explained where the building was, that she would call to let them know Andy was coming, and that everything would be O.K. Throughout all of this Andy sat, quietly, not saying anything or moving, hands in lap, sunglasses affixed.

At 3:20, niece and nephew, with Andy, arrived at the dormitory building, met at the door by the nurse supervisor. The family was taken to Ward 3, Andy's new home. It was a pleasant-appearing environment. At the far end was the day room, which looked more like a solarium. There were potted plants covering the entire area along the window ledges on the three walls. There were fall decorations on the windows and a few fall-like mobiles. Those residents that could be observed were quietly sitting, rocking, or resting. Upon entering, the nurse guided the family to the end bed, which was to be Andy's. She explained that this was to be his bed and that his dresser, and he had this rocker next to his bed to sit in. The niece and nephew, then, spoke to Andy, explaining that this was where he will stay, and that they would try to come and visit him when they could. They both said goodbye to him and went down the hall with the nurse. At 3:25, Andy could be observed sitting in the rocker, rocking, alone. By 3:35, one of the patients went over to Andy and touched him. There was no verbalization from Andy. He sat and watched. He continued to rock. Another man came over to the bed opposite Andy's and made it, taking the old sheet off and putting a new one on. He did the job well, although he was apparently blind. After making the bed, about five minutes later, he walked over to Andy to hold his hand (as if in greeting) and then went back to his bed. At 3:50, another man went over to Andy. Andy said something to him.

People came and went, passing Andy rocking, once in a while stopping to say a word. At 4:07, a man came over, moved Andy's pillow, and left. Andy twisted around in his chair and looked toward the movement not, however, verbalizing anything. At 4:10, two men came by. One sat down to talk to Andy, the other went to his dresser and put a hat that was on top into the drawer. He went to get some towels and placed them behind the dresser.

At 4:15, Andy took a handkerchief from his pocket, wiped his eyes, and put the handkerchief away. He continued rocking, alone.

Final Comment

"The heart is a lonely hunter," and civilized man is capable of making it ever so much lonelier.

chapter 9

ONE DAY AND NIGHT

I believe that the most efficient and understandable way to explain what Karen Arentzen did and why she did it is to begin with an anecdote that discusses an experience we had several weeks ago, then refer to a recent newspaper account, and—finally—permit Karen to relate, in her manner, what she did. It must be the reader's responsibility to determine, for himself, why she did what she did and what effect this might have on the nature of things.

A colleague and I have a research seminar with a small group of graduate students in special education. Several weeks ago, we became involved in analyzing and debating the relative merits of such global observational studies as Phillip Jackson's *Life in the Classrooms,* as contrasted with very carefully constructed laboratory studies, where all known variables are accounted for and controlled. The debate raged, literally, back and forth between the "carefully controlled laboratory" school and the "relatively dirty field study" school. After a considerable period of time, when all passions appeared to be exhausted and after all needs—both scientific and cathartic—appeared to be fulfilled, my colleague (chalk in hand) strode to the blackboard. He drew two horizontal, parallel lines that appeared to be of equal length.

He asked, "Which line is longer?" Some answered that the top line was longer; others, that the bottom line was longer. Still others argued that both lines were of equal length. One student said he didn't know and another student said he didn't care. The ensuing discussion, revolving around the tactics of research, was an enlightening and rewarding experience for all of us who participated in it.

It became clear, quickly, that an accurate answer to my colleague's question was difficult, if not impossible, to provide. It became clear that one line *had* to be longer than another and those who claimed the lines were of equal size were denying a difference they knew existed but was unimportant to them or, for whatever reasons they had, they preferred to deny the existence of the difference. It became clear that an ordinary ruler would not help us answer the question; the difference between both lines was too small to be measured by an ordinary ruler. Several alternative proposals were examined: (1) assume there is no difference between the length of each line; (2) make the best estimate with the measuring tools available to us; (3) not bother about the difference.

No one suggested that we buy or rent some sort of electronic hardware that could certify the exact length of each line. But, some questioned the importance of the problem, even if it could be satisfactorily resolved. For, we must all agree, the problem is a rather silly one, the importance of which escapes me—and, I hope, you too.

Although we can all agree that the aforementioned problem, as a problem, is trivial, I do not believe that we should conclude hastily that the questions one asks concerning such problems are trivial. This is to say, it seems terribly important to me—when confronted with a problem—to ask such questions as:

1. Am I denying the existence of a problem, or a difference, because I do not know how to go about seeking an answer or I do not care whether or not I find an answer?
2. Isn't it possible that, even though differences exist between variables, it is unimportant to either find them or describe them?
3. When the instrumentation that is designed for research exceeds in cost and effort the value of the problem itself, does the investigator need to re-examine his overall research strategy?

In preparation for writing this book, I read literally scores of research studies and reports concerned with institutions for the mentally retarded. I reviewed carefully controlled studies that purported to demonstrate that institutionalization has a depressing effect on the intellectual functioning of retarded children. Other reports demonstrated that institutionalization has a depressing effect upon young children but not upon adolescents or adults. Other reports concluded that institutionalization affects the personality more than it does the intellect, while still others concluded that the personality is the intellect. Some studies compared residents of large institutions with those in small "home-like" centers, while other studies compared those in institutions with those living in their natural or foster homes. Although many of the above kinds of studies have been very valuable to those of us who are trying to better comprehend institutions, I must confess that I have found too many others about as trivial in concept and conclusion as the blackboard problem. They have provided answers to research questions; but have the answers been worth the cost and the effort? Have the answers been accurate answers or have they been merely estimates, derived from the utilization of gross measuring instruments applied to very sensitive and complex interactions?

For quite some time, I have believed that the kinds of research problems we are interested in require us to study gross differences between settings or samples or phenomena, not subtle differences. Given the research tools available to us, we must maximize differences between groups and treatments to be studied or we will find ourselves confronting a "blackboard problem"—one that neither could nor should be resolved. Given the resources available to us, the manpower and time and funds, every research program—however well it is supported—is confronted with a decision concerning the number of variables and the size of sample to be studied. That is, to the degree that the researcher does not restrict the variables of the study, he will have to restrict his sample, or vice versa. My own preference is to restrict samples rather than variables. In studying so complicated a problem as residents in state institutions, the suppression of variables to be examined and accounted for may result in a kind of distorted impression of the study results that may mislead the researcher or tell him very little about that which he has so diligently attempted to investigate. Therefore, although it is desirable to recruit as large, as unbiased, and as representative a sample as possible—especially if one is interested in the generalizability that a study may provide—I cannot help but recommend that the research payoff will be greater if compromises are made with sample size rather than variable size. Lastly, and leading from the above discussion, we are just beginning to appreciate the dictum that, before the researcher attempts to manipulate variables, he should first describe the natural setting. The recent work of Oscar Lewis and Erving Goffman in sociology and Phillip Jackson and Seymour Sarason in psychology and education shows hopeful signs that times are changing, if grudgingly.

To summarize my long developing research strategy and, certainly, the research focus of this book: if the previously illustrated lines represent the kinds of studies I have not engaged in and I have little regard for, in light of the kinds of problems I am interested in, the lines that follow represent the kinds of studies I have been doing and those that I believe we must continue to engage ourselves in, at least until such time as we understand better and can measure more accurately the variables and interactions of variables crucial to an institutional setting.

As illustrated above, I am concerned with gross differences between groups and treatments. I believe we are at a stage in our understanding that requires us to study and attempt to understand important and obvious and meaningful differences, differences that should not cause us to argue whether they exist or not, but only why they exist or how they exist or how we can alter them.

I must remain convinced that, if we can portray clearly and honestly, the day-by-day and hour-by-hour and minute-by-minute disaster and disgrace imprisoning those who are residents in back wards of our state institutions, thoughtful people will not turn away from their plight —and, in fundamental ways—the plight of all humanity and all civilization. Thoughtful people will view the disgrace of our institutions with as much compassion and resolve as thoughtful animal lovers view, with abhorrence, the needless cruelty perpetrated upon animals.

A number of years ago, I became convinced that there is a dearth of adequate descriptions of what takes place in institutions for the mentally retarded. What appeared so necessary before we could identify problems more clearly than heretofore, and before we could begin to engage ourselves in the careful research so many naive people are calling for, were descriptions of the natural settings of state institutions. Karen Arentzen's report is that kind of description.

Karen Arentzen took her bachelor's degree with me at Boston University and, during my year with the Department of Mental Health, I hired her to work with our central office staff. As she mentions in her first sentence, she developed a plan to observe in a building in one of our state schools. The actual visit was not made until shortly after I returned to Boston University. With some very minor editing, this is her report, written shortly after her visit and prepared from lengthy notes taken throughout her edifying, yet terrible, ordeal.

> During the summer of 1968, I thought of staying in one building at a state school for the mentally retarded for a minimum of 24 hours, as an attempt to increase my sensitivity to what happens to average residents during a single day.
>
> Dr. _____ and I arrived at the state school at 11 o'clock. The superintendent met with us for approximately 20 minutes. The superintendent informed both visitors that, "A Building houses the 'lowest grade' idiot females, while K (A's counterpart) is for the 'lowest grade' idiot males."

Mrs. _____, an LPN attendant, was our guide. When we arrived at A Building, the residents were ready to go downstairs for their noon meal. We toured the building, first to the back part of the ground floor, where the "lowest grade" residents are housed—that is, where they sleep, eat, and spend much of their day. As we entered, residents were eating pots of mush. Several were being fed. Many were unclothed, restrained to benches by strips of sheets or cloth. One woman sat on a bench, covered with urine and feces, while eating. Two other women were in an isolation room nude, smeared with feces, while sitting and eating mush.

I had to swallow gulps of air, since the smell was unbearable. For a few minutes I thought I could not play the part of the so-called dispassionate observer.

The other residents were in the dining area located in the basement. They also had pots and spoons. The food in the pots looked like a stirred-up combination of ingredients and smelled something like tuna. The charge matron, a 21-year veteran of the building, was the only employee in the dining room. There was another attendant in the kitchen preparing the food. The kitchen and utensils appeared in need of a strong detergent. Workers (residents) were responsible for washing the dishes and running the small dish washer. The workers ate in a separate group and received extra cake.

After the meal, the residents were marched single file to the Day Room. There, approximately 90 people roam from noon until dinner time at 5 o'clock or 5:30. There is one attendant in the Day Room. There is always a crowd at the toilets, since there are only five toilets, directly off the Day Room, for a minimum of 90 individuals. The existing toilets are without seats or partitions between them. After a meal, residents who are accustomed to using toilet facilities drift there, always finding a line. Several of those in line are unable to wait until they get to the toilet and lose control of themselves, settling for the floor. The entrance into the toilet area is minus a door. There is a slant or dip from the shower stall and toilets to the doorway and, following the laws of gravity, the overflow gathers in the doorway. Since there is not a drain, residents wade through this to enter and leave the toilet. It was observed that toilet paper was not available. There were no sinks in working order in which the residents could wash their hands.

After watching this for awhile, I propped myself against a wall and looked around. Directly in front of me was a young woman, who pulled her dress up to show what she was wearing. Another woman was sitting under the table, her head nodding and nodding as she snored. Another was stretched out on the blood-stained floor, sleeping. Others sat sorting laundry that lay on the Day Room floor in huge bundles.

I asked the attendant LPN if there was a ladies' room for employees that I could use. She gave me directions and her keys. In order to go from the Day Room to the hall, a key is necessary to open the door. The ladies' room doubles as a utility closet with pails (of dirty water), brooms, and a toilet, without paper.

On one walk, we saw one of the two girls who were still in the isolation room laying on a bare feces-smeared floor. The LPN claimed that the girl was a biter. On another walk we watched the "barbers" of the state school give residents the dutch boy bob. Several of the "lowest grade" residents sat throughout the afternoon hours restrained to the benches. One resident was restrained to a pole by a strip of sheeting and she strolled around it with brief, catatonic-like pauses.

After spending the 3–11 evening shift and almost all of the night shift in K, we returned to A. By then we asked several questions, including: What do you need most in this building? Mrs. _____ replied, "Four or five more isolation rooms."

On a trip through A Building we saw one resident in an isolation room on the second floor—the same one we had observed at 4 o'clock the day before. The floor was covered with feces. We asked if she had been there all night: The reply, "If she wasn't she would take the mops (out of an unlocked closet) and hit other residents or eat the mop heads."

Shortly after the 3–11 shift began, Dr. _____ and I transferred ourselves from A to K. The person in charge there greeted us with apprehension, especially because of the presence of a female in the male Day Room. In the Day Room there were 40 or 43 denuded men, along with a few "selected workers." Chairs were brought for us and sheets placed on them. The sheets were to serve as protection for our clothing.

Some residents sat nude in corners in catatonic, ritualistic states, defecating at random. Some, who were dressed and used audible speech, were playing ball. The T.V. blared, but no one appeared to be watching it. When I entered the Day Room, one resident approached us, knelt on the floor to look at my clothes, and reached out to touch me. The charge matron told me to watch him, and not to turn my back on him. For an hour or so I was fascinated by his ritual of advancing toward me with a "finger dance" and being chased away by a "selected worker" or just a glance from me. Finally I decided he was harmless and interesting. I continued to watch him throughout the observation.

At 5 o'clock the residents were moved from the Day Room to the eating areas. The "lowest grade" residents were herded in a state of absolute nudity to the dining area on the first floor. Two residents who were unable to walk were carried by an attendant and a worker, in hooked arm fashion. There, the residents sat on steel chairs, at tables, without getting up for 45 minutes. According to the attendant, two residents were placed away from the other tables for disciplinary reasons. When Dr. _____ asked why they were nude, the following answers were given: "The laundry complains because there are too many food stains on the clothing from K and the stains are too hard to get out. And they will not keep clothes on, so why bother?"

At 5:20 or so, one attendant returns from his dinner and starts to prepare the pots of food. These are the contents, layer by layer:

1. a layer of bread crumbs
2. a layer of ground meat or chicken
3. a layer of mashed potatoes

4. a layer of white soup
5. a layer of orange soup
6. a layer of milk
7. sliced carrots

Then the pots and spoons are distributed to the residents. One Negro sang a chant-like melody, mixed with "freedom songs." A "selected worker" yelled at him to shut up.

There were several feeders, residents who were spoon fed by "selected workers." The worker held the pot near the resident's mouth and shoveled the food in. There was hardly time for the residents to breathe. Many of them gagged.

One man picked the carrots out with his spoon, removed them from the spoon with his fingers, and placed them in his mouth. He then looked for other solid food. When his pot was empty of solid food, he snatched another pot. While he was snatching another pot, someone else was snatching his. Pots rotated around the table. As he finally began to eat the mushy part, his pot was collected.

As soon as the pots were collected, the residents were herded out to await the shower procedure. They were placed in groups. Quite a few were herded directly into the bathroom; others were blocked in a corner by a bench in the Day Room. The Icebox Man, a "selected worker," washed the residents. I was unable to observe this directly, but I did see a hose nozzle and a scrub brush. The "selected workers" are residents whom the attendant permits to help him with his work. Icebox Man is a resident whom the attendants claim was placed in the state school for putting his sister in an icebox. However, the Icebox Man claims that his father did it—and that this father is 28 years old, while the resident himself is 32 years old.

During the showers, we observed at the dining hall for the other, "higher level," residents. To eat downstairs, it is necessary that the resident be continent and wear clothes, as there is a female kitchen aide downstairs. Individuals eating downstairs were given real food—chicken with bones. Several residents were trying to put the chicken leg bone between two slices of bread.

After the showers, the "lowest grade" residents—43 men—were put to bed. At 7 o'clock, they received nightly medication from a communal water cup. Many did not fall asleep until nearly 10 o'clock. During this time we talked to residents and, according to their stories, one was relocated in K after being involved in stealing a state car. The superintendent placed him in K supposedly for punishment. His father was a World War II veteran who has passed away. This resident approached us asking how he could get out and/or get additional education. Another resident was supposedly a "Peeping Tom," who had frightened some female in one of the cottages. The resident claimed that he was looking in the trash cans for old electrical equipment to fix and, when he heard someone coming, he hid to avoid being caught. This resident, age 27, was put in the "dog house," as he called it, for three days. He too claims that the Superintendent placed him in there for the purpose of punishment. Prior to his placement in K, this resident fixed electrical equipment.

Another resident appeared interested in us, and talked of his work as a shoe maker. We went to see his workshop. Unfortunately, he was orthopedically handicapped and had no orthopedic shoes. He asked if we could help him get a job so he could buy a pair of shoes.

The night was uneventful, with the exception of our need to smash roaches. There were many night sounds, such as the noise of a blind resident who sat up to figure out where noises were coming from. One resident rocked on a metal spring bed. There was the sound of a resident tearing his sheets. There was the sound of another resident unweaving a bedspread with his teeth. There were screams of residents. One man kept waking up and, at 1:45 or 2:00, the LPN repeated his medication order, but he did not go to sleep for several hours. The LPN did not write down the time of the medication and asked us when he had given the medication.

The residents on the first floor went to bed without night clothes on and, at 10 o'clock, the evening shift stripped the bottom sheets of the incontinent men and placed night clothes on them. They did not, however, clean the feces off the men. Not all of the incontinent residents were awakened. The reason behind this was simple. If the evening shift awakened all the residents, the night shift would be irritated because they would have to quiet them down.

A resident that slept on the second floor, one whom the attendants call a "homo," asked to be put in an isolation room so that others would not bother him. This was not done. Later in the morning, the "selected workers" began to awaken. There was some disturbance upstairs and I wandered into the hallway; I saw the attendant striking a resident with his foot.

As the men from the "lowest" wards awakened, they wandered straight to the Day Room, where they defecated on the floor while walking around.

"Selected workers" walked with one shoe on and the other shoe in hand, occasionally using the shoe to rap other residents.

After this, need anything further be said? I used to think not. However, I am not quite as optimistic that, once something is said clearly, enough has been said about the matter. I have greater faith than ever before in the power of these kinds of reports and the eventual good they will do. However, it has taken many generations to bring us to this state of pandemonium, and the struggle for reform has consumed and extinguished the passions of countless humanitarians. Before the struggle is really overcome, before every resident in a state school for the mentally retarded is guaranteed humane care and treatment, before the reformation changes conditions rather than labels and slogans, a great many more descriptions will be needed and a great many more Karen Arentzens will be required to suffer through their dispassionate note takings while the world immediately around them is mad and the world that caused this madness is yet madder.

chapter 10

LIFE WITH THE DECISION-MAKERS

It is within and around 15 Ashburton Place that many of the long-range and long-lasting decisions are made relating to the care and treatment of the mentally retarded in our Commonwealth.[1] This is where the "action" is. The Massachusetts Department of Mental Health, centered on 15 Ashburton Place, together with the State House, is a complex of authority, action and inaction, good deeds and bad deeds—but always power and influence. Life in this complex is always strange to the newly initiated, especially to one whose previous professional life was almost solely academic. The following is my attempt to bring some illumination to those who haven't experienced "government from the inside."

Admittedly, I take a very narrow view of things and have had very limited experience. To the degree that the reader finds me fair or unfair to certain kinds of individuals or operations, he will better understand that in a system such as I am describing it is not unusual to be both fair and unfair and to be treated both fairly and unfairly. Therefore, at the outset, I want to share my conviction that, in this particular system, decision-making is a reflection of the System and its capacity to initiate good deeds or poor deeds, rather than of individuals and their attributes. It is my impression that the System does more to change individuals than individuals do toward changing the system. Yet it is not possible for me to discuss the System other than in terms of individuals. In this regard, I must maintain that whatever is expressed in

---

[1] Quite recently, and after this manuscript was delivered to the publisher, the Department of Mental Health moved to larger and more comfortable quarters at 190 Portland Street, Boston.

105

this chapter and whatever approaches the reader uses to evaluate the origins of the pandemonium described elsewhere in the book, it would be erroneous in the extreme to place primary responsibility for these evils on certain individuals or types of individuals. We could continuously replace people or add new people or create new positions and not—in any but trivial ways—change the conditions we agree must be changed. For, in fact, it is very probable that the people replaced were as anxious to change conditions as those who had been pressing for their replacement. Adding new "good" people to a sick System does not make the System appreciably healthier, but it does infect the "good" people and they, eventually, behave in much the same ways as those they've replaced. Our goal, then, should be to change a System which promotes inadequate and inhuman care and treatment. Whereas, till now, our goal has been to change the people and, thus, rescue a System which is, in fact, without hope.

The Defensive Moat: Sophists' Paradise

A man can get along, quite adequately and for many years, on the elegance of his language and the passion and conviction of his speech. One would suppose that this is the hallmark of the university professor, and so it may be. However, I have observed sophistry and pedantries much more frequently in 15 Ashburton Place and its tentacles than in the halls of ivy. Very few people at 15 Ashburton Place *must* make decisions, if they do not wish to make them. The Commissioner of Mental Health must, as he is the Appointed Authority over all programs sponsored by the Department. The Business Office must, because they are responsible for both payrolls and hardware, items that are quickly missed if they are not delivered on time. Most other people—some high-ranking professionals included—do not have to make decisions, if they do not wish to. Obviously, many choose to make decisions, but they elect to decide and are not required to decide. For some, departmental activities are one grand round of debating, discussion, more debating, and more discussion. The payoff for sophistry is rather good, considering the investment. Men have been promoted on the passion of their verbal convictions, rarely having been required to influence the life of one child, but having persuasively proclaimed their regard for the lives of all children. Further, the System is such that one learns quickly of the peril of making certain decisions and the impossibility of making others. Rather than torment oneself with the uselessness of trying to "buck the System" (and one hears this time and time again), many men make their peace with it. They give expression to their good intentions, good training, and anger in activities that appear vigorous and dynamic but are empty repetitions, which are heard by no one of any importance or influence, but reassure the speaker that he is doing his job and that he is on the side of the "good" people. (We should not discount the cathartic effect such activities provide the speaker.)

Decision-Making and Accountability

Few people are forced to make decisions because few people are accountable for specific programs or activities. Obviously, those people who are accountable for specific activities must make decisions. How are these decisions made? A better question might be, "What causes an individual to make one decision rather than another?" For many months, my experiences at 15 Ashburton Place puzzled me because I was completely unable to "read" the System vis-à-vis decision-making. For example, several of what I considered to be very reasonable requests were denied by various business offices without explanation or apparent reason. Other requests were ignored. Still others were quickly and categorically honored to our complete satisfaction. There was no apparent logic to these responses. It seemed as if some mad table of random numbers was at work here, approving one thing, denying another, and ignoring the third. It must be admitted that, in each instance when I did require an explanation for a decision, there was some law or regulation or policy that seemed to lend credulence and wisdom to the decision. However, on other occasions, similar requests—in equal violation of the regulation or policy—would be granted. All one can do is speculate about the basis for decision-making at 15 Ashburton Place—as, obviously, one can't read the decision-maker's mind and there seems no logical pattern to his activities. My speculations have led me to three insecure and tentative conclusions: (1) It is thought much simpler and less perilous to make no decision, or to decide negatively, than to decide positively. (2) The System makes it more satisfying to decide negatively than to decide positively. (3) The process of working with laws, regulations, and policies encourages their utilization to prohibit activities and developments rather than to promulgate such activities and developments.

Because so few people have accountability and, consequently, so few people may make a final decision about a matter, most requests for one thing or another pass through several hands if, eventually, they are to be approved. With the exception of upper echelon business office personnel, there are few so-called "middle management" professionals who make final *positive* decisions. In innumerable situations, these individuals may make final *negative* decisions, i.e. they have the authority to ignore or deny a request but do not have the authority (or do not believe they have the authority) to approve it. Further, to approve a request for funds, personnel, a specific program, a transfer of personnel, or some other change from the "usual" is to—in effect—approve the wisdom of that action and certify the legality of that action. To ignore or deny the request permits the decision-maker freedom from accountability for his decision, yet permits him to make a decision. Inasmuch as the laws, the regulations, and the policies are not always without ambiguity and discrepancies and are, in fact, frequently open to multiple interpretations, one can more easily find his safety in that part of the law or policy that permits the decision-maker to ignore or deny than in that part that permits him to approve and, thus, requires him to stand behind his decision.

Whatever the central cause or causes are, there are many more negative than positive decisions made at 15 Ashburton Place.

As in the System the decision-maker rarely has the authority to approve, he is caught continuously in the frustration of "shuffling papers" from his desk to a higher desk, and of getting entangled in the red tape, bureaucracy, and inertia that are companion to such activities. It appears to be so much "cleaner," manly, and authoritative to deny a request than to involve oneself in the frustrations implicit in passing on this request to higher authority. It is, therefore, not difficult to surmise that there are negative decisions made whose sole purpose is to "satisfy" the decision-maker. And further, this narcissistic behavior is understandable, if not completely forgivable, in light of the untenable position most decision-makers are forced into. That is to say, most decision-makers may make *no* decision or a "no" decision but very infrequently have the option to make a positive decision. It is this set of circumstances that, I believe, causes more unhappiness and job dissatisfaction, frustration, and mutual ill will at 15 Ashburton Place than any other—including such problems involving salaries, working conditions, job pensions, and the enormity and complexity of the departmental mission.

Lastly, the innumerable frustrations and roadblocks one encounters in the decision-making process must eventually wear down a man's will to move things along in the proper direction and to make the proper decisions. From my limited observations, it appears that the Commonwealth laws and the Departmental regulations and policies are used— not to facilitate or permit positive decisions to be made—but to determine if it is legally possible or departmentally justifiable if a positive decision should be made. Essentially, and I know there is a fine line of distinction here between what may be and may not be legal or prudent, the departmental *modus operandi* is to, first, find something in the laws or regulations or policies that prohibit one from doing something rather than view these statutes for the purpose of finding justification for doing something. I have observed that departmental officials do not comb the statutes to find new opportunities to offer services and facilities, but they do comb the statutes for any prohibitions or incumbrances to a request that has been presented to them. Laws and regulations and policies being what they are—and Massachusetts being a Commonwealth long in the mental health business—it is often very difficult to "get something done" in the face of governmental and departmental restrictions, precedents, and inertia. I do not wish to communicate the impression that I am advocating flagrant violation of laws or regulations. Nor do I believe it unwise to proceed carefully and thoughtfully before decisions are made that affect the lives of patients or the careers of personnel. However, if a System is based on convictions and standards and precedents that make it easier, less perilous, and more satisfying to make negative decisions than to make positive decisions, to the degree that this assumption is true laws, regulations and policies will be interpreted in the light of their prohibitionary powers rather than in the light of their enabling powers.

The "We-They" Syndrome

There are a good many "we-they" dichotomies emanating from and funneling to 15 Ashburton Place. My observations lead me to believe that these dichotomies are always pragmatically real yet, in essence, artificial, more destructive than constructive, and usually based on various forms of bigotry, ignorance, and disrespect for particular "types" of individuals, their jobs or training, or their location of employment. To illustrate the "We-They" Syndrome, it may be helpful to discuss some of the common distinctions, or labels, used in the department, like: "Across the Street," "Professional Staff–Business Staff," "Unions," "Central Office–The Field," "Mental Health–Mental Retardation," "Parents–Professionals," "Physicians–Non-Physicians," and "Ethnic Mafias."

At 15 Ashburton Place, "Across the Street" *always* refers to the State House, the executive government, and employees in the executive branch. The people "Across the Street" include everyone from the governor to individual legislators to personnel in the various divisions of the executive branch. In one form or another, I suspect that every department of state or federal government has its "Across the Street." In some state capitols, "Across the Street" may be cross town and, obviously, the term used at 15 Ashburton Place would not be appropriate. However, it is unlikely that a "We-They" feeling does not exist between every department of state government and those in the executive branch who guide the legislation, promulgate the budgets, and make other vital executive decisions. There are various ways staff members of state departments attempt to deal with the people "Across the Street." Some spend a great deal of time "Across the Street," many of these on official business representing the commissioner or on request to appear before a legislative committee or at an executive office. Others, however, spend a good deal of time "Across the Street," doing errands for legislators or executive personnel, establishing and confirming their "ins," and currying one kind of favor or another. Still other members of a state department avoid "Crossing the Street," almost at any cost. They have learned that the risks are greater than the possible benefits. No doubt as a reflection of my own personality and style of behavior, during my year with the Department of Mental Health, not once did I walk "Across the Street" without either being asked by "them" or sent by "us." Rightly or wrongly, I concluded that a state official who is responsible for the placement of citizens in state institutions—where the waiting lists are interminably long and, therefore, there are no waiting lists—should not become too friendly with legislators and should never be in their debt. I entered state service with the impression (from the many stories I had heard) that the "only way" to receive approval for the placement of a person in a state school for the mentally retarded was to enlist the support of a prominent legislator who, in turn, would request such placement through his friends at the Department of Mental Health. Although, during the year, I had numerous such requests from legislators and other state officials, I can honestly claim that *no* person was placed during that year *because* a legislator requested or demanded such placement. Further, at no time did I receive abuse or any form of argumentation from a legislator after we explained to him why an individual should not be placed in the state school or why it was not possible to place that person at that particular time. After it was clearly established how people were to be placed and what the situation was in each state school, we were never confronted with unreasonable demands or requests for special services or special considerations for constituents of specific legislators. I learned that most legislators are very reasonable people and, once the facts of a situation are explained to them and they are satisfied that every possible effort has been or will be extended in behalf of their constituents, they are satisfied to permit the Department to do what it can—whatever that might be—for those for whom they are seeking help. Lastly, I have found that if legislators or other state officials are guaranteed (by your own behavior and reputation) that your office will treat *everyone* equally and without special advantage, they will not press you with demands for unfair consideration. All of the above is to suggest, at least from my viewpoint, that whatever ill will and mistrust exists between one side of our street and the other, much of it is due to a prejudice and ignorance about the other side. My infrequent contacts with the people "Across the Street" found them surprisingly like those on our side of the street, just as reasonable and equally concerned with the distressful conditions confronting us.

It's possible that our office was able to achieve this "state of things" because, not only did we not give special favors, we never asked for them. However, I truly believe that we did achieve this condition— which I believe to have been one of our important achievements that year—because, essentially, executive officers and people in the legislature are, as human beings, no better or worse than other state employees. There is such a complex as "Across the Street" because, I think, people huddle in their own little worlds afraid of the unknown other person and not daring to discover that he is, just, another person.

There exists a dichotomy between the professional staff and the business staff of the department. It is not an "Across the Street" dichotomy but it is an "Upstairs-Downstairs" one. The "Boys Upstairs" are the business office people and "Downstairs"—anywhere or everywhere or "never to be found"—are the "Doctors," the professional people. The differences between these two groups are many and very subtle, and it is neither possible to understand all of these nor possible to adequately discuss the few I do understand. However, it is well known that most professional staff members are on higher salary levels than the business staff and, on the other hand, the business staff have major control of such items as purchasing, new positions, and the interpretation of state and departmental laws and regulations. Many central office professional staff are not "tied down" to a nine-to-five office schedule and, consequently, their whereabouts or activities are varied—some comment, "to say the least." Undoubtedly, suspicion exists among those people who are required to spend most of their working hours at 15 Ashburton Place that some professional staff do not spend all of their required working hours on behalf of the Department of Mental Health and in discharging their responsibilities as state employees. Every now and then, one hears such terms as "private practice," "consulting," "salary supplementation," and "goofing off." At least equally, professional staff members distrust business staff. However, their criticisms run along different directions. Mainly, the professionals whisper or rage about "favoritism," "capriciousness," "unilateral decisions," "high-handedness," "bureaucracy," "paper shuffling," and on and on it goes. To be sure, there are some professional staff (as there are such people everywhere) who abuse their privileges and shamefully neglect their responsibilities. Also, the department has its share (but no more than its share) of bureaucrats, paper shufflers, and those who are plainly unfair. However, I believe that the important controversy (if there is one, and I should hasten to add that there are some who do not believe there is) between professional and business staff in the department revolves about the superior job status of the one group and the superior decision-making authority of the other. I do not know how to go about developing better relationships between these two groups. However, I do believe that, if such relationships are to be developed, the first step is to find more adequate ways to encourage individuals from downstairs and upstairs to interact.

Mental health is an industry and, as with all industries today, it has its unions and union problems. If it would serve a clear purpose, one could relate story after story—true stories that I witnessed or was, in some way, a participant in—concerning the evil influence of unions and union members on our mental health and mental retardation programs. It would be grist for those who buy from the anti-union mill to hear about malfeasance or misfeasance or nonfeasance that was attributable directly to union influence or union members. On the other hand, one can relate equally compelling anecdotes about management and management staff in mental health. Albeit very interesting and extraordinarily entertaining, such stories rarely do any good or shed any light on a situation. It is enough for me to say that I do not view the development of unions in the field of mental health as unmixed blessings; on the other hand, I neither view all of our management or management practices as unmixed blessings. My conviction about the union-management dichotomy is that to the degree unions have taken advantage of management in mental health, management bodies have taken equal advantage of unions. Whether one group is more right or more wrong is both a specious and senseless question. Certainly, there are differences between the two groups. However, I do not believe that these are so much differences between people as they are differences in objectives and, to some extent, differences in means to attain objectives. Certainly, as a group, management is better educated, more highly trained, and better compensated than labor. Certainly, as a group, labor provides more direct resident care and has more resident contact than management. These, and innumerable other differences, we can agree upon. However, I don't believe these are the differences that cause the deep undercurrent of labor unhappiness and distrust and management hostility and fearfulness. On two occasions, I invited the chief state union executive, members of his staff, and union representatives to meet with our central office staff and our superintendents and directors of facilities for the mentally retarded. What was confirmed for me, during these and other meetings, was the continuing theme in all dialogues I've participated in with union members. It isn't higher salaries that they are asking for, not because they don't want (or deserve) higher salaries; salaries are fixed by the legislature, and state departments have absolutely no control of this matter. What union members ask for—continuously—in one way or another, using one type of verbiage or another, is: respect, fair treatment, and honesty in mutual dealings. Time and time again, I listened to union members asking only to be treated with dignity, as human beings, and with appreciation for their efforts and accomplishments. Ironically—possibly, predictably—management is asking for exactly the same things: respect, fair treatment, and honesty in mutual dealings. I have met some union members and local union officials who offend or annoy me. However, so do a few of the so-called management team. While, on the one hand, I have been aghast at certain union stances and practices, I developed, on the other hand, after but one or two meetings a deep respect and trust for the highest state union official in our Commonwealth. I imagine that management will always resist labor and vice versa—and, further, some believe that this is the way things should be in the best of all worlds—but this resistance should be limited to single issues and not be fed by some false image that the other side is "different" and must be treated as an enemy.

In our department, as in all departments that have both consultative and direct service responsibilities, a dichotomy exists between the central office (or regional office) and the field. There are those of us who are responsible for overall supervision, coordination, interdepartmental liaison, and statewide planning. There are others among us who have direct supervisory responsibility for clients or patients. The dichotomy is strong and often heated. Sometimes differences are put in terms of line-staff authority. Less charitably, they are discussed in terms of those who coordinate versus those who do things for people. Superintendents have complained to me that they are on duty seven days a week for 24 hours a day (which, in reality, is impossible) while central office or regional staff are on duty five days a week for eight hours a day. Central office staff claim they must administer and supervise all state programs and all facets of these programs that they are responsible for (which, in reality, is impossible) while superintendents have responsibility for only very limited programs and areas. Essentially, this dichotomy is very similar to the problem continuously facing the researcher with a limited (however generous) budget and resources. To the degree he restricts his sample, he may study more variables and, to the degree he restricts his variables, he may increase his sample. However, there must always be a compromise between the size of the sample one is studying or treating and the extent of involvement with those he is studying or treating. It became clear to me that the true dichotomy between the so-called field and the central office was not one involving different degrees of dedication, responsibility, or hours worked, but one involving small samples versus the entire population, on the one hand, and intensive involvement versus superficial or indirect involvement, on the other hand. If we, in the central office and in the field, could but make our peace with, and understand, the inevitable need to either restrict samples or restrict variables—much as the researcher has made his peace—we might learn that the central office–field dichotomy is, at best, a trivial one and, sometimes, a destructive one. Insofar as I understand the dichotomy of central office–field or staff-line, the important difference is not that one group does "better than" or "more" than does the other group. The important difference is that one group works a little bit for everyone and the other a great deal for a few. There is but a finite amount of time, energy, and talent each man can bring to his work and to his mission. It would seem that, by this time, we could agree that the world is a big place and there should be enough room for anyone who has a serious purpose and a dedication to that purpose.

There are other dichotomies that flow from or to the Department of Mental Health. The separation of the field of mental health from the field of mental retardation is a serious one and, often, causes many problems. Later in this book, a chapter is devoted exclusively to this problem. A similar separation involves the distinction between those who are physicians and those who aren't. This, too, will be treated in the later chapter. At this time, it might be sufficient to relate an illuminating incident. Several years ago, before assuming my position with the department, I was asked by the then Commissioner of Mental Health to serve on a "blue ribbon" committee charged with the development of a plan for a diagnostic and research center in mental retardation for the city of Boston. A member of the committee was one of the most distinguished psychologists in the world, a man whose work I have admired for many, many years. The one contribution he made to our joint effort that I will always remember was the recommendation that this center be constructed adjacent to a medical school and that ramps be built leading from the medical school to the center. Our colleague attempted to impress upon us that, without this contiguity, we could not (nor should not) expect any involvement by medical faculty in this program. He indicated that it was not terribly important whether the center was constructed within easy commuting distance of graduate schools or schools of education or schools of social work. It *had* to be constructed contiguous to a medical center. I do not want to belabor this dichotomy between physicians and non-physicians; nor do I consider myself prejudiced against the medical profession. Having been brought up in a culture that reveres medicine, if anything, I am usually blind to the imperfections in this field that are continuously pointed out to me by much more jaundiced colleagues. Yet I am uneasy sometimes, especially when faced with the kind of situation that occurred recently. In a program quite apart from mental health and mental retardation, several colleagues and I have been studying the education of psychiatrists. As part of this project, we arranged for the supervision of psychiatry residents in a program preparing them to teach. For reasons that are not important to this discussion, it was necessary for a distinguished professor of education to meet with one of the psychiatry residents. The professor of psychiatry suggested to the professor of education that *he* come to the medical school to meet with this student, in view of the student's heavy schedule.

I have heard, time and time again, about differences between parents and professionals. Again, this is undoubtedly a reflection of my own personality and experiences, but I can say very truthfully, that during this past year and—in fact—during my twenty-year career in mental retardation, I have never been confronted by parents' groups with unreasonable requests and I have rarely been confronted by individual parents with unreasonable requests. My experience has been that there are no more—and no fewer—unreasonable parents than there are unreasonable professionals or unreasonable any other group of people.

The most interesting "we-they" phenomenon that I observed during the past year was the "Insider-Outsider" division that is associated with ethnic power. In every large city, where great numbers of immigrant families settled, particular ethnic groups sought opportunities and developed strength in certain professions and with certain departments of civil government or sectors of private industry. As such groups broke down the barriers of discrimination and hostility, their co-religionists or national brethren followed in the footsteps of those who led the way. Thus, in New York City, most of the school teachers and most of the school principals and administrators are Jewish—first, because there are many Jews living in New York City and, second, because the school department was a receptive and "upward mobility" type of organization that the children in the ghetto would predictably aspire toward. In a similar fashion, the Irish came to dominate politics and state civil service in Massachusetts. The Pole has his "bag" in Chicago and the Japanese his in San Francisco. And, yet, saying these words so rationally, and truly believing that we understand them, does not prevent men from discussing the New York City school crisis in terms of Jewish domination and control and does not prevent men from setting black against Jew (lunatic as that sounds) and Jewish teachers against blacks (after the evidence, still absolutely unbelievable). In Massachusetts, we are reputed to have our "Irish Mafia." I believe it exists to the degree that Jewish teachers control the public schools in New York and Japanese grape growers control the valleys of the west coast. In fact or not, however, believing that such an Irish Mafia exists causes the same kinds of difficulty—on both sides of the ethnic fence—as believing Jews control the New York City schools.

It will be no surprise to those who are acquainted with my work to read again that I do not believe men are very different, one from another. I believe that we are different to the degree that living with each other is interesting, more than that, necessary, but not so different that living with each other should ever lead to irreconcilable conflict. Possibly, the following letter, received by me in January of 1969 illustrates the essential interdependence of man and the essential goodness that is found in man—in both the most commonly expected and surprisingly unpredictable places. Possibly, men such as Jim C_____ will, in our generations, teach us the fallacy of the "we-they" syndrome:

Dear Sir:

I am writing to you in response to your most anguishing article. That you published it incomplete, when you obviously had more information should be causing great concern and torment among the mothers, fathers, brothers, and sisters. You have told of and shown me a spectre of horror almost beyond the average person's grasp. I wonder how many people asked, was that my Tommy he saw, was that him cowed and neglected in that cell. Was that my boy that he stood and watched being kicked repeatedly or do they ask as I do, did you see my brother sitting on those bleachers staring at a blank T.V. waiting. . . . It's entirely possible, for my brother is in an institution for the mentally retarded in _____. What is it like there, Doctor. When you, or I should say, when I ask them how he is doing, they assure me that he is getting the best possible care. Just what is the best "possible" care that the State of _____ affords as to the following: hygiene, pleasant surroundings, schools, and training facilities with recreation areas with abundant equipment, competence of the staff as opposed to their position, volunteer organizations, is the administrator politically appointed or the result of competitive examination by a Civil Service board, brutality or unusual "punishment" (i.e., restraint), ratio of staff actually involved directly with the care and supervision of patients to the number of patients. You see, sir, before he was placed or to put it more accurately, railroaded and abandoned for some nebulous reason that my parents are procrastinating about, well, anyway, they put him in _____ Mental Hospital, _____ and I still don't know why. He wasn't violent or hard to handle, although you had to watch him pretty close or he would be into something which would be normal for a child of his mentality. Well I suppose that you are familiar with _____'s mental health program. It's the best going. How do you think of moving him from a known pleasant and healthy environment to _____? I think that if it is not a progressive institution where he will be loved and cared for properly I can put enough pressure on my parents to get him out. I'm in a pretty bad place myself, and I'll be here for a long time, but as they say, I brought it on myself. But any hell that my brother is going through is because of my parents and not because he did anything wrong. Obviously I'm not in any position to demand anything, though I am a criminal and must live behind walls of stone and steel, I still have feelings. I still believe in justice. I still believe in helping those who can't help themselves. I laugh, I cry, I feel compassion, tenderness, hurt and shame though I am a crook, a criminal, and the scum of the earth in the eyes of God and common man. I guess I'm still human too. For I want to help my brother if he needs help, but not only him, but the tens of thousands of others less fortunate than myself. I can't do much, I suppose, compared to others, but I can do something. Thank you for reading my letter. Let me know what I can do to help.

Respectfully yours,
Jim C_____

The Meretricious System and Uncivil Service

The beautiful concepts of the merit system and the civil service, concepts that are basic to our fundamental form of democratic government, have fallen on evil days. There is not very much I want to, or can, say about merit in state government and the civil service system. However, I do believe that we must find a better way to recruit, select, promote, and encourage state civil servants—from the most unskilled level to positions requiring highest attainments in education and experience. We must face squarely the knowledge that time is always on the side of the mediocre and a system based on "putting in one's time" for promotion, more favorable assignments and duties, and other benefits is a system that promotes mediocrity; it is a system that programs for and reinforces slothfulness and inefficiency and, consequently, these are the products it deserves. Why should having served in the military for 25 years have anything to do with one's standing on a civil service list for chief social worker or chief psychologist? Does a system make sense that requires all new attendant employees to work every weekend, every holiday, and the least attractive "shifts" so that employees with seniority may receive all weekends and holidays off and may work the most desirable shifts? Especially, in the face of severe staff shortages at our state schools, can such a system be justified when prospective employees are eager to accept positions but not under conditions they deem intolerable. Yet, we continue to permit these policies, on the one hand, and decry the sixty vacancies for attendants at the state school, on the other hand. I don't have any better answers to these problems than other people have proposed. Further, in principle, I support a merit system and the concepts of civil service. However, I do not believe that our system today has merit— both as a system and as a way to reward deserving employees. Nor do I believe that the civil service is anything but another kind of spoils system, one that's different from Boss Tweed's but one that is now based on similar operating principles for the purpose of achieving similar objectives

Defining Governmental Utopia

I worry for planners who plan for a livelihood, that is those whose major assignments are to plan. All too often, I have observed and participated with them in planning changes in our state programs for the mentally retarded, and found they are given neither the resources nor encouragement to implement these changes. As a result, we have a great many thoughtful, oftentimes exquisite, plans that lie fallow gathering dust on administrators' bookshelves or on desks buried under avalanches of reports of commissions and reports of advisory boards. The life of decision-makers would be happier and more productive if they had environments at their disposal that permitted both planning *and* implementation. All organizations are in a constant flux and, at any one time, represent a balance between the stability of the System and the pressure for change. To me, governmental utopia would provide a System that is stable—i.e., a System that is reliable and tested, one that can be counted upon to deliver goods and services—while it would always have at its command options to change parts of the System radically or the entire structure of the System evolutionally. For me, governmental utopia means stability and comfort and reliance, on the one hand, and options and dynamism, on the other hand. While it is quite understandable that we have not achieved utopia, it is regrettable, to the extreme, that we are barely on the right road. Our optimism must lie in the knowledge that now, at least, we may have stumbled onto that road. I believe we have, or people such as myself would never have been permitted to study the things we have studied and say the things we are saying.

chapter 11

LEAVES FROM A EUROPEAN DIARY[1]

August 27, 1968: 2:00 A.M. Natick, Mass.   One year ago today, Edward (then aged 13), Steven (10), Michael (7), my wife Ethel and I, boarded a plane for return home to Natick, Massachusetts. Our trip had begun on June 11, and during the ensuing eleven weeks we visited the Scandinavian countries, the British Isles, Luxemburg, France, Austria and, for seven weeks, West Germany. Of all the places on Earth, why should we set foot in that dread land, that inspired Dachau, Auschwitz, Treblinka, and ONE HUNDRED OTHERS?

Several years ago, Boston University developed overseas graduate programs in a few selected fields, primarily for servicemen and teachers assigned to American dependent schools in the European theater. One such program is in the field of education and I had been asked to teach my course "Nature and Needs of the Mentally Retarded" during one of the summer sessions sponsored in Germany. After considerable family discussion, over a period of several months, we agreed to participate in this program. The plan was for all of us to travel to Munich for a briefing period early in June,

---

1 Some readers, mostly younger ones, may be puzzled about the inclusion of a chapter concerning a summer trip to Germany in a book on human abuse. Although they have read about Nazi Germany, the Holocaust is about as removed from their lives as the American Revolution is from ours. Those readers, the author asks to accept—on faith—the logic supporting such inclusion.

119

drive to Heidelberg for participation in the graduation ceremonies for the preceding year's students, teach a three week intensive course in Stuttgart, and return to Munich for a repeat of the Stuttgart course. At the conclusion of that assignment, we would have one full month remaining for travel through Scandinavia and the British Isles.

What were the advantages, as we envisioned them then, and what were the liabilities of such a plan? The opportunity presented would permit our family to spend three months together, much of this time free to explore, to visit the museums, to enjoy the scenery and countryside. This opportunity would permit a retreat, albeit temporary, from what had been a very rigorous year and what was expected to be a continuation of work pressure and personal demands once the new academic calendar and schedule dominated the fall season.

Why did we hold back, have reservations about this trip, refuse an identical invitation of the previous year? It was Germany! Why couldn't we be asked to teach in France, or England, or—better yet—Israel? That which at first had made us hesitant about going to Germany later made me resolute, determined to live for a period of time in that land. I must admit that my determination to go to Germany, once I had made up my mind, was a minority position in our household, as well as a selfish one. Further, my reasons for this determination did not fully crystallize until we were firmly ensconced in that country. From the time when the possibility of a summer in Germany first presented itself until our plane landed in Munich, I had been slowly—but increasingly —developing the notion that it would be important for me to observe and study the German people, in light of the holocaust of the 30's and 40's, a period in history to which I had become morbidly attached. It was not until several weeks after our arrival that I began to think seriously, in fact regularly, about the striking correlates of Nazi Germany and its concentration camps and American mental health and its institutions for the retarded. That summer in Europe gave me a perspective of things that increases in importance as I review them.

It is hoped that this presentation of selected passages from that summer's diary—impressions recorded not with any thought for eventual publication but in keeping with the roles we were assuming as travelers and tourists—will contribute something toward comprehending mankind's capabilities for destruction, and the conditions that appear to be present during these periodic barbarisms in which human beings participate. I had already spent considerable time observing attendants in some of our most wretched back wards. I have spoken to these men and women, calmly and rationally, eye to eye. Now, I wanted to observe the German citizen, speak to him calmly and rationally, eye to eye. I wanted to visit Dachau and try to understand what was then—and now—an incomprehensible and fiendish period of inhuman history. Certainly, these excerpts can make no pretension insofar as unraveling the puzzle of The Third Reich or understanding the German culture as it is known today. Far more sophisticated and erudite attempts toward these kinds of understandings are available to the reader. However, these impressions may be useful within the context of a book on human abuse. There is no doubt in my mind, after reading too many histories and personal accounts of the German death camps, that the Germany of our generations will be recorded as the most savage, inhuman, ungodlike tribe ever to inhabit this Earth, the likes of which we pray will never be seen again. For one interested in the foundations of human abuse, in retrospect, it seems clear that the German people should be studied from every angle possible, with even an *ex post facto* analysis likely to prove valuable.

June 17, 1967: 6:15 P.M. Bayrischer Hauf, Heidelberg

Most aspiring Germans carry briefcases. I am told these are used to store lunch and other necessities. Usually, middle class workers—both male and female—carry these briefcases, although some blue collar workers also find them valuable accessories. Those blue collar workers that do not carry briefcases, oftentimes an "old time factory hand" or "laborer," generally wear what we in America call "laboratory coats." Some workers wear boots and knickerbockers. All bellhops wear green aprons and bus and street car conductors have uniforms identical to my stereotyped conception of a German military officer. It must be an overreaction, but my impressions lead to the conclusion that there is some design to all of this.

June 20,
1967:
3:45 P.M.
Robinson
Kaserne,
Stuttgart

From a few discussions and observations, it is clear that the Germans build private homes to last at least a hundred years. It isn't unusual for a family to buy a modest home, which is terribly expensive, after many years of saving. Unfortunately, the family cannot possibly keep up the mortgage payments with their family income. So they buy the house to rent it, using income from the rental to meet mortgage payments. During these many years of mortgage obligations, the family that owns the home lives in a small apartment elsewhere or in a small section of the house, oftentimes the basement. The plan is to complete the mortgage payments sometime before the retirement of the head of the household when, at that time, the family moves into their "new home."

One may ask why this is necessary in order, eventually, to own a home. And why is housing so expensive? One would think that the Germans—especially the Germans—would have the affluence to be able to afford to purchase, and live in, homes in the same way that Americans do. I don't have the depth to understand the so-called German mentality, if there is such a special mentality. However, I do know that their homes are built to last many generations. The walls are very thick, the doors appear to be designed for banks, the window sashes and other woodwork are hand cut on the building site. It seems that, in order to sell a home in Deutschland, the builder must: make it strong, thick, aplastic, sensible, dark, and functional. Don't make it fragile, elegant, or graceful. What that country might need is a Levitt and a Levittown. It seems to me that, especially in Germany, less permanent-type homes would be an appealing economy. There doesn't seem to be much point in building a home to last a hundred years, while, at the same time, preparing for or waging wars that destroy the homes every thirty years.

June 23,
1967:
1:15 A.M.
77 Lembach
Strasse,
Stuttgart

We spent the best part of a beautiful day in Killesberg Park, a short walk from our house. This park is dedicated to the millions of Jews killed in German concentration camps and, ironically, it must be the most beautiful park we had ever been in. The Germans enjoy and take care of their parks, which are very safe and comforting. Everywhere around us is kindness, consideration, dignity, and contentment. The Germans are not arrogant about their language. Unlike the

French (so we've been told) they will try to understand you and help you if you make an attempt to speak their language. They have no false pride, so it seems, when confronted with a fumbling tourist who is trying to communicate while relying on long forgotten high school German and faint remembrances of a grand-mother's Yiddish. How could these kind, thrifty, and bright people have participated in such horror? Killes-berg Park, and the people we encountered there, do not make sense in the light of history.

July 8, 1967:
7:00 P.M.
The Grand
Hotel,
Nuremberg

In this city where the Trials were held, I compared my daily observations of black GI's with the riots and troubles in the States that are reported here daily. I have noticed—possibly wrongly—that the black GI in Germany is less alienated, less alone, more integrated in the Army than in Boston, Massachusetts, or any-where else in civilian life with which I am acquainted. I have noticed no special groups of black GI's, but rather, blacks and whites together. I don't want this reaction to appear to be something it shouldn't. However, com-pared to what I have seen in the United States, black GI's in Germany seem to have a better deal than black civilians in New Jersey.

Why do we have prejudice? This diary, now to the point of embarrassment, continues to disclaim any special insights or depth concerning the questions raised. However, I have noticed that most of the pov-erty, misery, and suffering in the world is in the South-ern Hemisphere. So-called "civilization" is in the North-ern Hemisphere. Color seems to be less important as a determiner of either income or racial bias than is place of residence. Men of color populate the Northern Hem-isphere and are not viewed—because of their color—in pejorative ways, e.g. the Chinese and Japanese. It al-most seems as if color isn't inferior; the South is or the heat is. White isn't superior; the cold is. What might be needed is not more civil rights legislation but a good cold wave in the Southern Hemisphere or continent-to-continent air-conditioning.

What are the trappings of the favored? Geograph-ically, living in the temperate zone is tremendously im-portant, probably necessary. We must also include such items as: a religion, preferably Christianity; whiteness; cleanliness; the written word, monogamy; and taking the past seriously (e.g. museums, antiques, catalogues, tours). Symptoms of the favored are ties, briefcases, symbolic expressions of wealth, Culture. Most of the favored can be located in Western Europe, the British Isles, North America (with the possible exception of Mexico), and Japan, which is becoming White in attitude. The USSR will soon be as favored as any nation and is now, practically "White." China is "Red." Soon they will be colored "White." Find a little "Blue" and you have Old Glory, McCarran Act and all.

July 11, 1967:
5:15 P.M.
McGraw
Kaserne,
Munich

We went to Dachau today. It's a short, pleasant drive on the autobahn from Munich to Dachau, really just a few kilometers before reaching the autobahn exit sign "Dachau." After a drive of about four kilometers through level farmland, you arrive in the middle of the town. We stopped a passing pedestrian, asking, "Pardon, wo ist der koncentrazion kamp?" in our best school German and pidgin Yiddish-English-gesture. No response! Possibly, the pedestrian was a stranger in Dachau or didn't understand you. So, you ask again, and again, and again. You don't give up. You ask, in a German dialect that had been very well understood until now, "Where is the concentration camp where 200,000 Jews, French, and clergymen from many nations were tortured during the years 1933–1945?" You ask, "Where in your town are the crematorium and mass graves?" Finally there is an answer from a man you were able to intimidate sufficiently to respond to your, by now, enraged questions. "Ah! Sie gehen zu dem Americana kamp!" You don't understand the answer but you get the directions and, within a kilometer or two, you are standing at the entrance to the infamous Dachau KZ.

Certain things must be cleared up. Is this Kamp so unknown to the local population or is our German so poor that our inability to locate the camp was the result of unintentional roadblocks—nonfeasance rather than malfeasance? What did my informer mean by "the Americana kamp"? I'll try to answer those questions, and hopefully unravel a number of puzzles that confronted us this morning in Dachau. First, anyone who lives in Dachau must know exactly where the concentration camp is and how to get there. Literally, one can see the camp from parts of the town. Secondly, to date, more than 300,000 people from 30 different countries have visited the camp. Since the camp had been developed as a memorial and museum, it appeared impossible that any citizen of this small town had not been asked directions to the camp on innumerable occasions. The most frequent answer I received to my question for directions to the Kamp was, "Es gibt kein koncentrazion kamp hier in Dachau." ("There is no camp . . .") Lastly, the Kamp is called the "Americana Kamp" by the townspeople because, after World War II, our army occupied Germany and, to this date, we have not returned this camp to the German Republic. That is, in a legal and technical sense, the Dachau Concentration Camp is an American camp. This is one instance where changing the label cannot remove the history or the stench of the product.

July 12, 1967:
10:35 A.M.
17 Badel-
schwingh
Strasse,
Munich

More on Dachau. The first German concentration camp was opened here on March 22, 1933. During the ensuing 12 years, 13 million defenseless human beings were slaughtered by the flower of Germany. There is little I can say that hasn't already been much more eloquently said. What struck us, really hit us hard, was the list in the museum of all the concentration camps and the destruction each had wrought. Imagine, over 100 such hells strategically placed both in Germany and conquered nations! As you visit the crematorium, the grave sites, and the memorials—as you examine the documents on display in the museum—over and over is the reminder "Remember us. Do not forget." You see a warning to the living, for all time to come or until there are no longer any people, "Help us to testify of the past. Help us to protect the future." And as you see pictures that, two generations later, can torture, you ask "How can anyone have participated in such barbarism?" And when you look out across the bucolic splendor of Bavaria, passing idle moments in pleasant conversation with a good man, a decent and honest German, answers don't come easily.

How can these good Germans continue to live in the town of Dachau, with a constant reminder of their inhuman past? How can a young family move into a new garden apartment, a couple of hundred yards from the entrance to the concentration camp? How can the townspeople claim ignorance of what transpired in a camp located on Route 471 that existed for a dozen years, almost in the middle of the town? How can they plead ignorance and why do we believe them? It's too frightening to remember the terror they participated in and it's too frightening for us to disclaim their inocence. Human beings can understand—even tolerate—pathology or sickness among some of our less fortunate. However, it is probably too terrible to contemplate an evil such as Germany perpetrated. A conspiracy of the sick and degenerate and psychopathic is unpleasant but manageable. We must remove these sick ones from the mass, the healthy, the group that can be called human beings. A conspiracy of this kind led by the cream of the nation, the harvest of its years of toil and drudgery, is an affront to all mankind. It is an assault on our personal eminence as human beings and it demonstrates what man is capable of, given certain conditions and opportunities.

To understand Nazi Germany—to comprehend what drove them to their terrible misdeeds—will lead to our understanding the treatment of blacks in the United States, our past treatment of the American Indians, and the care we provide for the mentally retarded in the back wards of our state institutions. To understand Nazi Germany, or to understand the background to any of the evils mentioned, is to help unravel what I consider the most important and basic problem known to man. What are the conditions required before a man can abuse another man? I cannot believe that the abuse of individuals or, for that matter, the abuse of groups proceeds in a random or haphazard manner. I believe that the proper study of human abuse will reveal a theory leading to understanding the factors that give rise to it. The results of this study may, some day, provide us with ways to prevent human abuse or—at the very least—sublimate or mitigate mankind's apparent need to inflict pain and cruelty.

July 17, 1967:
9:20 A.M.
Bachelor
Officer's
Quarters,
Garmish

We were invited to the Casa Carioca International Ice Review last night by two friends we had met in the States. After what really was a most enjoyable ice show, all of us went to a local restaurant for coffee. We talked about many things, including responsibility, even had a mild argument. The husband is an unusual man who has remained a classroom teacher for many years despite strong pressures from government school authorities to promote him to one or another administrative post. I understand completely his decision in this matter, and both congratulate him and agree with his logic. However, the point I made to him was that if part of his decision were dictated by an absence of any personal ambition, then I should understand with reluctance and regret. People who have little personal ambition may be as dangerous to society, possibly more so, as those who have driving personal ambition. People without ambition, but with talent, abrogate the positions they should have taken (or sought) to those with the ambition (but not always with the talent). One shouldn't overstate the line of this logic but, in these troubled times, one must at least raise the question as to how much individual freedom a man has in accepting or rejecting responsibility. There may be a kind of collective concern that each individual must respect with whatever insight he has to bring to bear on the decision.

We discussed Dachau with them; the husband had visited there, and his German wife had lived in Munich during the war. His wife, who is a wonderful woman, doesn't appear to feel any more personal guilt about such places as Dachau than most Americans would feel about institutions in the States where atrocities have been known to occur. I believe she feels a kind of responsibility as a citizen of the Third Reich. However, I don't believe she feels any individual responsibility for Hitler, the KZ, or the 13 million humans slaughtered. Who can fault her? The ambivalence and vacillation between the horror I saw at Dachau and the horrors I am acquainted with in the United States trouble me and, at the same time, permit me to understand something about how abusive situations are allowed to arise and to continue unchecked by "civilized" people. Don't most of us in the United States deny any individual responsibility for the "black problem," the "migrant worker problem," and the problem of back wards in state institutions?

July 20, 1967:
11:30 A.M.
17 Badel-
schwingh
Strasse,
Munich

We had a marvelous day yesterday visiting the great Munich art museum, Alte Pinakothek, with George and Julie Tsiramokes. George is a major in the Air Force, stationed with the American consulate in Munich. Some random thoughts: (1) Why are we surprised with reports of brutality, murder, and terror coming from the emerging African countries? After spending a day at the incredible Alte Pinakothek, one must become convinced that the relationship between Culture and Decency is a very obscure one, if it exists at all. It is probably true that the Germans weren't cannibals. Their industrial inventiveness led them to manufacture lamp shades. (2) Toilets in public places are sometimes free to the user, but more often there is a charge of ten to twenty pfennigs. At such public toilets where there is a charge, the attendant on duty is usually an old lady. This woman, anywhere from seventy to eighty years old, lurches about the foul smelling men's room, placing the fees collected in nondescript, grubby looking folds of clothing. It seems to be an affront to the dignity of old age to permit someone (anyone) to work at this occupation. First, the smell is horrid (which questions the tradition of German cleanliness). Second, it desexualizes this woman who, by the very nature of her work, is either a disinterested observer of male genitalia or a female voyeur (a neat trick at eighty). On the other hand, after occasional visits to nursing homes in the United States, it is difficult to decide which of the two would be the more appealing existence. (3) Every day, I have been reading reports of riots in Newark and Detroit and New York. Today, suburbia is good; the city is not good. It hasn't always been that way. Most of us can remember when the "poor" countryman left the farm for the luxury and richness of the city. When he came in sufficient numbers to the city, the wealthy cityman (whom the countryman came to emulate) moved to the country. Now certain urbanologists are suggesting that we take undeveloped suburban areas and plan housing for the poor. If this succeeds too well, it will only drive the middle and upper classes back to the city. The favored land is where the favored are, not necessarily where the birds are.

July 25, 1967:
3:00 P.M.
17 Badel-
schwingh
Strasse,
Munich

We will be leaving Germany in less than forty-eight hours for Scandinavia and, then, on to the British Isles. What has it been like to spend seven weeks in Germany? Our daily existence forgives the Germans for what they have done. Our hearts and our minds—even our so-called logic—can't forgive. We play the part as they, in another way, play theirs. We are civilized to them, engage them in pleasant conversation, feel—for the moment—very warmly towards them. They have been the most polite of all the Europeans during our limited experience here. Surprisingly, we have been most comfortable with them. They are not arrogant about their language and customs, easily forgive the frequent mistakes that tourists are wont to make, and are honest and reliable people.

But, we must never forget what they did. We may forgive individuals but we must never forgive the Third Reich. We must be remorseless and relentless. No one can give us a "testament" to insure remembrance, as others have been given testaments to insure other thoughts and deeds for all the ages. Our individual zeal to remember and to pass on what transpired here must be in our "mortal to mortal" and, thus, "immortal" insurance.

August 30, 1968: Natick, Mass.

I have just completed the preparation of this chapter taken from my diary of last summer in Europe. One particular thought keeps returning to my mind, a thought I heard chanted continuously two nights ago. "The whole world is watching, the whole world is watching." Those brave words, chanted by the demonstrators on the Chicago streets as the television cameras recorded it all, did not stop the policemen's clubs, the gas, and the strong-armed forces of Mayor Daley's order, if not law. Now that the whole world has observed, what will we do? History has taught me that the chances are excellent we will do nothing. Good German citizens did nothing. The Northern White liberal did nothing. The humanitarian Chicagoan will do nothing. I am fearful that the administrator of the back ward will do nothing.

The more I study the problem of human abuse, the more convinced I become that the ancient Chinese proverb, "Virtue is not knowing, but doing," is as profound as any words put together by man. Further, I am persuaded that unless we find better ways to convince the man-who-knows that knowing isn't enough, our children's children will pay homage to memorials yet to be conceived, protesting horrors yet to be imagined. For too long, the good people have sought solace from human outrage in their religions or have told their troubles to the wall. Possibly, this is the time we might convince ourselves that our protection and salvation on Earth is with each other. We must tell each other and must act on behalf of each other.

chapter 12
JIMMY[1]

In early December of 1965, a professional matter required my presence at a state school. For reasons that are not germane to this report, my specific purpose was to observe in the "back wards." I met Jimmy during that visit. He was a resident of the dormitory housing the most severely retarded male adult ambulatory residents. It was a visit that I do not expect to ever forget. However, unlike so many other visits I made, it had a very happy ending.

An attendant was our guide during that tour of K Building. I noticed that few residents were on the ground floor or the dormitory floor above. I asked the attendant where all of the other people were and she said, "Have patience. We're going to see them now." We descended a flight of stairs, walked along a dark passageway and came to a heavy metal locked door. In an instant, out came the inevitable key chain and ring of keys, a wrist turned, we bolted forward, the door closed behind us, and—in an instant—I observed the transmogrification of the sane and stable world I knew to the Day Room of K Building. I had been to many back wards and many Day Rooms but never before, or never since, had I ever seen or felt or smelled the clamor, the grotesqueness, the animal-like environment of this Day Room.

It is a large room, possibly 50′ x 50′, maybe larger, maybe smaller. The walls are made of a grayish white tile, the kind you see in hospitals or other Day Rooms. The windows are glass bricks, not really opaque

1 The author is grateful to Sumner Rotman, who, during much of Jimmy's recent development, was principal psychologist at the state school, and Dr. Edward Meshorer, superintendent there. Both encouraged me to learn more about their Hospital Improvement Program and provided the case material necessary to prepare this chapter.

but, on the other hand, permitting only light to pass through. The floor is constructed of a terrazzo-like substance. I remember that there is a metal pole rising from the floor to the ceiling, somewhere near the center of the Day Room. In recent days, during the preparation of this chapter, I have been haunted by my complete inability to remember anything more about this pole—except, to think now, how ludicrous it seems to construct a metal pole in the center of a Day Room for severely retarded residents. Along the walls of the Day Room are several wooden benches, very sturdily constructed and each capable of seating five to six adults.

Sitting on benches, standing around, sitting on the floor, pacing back and forth, lying on the floor, huddled in corners, standing by the door, mumbling, shrieking, laughing, crying, stony silent, fifty to sixty residents were crowded into that Day Room. About half of these men were completely nude; about half wore some garment or another. Of the latter group, one man had a baggy pair of pants, a double-breasted sport coat, no shirt, no underwear, no socks or shoes. Another man wore pajama pants and a Harris Tweed sport jacket, 1930 vintage. A third man had another double-breasted sport coat, nothing else. Another man wore dungaree pants and, instead of a shirt, another pair of pants wrapped around his shoulders. Those that used belts had pieces of rope or neckties for this purpose. Some had shoes—or one shoe—without socks; some had socks and no shoes. One or two men wore hats, nothing else.

Standing to the side, taking distance and observing this scene whose scenario might have been written by Lewis Carroll or Maxim Gorky or Dante, were two attendants—one male and one female. Yes, reader, I too was startled to find a female attendant in this dormitory, although it is not surprising that this institution will employ women in such positions since staff are desperately hard to get.

Each in a spotless white uniform, the two attendants stood off to the side, staring imperiously at the residents and, after we had entered, at us too. They did not come forward to introduce themselves to us, their manner suggesting to me that there was no point to any gesture we might make in this vein. The two attendants stood rigid, indomitable, spotless, and unsullied by the chaos surrounding them or by our intrusion into their special world. After several minutes of wandering amid the debris of the Day Room, my eye caught a closed solid door. I turned the knob, trying to open it. It was locked. I walked the thirty or forty feet to the male attendant (some kind of embarrassment prevented me from meeting the eye of the female attendant, much less speaking with her). My first words, ever, to this attendant—we had not, in any way, been introduced to each other nor had our presence been acknowledged by either attendant—were, "What's on the other side of this door?". The attendant replied that the door led to a toilet facility. I asked him if he would open it. He told me that the door had to remain locked because, during the day, it served as a seclusion room for a very destructive and dangerous twenty-year-old resident. I asked the attendant to please open the door so that I might see this resident. He explained, with some exasperation, that Jimmy was an unmanageable, quite strong resident and it would be best not to unlock and open the door. In a mild, but stubborn, way I persisted and, reluctantly, the attendant unlocked and opened the door. Before the door could be opened fully, out streaked a completely nude man. He ran here, then there, then back here again, then to some other place. There did not appear to be any thought to his movement or any language to the sounds he was making. He was tall, well built, without any apparent organicity or physical stigmata—with one exception. He had an enormous tongue, which kept darting out and in much like a snake's. I never did learn the clinical syndrome associated with this anomaly, if there is such a syndrome. It is enough to say here that Jimmy's tongue was (and still is) the largest tongue I have ever seen and it would flabbergast me to ever see another one like it again.

Jimmy did not remain very long out of the toilet room. Unfortunately, soon after his release to the Day Room, he ran to a nude man who was sitting on one of the benches. I had singled out this resident before because he had an enormous ulcerated lesion on his shoulder. It was uncovered and without any apparent medication on it. The lesion was about four or five inches in diameter, quite bloody, and pus oozed from it. While the man sat, rocking back and forth on the bench, Jimmy snatched at his shoulder and began to suck on this festering ulcer, his tongue swilling up the cankerous rot. My companion and I viewed this in stark horror, he blanching and looking as if he was about to faint. I, not in very much better condition, turned away with a horrified look at the attendant. The attendant, immediately, walked to Jimmy and firmly, in a way gently, disengaged him from the rocking resident and guided him back to the toilet room, locking the door as he closed it.

After things had settled down, both attendants began to explain to us why they had to keep Jimmy locked up in the toilet room. The tones of their explanations made it very clear that, had we heeded their advice and minded our own business, this incident would never have happened—which is, obviously, quite true. We learned that Jimmy, now twenty years of age, was admitted to the state school at the age of three. On presentation to the state school, he was evaluated as "grossly retarded." The etiology was never clarified and he was classified as "undifferentiated etiology, functional diagnosis of idiot." We learned that, prior to his placement at the state school, Jimmy's early history was quite uneventful until his eighth month. At that time, he became quite hyperactive, chewed anything he could get his hands on, threw things out of the window, turned on gas jets, attacked other children and, literally, required twenty-four hour supervision and care. His bizarre behavior attracted so much adverse attention and notoriety that his mother was forced to move a number of times, being evicted from one apartment after another. By the age of three, his mother's health was at the breaking point and Jimmy was finally admitted to the state school. We learned, during this discussion with the dormitory attendants, that Jimmy's mother rarely visited him. In fact, in recent years he received no visitors at all.

I did not see Jimmy again until the spring of 1968. However, I had learned that shortly after my visit, the state school received a grant under the provisions of the federal Hospital Improvement Program. The purpose of the grant was to develop a program to maximize the functioning of 250 profoundly retarded residents, Jimmy included. Specifically, through the use of operant conditioning principles and techniques—including a graduated reward system from food reinforcement to token and vending machine reinforcement—individual resident programs were designed which emphasized the acquisition of eating, dressing, and toilet skills.

This program in behavior modification was spearheaded by two individuals at the state school—one the superintendent and, the other, the principal psychologist—who, to paraphrase Sarason, have a concept of human potential and an attitude toward innovation with the mentally retarded which is optimistic (not pessimistic) and who believe that all human beings have the potential to change and that all human beings—including people such as Jimmy—are capable of learning and improving their functional behavior. This superintendent, fairly recently appointed, and the principal psychologist rallied around them a group of dedicated and zealous workers, including one senior physician, the director of nurses, a nursing supervisor, and a teacher. For sixteen hours each day, the trainees (as these former back ward outcasts were now called) were given a great deal more attention than ever before, much more staff time and thoughtfulness, and a very special environment created for *their* needs. The barren Day Room of K Building was transformed into an activity room, where people spoke to one another and were clothed, where there was genuine human interaction, where gymnastic and other learning equipment was available and used, where there were books and records and things to do—and places to go and music to hear and something to learn. In the spring of 1968, I visited the state school to observe and discuss the progress these most severely retarded residents were making in the Hospital Improvement Program. I was especially interested in Jimmy, hoping that the reports I received periodically concerning him were not overly exaggerated and not daring to remember the circumstances surrounding my last observation of him. Before discussing that visit and a summary of Jimmy's activities in the Hospital Improvement Program, it may be helpful to review, in some modest detail, Jimmy's history at the state school between the years of his admission and his entrance into the Hospital Improvement Program in December of 1965.

Jimmy's History: 1948–1965

As mentioned previously, Jimmy was admitted to the state school in 1948, when he was three years and three months old, and diagnosed as having a mental age of one year and seven months and an I.Q. of 38. Initially, he was placed in a dormitory of so-called "crib cases," where he was regarded as a constant menace to the other children. One attendant recalled that Jimmy's crib was often turned upside down by an attendant, so as to protect the other residents from him. Probably, this was Jimmy's first acquaintance with seclusion although, undoubtedly, in subsequent years he experienced every form of seclusion, restraint, and punishment. Two years after admission to the state school, in 1950, he was re-tested, with a mental age now of seven months and an I.Q. of 11. Between that testing and 1966 (sixteen years later) he had not been evaluated, staffed, or programmed in any way that could be discerned from a review of his records or interview with staff members who had known Jimmy during those years.

The following comments were abstracted by the principal psychologist from reports and notations recorded, during the years, by physicians for inclusion in Jimmy's medical file. These vignettes provide an extraordinarily illuminating picture of Jimmy during that sixteen-year period, which he endured, and which others suffered through:

> 1948 . . . . A three-year-old colored boy brought to the school today by mother. Mother stated that child puts everything into his mouth, has no sense of danger and will deliberately run in front of automobiles.
>
> 1949 . . . . James requires supervision at all times, very untidy, no improvement.
>
> 1950 . . . . James likes to bother other children, does not go to school.
>
> 1951 . . . . Patient is a very active child, runs and yells most of the time, requires constant supervision, does not go to any entertainment.
>
> 1952 . . . . Jimmy is untidy and runs away from the building if not watched.
>
> 1953 . . . . Hard to manage, requires constant supervision.
>
> 1954 . . . . Will not keep clothes on. Requires care of an infant. Cannot talk, is noisy and cries a great deal. Cannot find his place at table or bed, runs and jumps all the time, licks walls, floors, or any furniture with tongue.
>
> 1955 . . . . Jumping and screaming, grabs for other boys.

1956 . . . . Very active, will not stay in bed or at the table while eating, will not keep clothes on.

1957 . . . . Hard to control him long enough to eat.

1958 . . . . Destroys everything in building. Getting more active and destructive.

1959 . . . . Jimmy continues to be a major problem in the building. Most staff members are afraid of him.

1960 . . . . Very active and destructive. "Colored boy idiot."

1961 . . . . Most destructive, no schooling, no change or improvement.

1962 . . . . Noisy, runs over and under beds, destroys blankets, hits his arms against his body and spanks his feet as he runs. He seems to be getting worse as he gets older and stronger.

1963 . . . . Pulls pillows, sweaters, anything made of wool, every chance he gets. Climbs out of shower unit window and jumps over the fence and runs around the grounds in the nude.

1964 . . . . Patient is kept secluded most of the day. Picks scabs from the other children and eats them. Runs wild and escapes over the fence if let out and goes to rubbish barrel. Pulls his tongue out of his mouth and likes to lick people.

1965 . . . . Jimmy bites other boys and sucks the blood from the wounds. He mostly has to be kept separated from the other patients. He is very hyperactive, has no speech and pays no attention to commands. Is not toilet trained.

1966 . . . . Numerous mannerisms, rituals, stamping of feet, licking of objects, pulling tongue twice as long as a normal tongue. For the first time has had a grand mal seizure; may have been due to medication. EEG report is not compatible with a seizure pattern.

I was made acutely aware of the variety and frequency of injuries that befall a resident in a back ward after reviewing a compilation of Jimmy's misfortunes, prepared by the aforementioned principal psychologist. On the other hand, knowing something about Jimmy and his behavior and something else again about the nature and quality of the supervision and attention given him during his years in K Building, the following documentation of Jimmy's "accidents and injuries" does not really surprise me, nor should it surprise any reader who has had even a limited experience observing in our so-called back wards:

July, 1955 . . . . Patient threw a hammer at Jimmy's right foot; deep laceration inner left ankle.

April, 1958 . . . . Contused right second toe, banged foot against a door.

October, 1958 . . . . Patient threw Jimmy against wall in shower area. Left upper central tooth missing.

December, 1958 . . . . Patient has two ecchymotic eyes (black and blue) that he did not have on November 29.

April, 1961 . . . . Patient under treatment. Infection inner aspect left thigh.

May, 1962 . . . . Patient admitted to hospital; fractured hip.

August, 1964 . . . . Edema of nose.

August, 1964 . . . . While playing in the ward, James fell on the floor and cut upper lip. Received a small cut inside of his upper lip.

October, 1964 . . . . James reported missing from building. A short time later found in locker room. Broke several bottles of creolin.

February, 1965 . . . . While jumping about, fell forward, knocking out upper right central and lateral incisors.

The above physicians' notations all were recorded between the year 1948, when he entered the state school, and his entrance into the Hospital Improvement Program in January of 1966. At the time of his placement in the H.I.P. program, Jimmy had been for many years a resident in K Building, where I had first observed him. Traditionally, this building housed adult male profoundly retarded residents and, in January of 1966, it had a complement of 135 residents cared for by twelve attendants. For those readers who are not acquainted with institutional shifts, days off, absences due to sicknesses, etc., a total complement of twelve attendants never permits any more than two or three attendants on duty in a building at any one time.

1966–1968

In January of 1966, Jimmy was one of the four most severely retarded adult residents at the state school selected to enter the Hospital Improvement Program. At the time, the staff of K Building evaluated him as unmanageable, destructive, denudative, and aggressive. He was unable to demonstrate any self-help skills involving eating, dressing, and toileting. He would defecate and urinate in the activity room and its surroundings, he would steal food in the dining room, he was completely and totally uncontrollable. The following are abstracted notations, prepared by the principal psychologist, covering the period from January, 1966 to February, 1968. It should be noted here—and will be revealed to the reader in a moment or two—that residents such as Jimmy, individuals who have started with so little and have suffered through so much, do not change very easily or quickly. However, change they do—at least, Jimmy did. (The parentheses in the following chronicle are this writer's, intended to either clarify the recorder's comment or explain why the staff member did or said a particular thing.)

January, 1966 . . . . Hyperactive, assaultive to trainees and employees, exploring with tongue.

February, 1966 . . . . Stealing food, banging with elbow and foot, assaultive during evening.

March, 1966 . . . . Stole food at breakfast, misbehaved all morning, settled down and became more cooperative, active but not hyperactive. Assaultive on afternoon shift. No supper, due to lack of tokens. (Tokens are used as rewards for desirable behaviors; trainees must earn sufficient number of tokens to "buy" meals; this writer does not wish to make any moral judgments or comments here about this procedure.)

April, 1966 . . . . Banging mirrors, stamping on furniture. Sodium amytal given, 7½ grains, 10:30 a.m. without effect.

May, 1966 . . . . Wanting to go to the store on various occasions. Stamping feet and crying if not allowed to go.

June, 1966 . . . . When I give Jimmy a token, I try to get him to put it in his pocket without licking or sticking it in his ear, or banging it on the wall. I think this will be very helpful in the long run because it will tend to civilize him a little bit more. It is crucial, however, that everybody else (other staff) do the same thing.

July, 1966 . . . . Active, stamping feet. Charged one token each time. Was rewarded too when he refrained from it any length of time. (Rewards are given for approximating desired behavior.)

August, 1966 . . . . He feels more at ease when he is around me and I am not quite as afraid to discipline him because I know just what limits he has. This brings up another point that I am discovering; each child has certain limits within which he will obey a person. In other words, if the screaming or stamping continues, you can be firm with him and get him to stop but you can only be so firm. If you are too strict with him, then he will simply become a lot worse than before.

September, 1966 . . . . I feel that in order to keep Jimmy's interest, it's necessary to take him to the store twice during activity period. I make sure, though, that Jimmy still has enough tokens for lunch.

October, 1966 . . . . To my amazement, James began crying real tears. Apparently he felt I had changed my opinion of him. He was pathetic. I tried to calm him down and he then became all right.

November, 1966 . . . . We started with the lacing boot. This was laced twice but he still refused to tie a bow. He put all the pieces back into the boot. He had some difficulty with the round piece. I let him experiment and he finally found it. He then worked with the nuts and bolts. He will always choose red before any of the colors. Second color appears to be yellow. He will not screw nuts and bolts on but will screw them off.

December, 1966 . . . . There are outbursts of temper when he is pushed too hard. This may be displayed by slaps and licking other patients.

January, 1967 . . . . Onset of afternoon, beginning with lunch, James became increasingly temperamental and peevish. He stole food and slapped Sophie. I still feel that it is his teeth which are bothering him.

February, 1967 . . . . Was wide awake at 6:45 a.m. Seemed to sense I was the only one in the room and began jumping from bed to bed on bureaus and radiators. Laughed when I couldn't catch him. I feel that to chase him was the wrong thing as he likes being chased. (Staff person ignores undesirable behavior, a common operant technique.)

March, 1967 . . . . Loud and lovable, that was James. What a character! He laughed and laughed for a solid 15 minutes. Enjoyed the mat (gym mat). It really looked as if he wanted to laugh because he forced himself. He's a "kook" but I love him.

April, 1967 . . . . James, being likable guy that he is, I have not heard one employee working with the children saying that they dislike him.

May, 1967 . . . . Jimmy is in the hospital having his teeth removed.

June, 1967 . . . . Wonderful day for Jimmy. He returned from the hospital and his joy knew no bounds. Laughed, smiled, and sang. No one ever saw a happier kid. He ate a good dinner consisting of mashed carrots, potatoes, gravy, pudding and tea.

July, 1967 . . . . On this day Jimmy and the group were taken to a nearby lake for a swimming outing. He conducted himself extremely well and was even able to get into a row boat. Several times throughout the afternoon Jimmy ran into the water, ducked himself and, in fact, splashed others. He undressed and dressed himself in the bedroom of a private home.

August, 1967 . . . . Out for a walk, went to E Building playground. Enjoyed himself. Seemed to single out the other Negro boys and stayed with them.

September, 1967 . . . . Jimmy has been very noisy and active the last few days. I think this is due to being stuck in one room. He needs to be outside or someplace where he can be more active. Was markedly noisy this afternoon because he wanted to go out. This couldn't be done because of lack of help.

October, 1967 . . . . After supper he was taken to the barn. He enjoyed the animals and also he "took to" a little kitten that was up in the barn. Laughing as he always does.

November, 1967 . . . . An experiment was conducted today with Jimmy. Aside from the usual walk in the afternoon, I opened the door and told Jimmy to go outside and take a walk by himself. After repeated requests to Jimmy, he soon left the dormitory and for two hours walked around the entire school. He slowly found his way to the school building. He went directly to the gym. Jimmy understands the importance of the gym because it is here where he uses the trampoline and other equipment so often.

December, 1967 . . . . At the Christmas party, Jimmy showed a momentary interest in toys; then he became a typical small child and played with ribbons and took a big interest in candy.

January, 1968 . . . . Jimmy dressed well this a.m. Ate both meals well. Went to the bathroom perfectly. Went to the gym and used the trampoline. Had refreshments at the Canteen. Excellent at both places.

On April 8, 1968, the principal psychologist evaluated Jimmy. Paraphrasing that report: Jimmy was observed in the dining room having lunch with a companion. He ate quietly, waiting for the various courses to be served to him, and using a spoon and fork correctly. Occasionally, he spilled very small quantities of food from his plate to the table. When he did this, he would glance furtively about, picking up the food with his fingers. Once, he picked up his plate and ate directly from it. However, he immediately stopped this activity when told to do so by the attendant. There was no food stealing observed, no ravenous eating, little use of his fingers in eating, no impatience between courses, and no improper use of food such as smearing or throwing. In quantitative terms, results of the Vineland Social Maturity Scale revealed a social age equivalent of three years and ten months, this in contrast to Jimmy's last evaluation (1950) where he received a mental age equivalent of seven months.

A Final Comment

On the day I visited the state school in the spring of 1968, I observed Jimmy in the Activity Room, sitting at a table with an instructor, listening to a story, and responding as appropriately as he could to the instructor's questions and comments. He was fully dressed, patient, well-mannered, and considerate of both the instructor and other trainees in the room. At that time, I commented to the principal psychologist and the superintendent that Jimmy represented, in my opinion, a remarkable demonstration of man's unquenchable human spirit and desire to live among men. I commented that, for me, Jimmy's progress is as important to understand and is as important for mankind to take seriously as other great documentations of the past: Victor, The Wild Boy of Aveyron; the lives of Helen Keller and Anne Sullivan; Rousseau's Emile; and May Seagoe's Paul. I mentioned that Jimmy's development is important for all human beings to rejoice in, as all human beings do when they learn that a man, once thought to be an irretrievable derelict, now walks among us, reborn a man again. Lastly, I mentioned that we—scholars and scientists and clinicians—could learn from such cases as we can learn from very few others. The concept of educability, the hypothesis that intelligence is plastic, the philosophy of optimism and faith and love, all of these concepts and ideas can be studied and better understood because some people had the motivation and faith to believe that Jimmy was capable of changing.

However, it was an offhand remark, made by an attendant to me that day, that washed away so many bitter memories and frustrations, and made so much seem worthwhile that seemed so foolish only the day before. As we were chatting, she mentioned to me that Jimmy's mother visits him regularly since he began to wear clothes and eat at the dining room table and "look" like a human being. The mother told this attendant, "After all of these years, I now have a son. I lost my child many years ago and you have helped me find him."

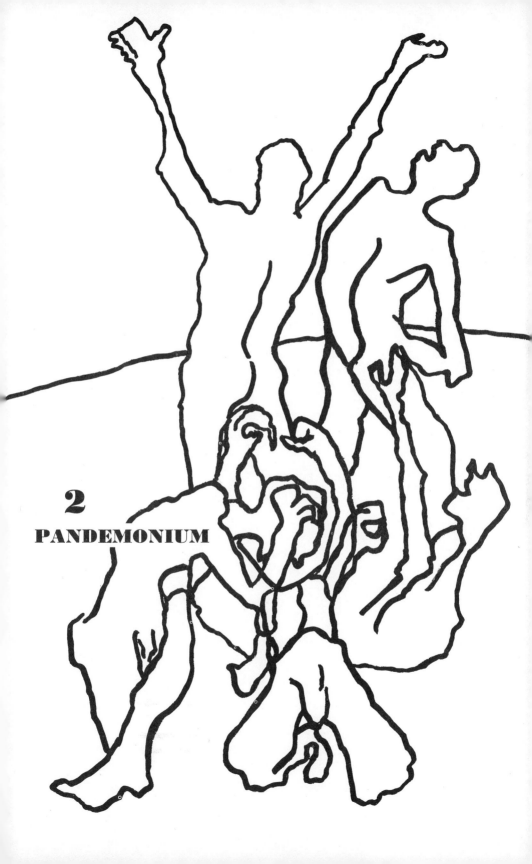

2
PANDEMONIUM

chapter 1

REFORMATION
OF PANDEMONIUM

Pandemonium is the capital of Hell. It is the fantasy of Milton, yet, to
many, it is the reality of being. One does not describe Pandemonium but
reacts to it. Book II reacts to the mentally retarded in Pandemonium
and the reformation that is attempting to return them from the
brutality of institutional back wards to the realm of human awareness,
compassion, and interrelatedness.

> In Pandemonium, there are many aliases: solitary
> confinement is therapeutic isolation; restraint is pro-
> tection; punishment is negative feedback; and
> indifference to all of these is thoughtfulness.
> In Pandemonium, a girl has seven healthy teeth
> extracted to prevent her from eating threads of the
> day-room rug.
> In Pandemonium, the physically handicapped become
> more disabled as each day passes each identical
> day and as each old contracture is the cause of new
> contractures, and as both old and new are the
> effects of indifference and ineptitude.
> In Pandemonium, we appropriate such progressive
> terms as "comprehensive," "community," "regional,"
> and "prevention," but nothing changes,
> or we wouldn't be in Pandemonium.

In Pandemonium, there is little drug addiction, but there
is pervasive, more destructive, environmental
addiction with its accompanying withdrawal
syndrome and sickness.

143

In Pandemonium, the cry of the anguished is, "I am
here!"

In Pandemonium, children are locked and forgotten in
solitary confinement cells for such crimes as
breaking a window or speaking disrespectfully to
an attendant.
In Pandemonium, the tunnel is endless, the darkness
unendurable, the light extinguished.

In Pandemonium, weakness is strength and strength
is weakness.
In Pandemonium, causing nothing to change is Power.
In Pandemonium, trivial questions are answered
erroneously while meaningful ones are
never asked.

In Pandemonium, Utopia is anywhere else.
In Pandemonium, humanists dislike people.
In Pandemonium, both labor and management are
represented by one collective negotiator,
the devil.
In Pandemonium, we find new ways to express horror
and debasement.
In Pandemonium, to embrace life is to kiss death.
In Pandemonium, the humanists are inhuman,
the theists are atheists, the lovers are
haters.

In Pandemonium, you die before you live; the end
precedes a beginning.
In Pandemonium, the luxury of life is death.
In Pandemonium, labeling someone or something
makes it fact.
In Pandemonium you are in the eye of the eye
of that mischief named hell.

Pandemonium is the sophist's paradise.
Pandemonium disguises inertia as reasonableness.
Pandemonium demonstrates the tautology of the "evil
of massive institutions" and the non sequitur in
"excellent large institutions."
Pandemonium is entranced with medical curiosities
rather than concerned with human necessities.
Pandemonium is a phantasmagoria which is
real.

Pandemonium proves the gnostics' thesis that man is
wicked and the world is an evil place.

Pandemonians hope for their nightmares to end while
knowing their terror is permanent, for the
floods to subside while expecting the deluge.
Pandemonians have learned that the meaninglessness
of one's question is only exceeded by the
valuelessness of its answer.
Pandemonians respect an equality that understands no
difference between "he" and "it."
Pandemonians have learned that the next hour will
be a greater catastrophe than the last.
Pandemonians who are deaf never speak, who
are palsied never walk, who are retarded never
think; in Pandemonium, the blind have
no eyes and the lame no feet.
Pandemonians know that life is war.

Good works are inherited from evil deeds in
Pandemonium.
We are trapped because the priest *does* practice what
he preaches in Pandemonium.
There is no need to talk through one's problem
as there is no shade of difference, just an omnipotent
MAN who proclaims what *is* in Pandemonium.

Artists distort reality to present reality; distortion is
the reality in Pandemonium.
Naïveté and innocence cannot survive in Pandemonium.
Subterfuge is the shortest distance between two
conspirators in Pandemonium.
One man lives in the future, another in the past, while
no one has either in Pandemonium.
Nothing changes, yet there is an illusion of
change, for things do not change differently, now,
from the way they have not changed before in
Pandemonium.
There are many liberals but few equalitarians
in Pandemonium.
No one is dehumanized *because* he is a man, but many
are dehumanized *because* they are residents
in Pandemonium.
Sick people live in a healthy culture and healthy
people live in a sick culture; the mix is Pandemonium.
Today is Doomsday in Pandemonium.

The law of Pandemonium is to know right and do
   wrong, think well and behave poorly.
The law of Pandemonium is to believe that nothing can
   be done so nothing need be attempted; the
   system is wrong while we are right.
The law of Pandemonium is to treat other humans as if
   they *weren't,* then treat ourselves as if we *were.*
The law of Pandemonium is to promote the
   administrator's pseudo-giftedness while he promotes
   the patients' pseudo-custodialness.
The law of Pandemonium is not to believe in the
   fulfillment of every human being.
The law of Pandemonium relates more to *ahumantia*
   than to *amentia.*
The law of Pandemonium is to present a public image
   that disguises closed systems as open systems.

The law of Pandemonium unfolds the animal
   ethos leading the human spirit.
The law of Pandemonium is to build ideational and
   physical tunnels to deny man the sensation
   of natural light and experience.
The law of Pandemonium is to learn geography while
   neglecting etiology.
The law of Pandemonium relies on the truth of its deceit,
   the courage of its cowardice, and the love of hate.
The law of Pandemonium is for the state to give the
   patient everything but he gets nothing.

Pandemoniacs destroy relationships.
Pandemoniacs respect chaos.
Pandemoniacs build evil.
Pandemoniacs exude unforgiveness.
Pandemoniacs induce pain.
Pandemoniacs cause mental retardation.
Pandemonaics revolt against competence.

What will the reformation of Pandemonium bring? We
will agree that mere intention is meaningless; mere
speech is noise; behavior is character. We are what
we do! And, we will question not only truth but
value!

In our relationship with humanity, we have learned that:
Love penetrates hate.

The heart moves mountains while the mind moves only
   the heart.
And the soul is man's ultimate triumph.

The saga of humanity has its glory in the human value.
The glory of humanity is its saga of humanhood.

In the cause for humanity, we must agree that:
All men are human beings.
All human beings are valuable.
And all the rest is commentary.

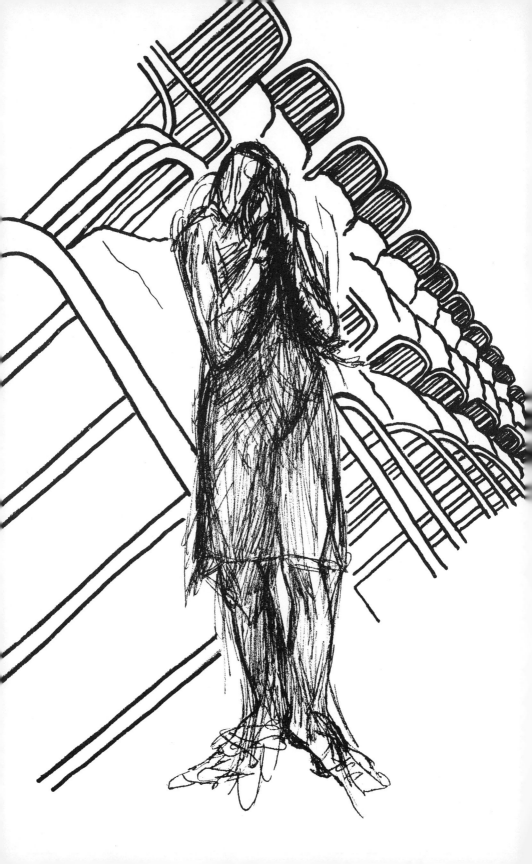

chapter 2

THE LONG WAIT

In the institution, everyone waits—patients, attendants, doctors, the superintendent. But, the patient's wait is longest: first, because it *is* longest and, second, because it usually is for no reason, toward no goal, no achievement. He waits for nothing. This is his destiny. And, if he is lucky, he is not surprised by its discovery.

One asks, "How long is endless?". It is an instant past the end, a shadow after meaning would have been comprehended, a shade of time later than too late.

In the institution, everyone waits. But, the patient's wait is longest. His wait is endless, having had a beginning long forgotten or never known, endless or senseless, dimensionless, a vacuum in time, a ghost in space—nothing, in nothing, for nothing.

Here, people are squeezed between the place and the system, less important than the former and subservient to the will of the latter.

It is a lucky and rare patient—and a sad one—who *knows* that The Long Wait leads to the next wait. I have found that *knowing* one is waiting for nothing, however long the wait, makes for a shorter wait than believing one is waiting for something to end so there may be, then, a new beginning. Being fully prepared to wait for nothing makes time pass quickly, much like a long, deep sleep. The lucky patient hardly ever realizes he's lived.

The Method
from Science to Metaphysics

The 20th century disrepute of Metaphysics, as a way
   to know, may be less because of factors concerning
   the value of Metaphysics, as a method, than factors
   associated with theories to which it has been applied
   —e.g. psychoanalysis.
That is, there may be more "error" in psychoanalysis,
   as a method, than in Metaphysics, as a way to
   study it.
There may be value in the belief that Science is but
   one way to know—the only way under certain
   circumstances, and no way under other circumstances.
I have found the Scientific Method to be inapplicable in
   confronting the incomprehensibility of the back
   ward.
However, I needed a grasp of the Scientific Method to
   arrive at that conclusion and to find and draw upon
   other ways to know and understand.
The application of Metaphysics without some roots in
   Science may be like having faith without religion—
   not that it is wrong, or that it makes it impossible to
   do some good—but there is no reason to it.

The Place

This book is a hybridization of facts (reality?) and
   illusion (reality?).
I had to write it this way because the institution is such
   an interbreed.

            The institution is both fact and illusion.
            It is real, but it can't be!

Back wards are one of mankind's few inventions that
   are categorical, unequivocal, neither relatively this
   or that—
All Bad, All Ways Bad, Always Bad!

       There are no peaceful days in the institution,
       Nor are there silent nights in the back wards.

        There are institutions,
        Where the weak become weaker,
        And the strong become weaker.

Data I have seen lead me to conclude that mortality
   rates at state institutions are lower than for those
   "on the outside."
If the choice were mine to make, gladly would I permit
   mortality rates to rise if these would improve, in some
   mysterious manner, living rates.

       We have never won anything of value for the
         institutions,
       For, essentially, they are little different than they were
         at the turn of this century—
       Except that, perhaps, they are now not as humane or as
         dedicated to human welfare as they were once.

Entering a back ward is very much like turning on the
   lights in a dirty kitchen at three a.m.
In the back ward, instead of cockroaches scurrying
   about at the least sign of life or activity, patients jump
   at the turn of a door handle—running here and there,
   without direction (except that it's toward the stimulus)
   and without purpose (except that it's for human
   contact).

       Institutions for the mentally retarded are "mental" to
         the degree that institutions for the delinquent are
         "correctional."
       The wish is stronger than the fulfillment.

My memoirs of being in institutions are tragedy piled
   upon tragedy piled upon tragedy.
For that reason, in spite of this book, they have not been
   written. I am not capable of writing them.

The People

Some Contemporary Champions
for Humane Residential Care

a very personal assessment

1. Niels Bank-Mikkelsen
2. Gunnar Dybwad
3. Fred Finn
4. Erving Goffman
5. Karl Grunewald
6. Robert Kugel
7. Leonard Mayo
8. Bengt Nirje
9. Thomas Szasz
10. Jack Tizard
11. Wolf Wolfensberger

Some Pioneers

1. Albert Deutsch
2. Dorothea L. Dix
3. Jean-Etienne-Dominique Esquirol
4. Johann Jakob Guggenbühl
5. Samuel Gridley Howe
6. Emil Kraepelin
7. Philippe Pinel
8. Ernest Roselle
9. Edouard Seguin
10. Henry B. Wilbur

Dante and Gorky should be here now to describe our
    back wards. They did so well without the benefit of
    site visits.

The blind do not become "blind with rage,"
The deaf do not "turn a deaf ear,"
The mentally ill do not "behave unfeelingly,"
And, the retarded do not "act stupidly."
Those are the weaknesses of ordinary men—
Who commit most of the world's extraordinary evil.

In one respect, institutional caretakers are alike. They
    give patients what they decide the patients should

have, not what patients want, or need. The price is
high—allegiance and obedience—a lot to pay for
shoddy unwanted merchandise.

> One is at leisure when, in making the choice between
> work and recreation, he chooses the latter. Without
> the choice to engage in meaningful work, leisure
> becomes idleness, peacefulness becomes deadli-
> ness, a beautiful change of pace becomes stultifying
> sameness.

There is little virtue that can be lost during the long
institutional wait.
For, in the institution, there is little virtue.
Possibly, the best among us—and the best that can be
said about us—test our virtue, risk losing it, to find
out if we have any to lose.
The temptation is not the pleasure from without, but the
uncertainty from within.

> As I study my colleagues, I must conclude that—
> The wisest among us, in the institution, *must* be
> arrogant—
> For, to remain there, arrogance is required for
> survival, in the face of one's wisdom and
> knowledge—
> A foolish man can remain there, and be humble, in
> his ignorance or self-deception.

The System

In our efforts to formulate a theory on human abuse, we
devote a great deal of attention to studying the
abused, but rarely—if ever, the abuser.
We have an enormous collection of data concerning
those who get "done in," and how.
All the more surprising, because we know so little—
and seem to care even less—about who's doing "the
doing," and why.

Feces and urine are not, themselves, problems
besieging mankind. In the main, we possess very
adequate ways to deal with these "necessary items."
Feces and urine become terrible problems when
human beings do not dispose of these "necessary
items" in the expected manner, time, or place.
All this is by way of saying that the basic disorder of
the back wards is not "feces and urine." The basic
disorder is that we have not found ways to organize
and conquer the feces and urine. The basic problem
is organizational, logistical, motivational, educational
—one involving understanding and faith—and requires solutions from such people as educators,
psychologists, theologians, sociologists, physicians,
and systems analysts—not from such people as
plumbers and sanitation engineers.
The basic problem involves, but isn't, feces and urine.
However, make no mistake; to make any real
progress in this matter, we must learn to deal, better
than heretofore, with feces and urine.
Men have built their castles on weaker foundations.

One interesting situation concerning institutions is that
many individuals and groups claim proprietorship—
e.g., superintendents, boards of trustees, commissioners, even parents' associations.
They say, "At my institution . . .," "Our school is
. . .," "My program . . .," "Our building . . ."
This would be an amusing state of affairs, if it were not
so discouraging, because very few of those people
claim primary responsibility, and few feel accountable
for institutional conditions.
Those people are wrong about such matters involving
proprietary rights and responsibility. Obviously, the
devil makes the strongest claim to ownership, and
just being a human being requires each man with a
knowledge of institutional conditions to hold himself
responsible for the conditions—and accountable to
his soul for their eradication.

We may have a chance to change the System when
better ways are found to include the Outsider, who
becomes part of, but apart from, the System.
We need people from the Outside who can take both
distance and, temporarily, exercise responsibility and
authority.

We need people from the Inside who can take both the
Outsider and themselves seriously.

It isn't necessary to proscribe behavior in the back
wards—
When the world is nothing, there is nothing to prohibit.

Many patients wait in nakedness. They enter the
institution with weak or little appreciated brains.
Once in, their spirits are eroded; their personal
effects are depersonalized; their clothes and most
anything else they have, they have temporarily, on
loan from the Commonwealth.
In London once, I had to go to the men's room while
visiting at a government building. *Each* square of
toilet paper bore the proclamation:
GOVERNMENT PROPERTY
My surprise is that we haven't thought to manufacture
such toilet paper for our institutions. We've thought
of virtually everything else.

A shame of our institutions is that Pyrrhic victories,
infrequently as *they* are achieved, are as treasured
and savored as the genuine triumphs of men "on
the Outside."

It is possible that this Movement will fail,
That there will be no reformation of state schools.
It will fail, if we have miscalculated and struggled for
reform when, all the while,
The need was to revolutionize.

chapter 3

GOOD AND EVIL

To distinguish Good from Evil, one must appreciate one from the other; to appreciate one from the other, one must believe in the Good in man —and must recognize the Evil he is capable of.

And, one must know that Evil is never very far from Good—but Good, therefore, always shadows Evil.

This chapter attempts to express some ways to recognize Good from Evil. It further attempts to express both the interrelationship and dependence of one to the other. One could not exist without the other. In a world without evil, we would not recognize goodness. In our world, and especially in our institutions, goodness glistens, almost obscenely.

The danger is not that goodness will be unrecognized, but that evil will—or is.

The good in man lives after him; the evil lived before and will remain generations after he departs. Evil accrues but, so it appears to me, good can generate and regenerate from its own resources.

To participate in evil requires a past. Good requires but a future.

Goodness can cease under its own volition; with evil, once begun, remission is slow and never under full human control.

Good is like the Phoenix, in spite of what we find in our institutions.

Some of us believe we can build from the ashes if we but begin, now, to do good for people.

By doing good, we may better recognize good from evil.

Few of us pretend to understand, truly, the origins of Good and Evil. But, some of us believe we sometimes know the difference—one from the other.

It's a beginning.

Good

There is a pervasive tension surrounding the good
    man who works in the institution. Like most men, his
    wish is to be left in peace, to do his job, to be like
    other men. He does not wish himself to be chosen
    for sacrifice, or martyrdom, or specialness.
Yet, with evil confronting him everywhere, he learns
    that he cannot go in peace, or be at peace with
    himself, unless he tries to be different, to be special
    —unless he chooses to lead the way.

He, who will sit down for a meal with residents of a
    back ward, is more than a Good man.
He is a person of genuine manners and impeccable
    upbringing.

No one who observes true goodness is embarrassed,
Puzzled and confused sometimes, but not embarrassed.

One of *my* problems may be that I have seen Evil when
    it wasn't there—because there was so much Evil
    surrounding me,
And, I may have missed Goodness when it was there—
    in bold relief—because I would not trust the obvious,
    not daring to believe that Goodness can exist in
    Pandemonium,
Not *really* believing that—especially in Pandemonium—
    Goodness must exist.

Evil

Most abuse committed in the institution is non-violent.
Evil is so tolerated and accepted, as a way of life, that
    violence is unnecessary, almost unthinkable, and
    certainly uncommon.

When you want to scream and you are forced to laugh,
When you have to throw-up and you are required to eat,
When you need to love and you have better reason to
   hate,
When you wish to leave and you have no place to go.
Where the servant to accomplishment is accident,
Where the handmaiden to love is opportunity,
Where things are taken because they are found,
Where no questions are asked and none are expected.

The sign on the Administration Building wall:

> NO VISITORS ARE
> PERMITTED ON HOLIDAYS

Irony and symbolism are lost in the blunted evil terror
   of the back ward. This is unfortunate, for there is so
   much of each there, and so much we can learn
   through these ways to learn.

Scratch an institution and pus oozes.

Pulling seven healthy teeth to prevent the patient from
    eating the day room rug.

Installing a sewer on the day room floor.

Toilets without seats,
And toilet stalls without enclosures.

Applying to human beings such words as "vegetable,"
    "basket case," "animal," and "sub-human,"
And, then, guaranteeing that such words become
    applicable for human beings.

Where the welfare and needs of the residents are
    considered last.
Where two attendants must "spoon feed" 60 severely
    retarded residents in one hour.
Where no resident owns a single article of clothing.

Physicians who are comptrollers more than physicians,
Comptrollers who make medical decisions,
And, Superintendents who make no decisions.

Permitting a family no alternative to the back ward.

What appears to be a puzzling aspect of institutions is
    that good men compete with each other in
    rationalizing abuse, and evil men compete with each
    other in extolling virtue and goodness.
I don't believe they do these things out of a spirit of
    cooperation or professionalism or in trying to "see
    the other fellow's problems and point of view"—
    although such motives should not be discounted
    completely.
I believe good men and evil men do these things out of
    an instinctual sense of self-preservation—be it moral,
    spiritual, psychological, economic, or whatever.

Knowing something about the history of institutions and
    their support, one must reserve some compassion
    and understanding even for those who are respon-
    sible for the evils perpetrated there.

chapter 4

MEANS AND ENDS

There are no ends without means, but there are means which are ends unto themselves. There are ways and there are ways, and these should be looked at.

There are ends upon ends, and these should be looked at. There are aims and purposes, objects to grasp and ideals to espouse. There are intentions and outcomes; there are expectations and results; there are coincidences and consequences. There are ends that provide a reason to do; and, there are ends that are no more than the final point, the end. There are ends that do no more than conclude, and there are those that offer a beginning. There are ends that become parts of other means and ends that become means.

There are ends that *may* justify means. Certainly, there are means that *do* justify ends.

There is process and there is object, and both should be commented on, in the absence of real ability to examine them carefully.

Means

A really unthinkable thought is to admit that most teachers, psychologists, social workers, and physicians are overtrained in respect to their everyday responsibilities.

A really unthinkable thought is to think that supervised bright high school graduates can teach, test,
counsel, and dose effectively.
A really unthinkable thought is to believe that
undergraduate-prepared people can supervise, and
that doctoral-prepared people are, probably,
in sufficient supply but misused in their current
occupations.
A really unthinkable thought is to have faith in the
power of educability, motivation, and faith itself.

Arthur Jensen, Rick Heber, and many more others notwithstanding,
we must believe and behave as if intelligence is plastic, is educable,
is a function of practice and training.

Possibly, Rosenthal and his associates were on this
track.
We must learn how to program the "Hawthorn Effect."

All humanitarians must love more than humanity.
They must love individuals.

Why is one person, or animal, abused and not another?
If this is understood, everything is understood. In the
face of greatly mounting criticism, one Canadian
official commented on the slaughter of 50,000 harp-
seal pups each year in the Maritime Provinces: "If
we could find a way to make pup seals look like
alligators, our problems would be over."

It was the job of Joseph Goebbels to make pup seals
look like alligators and Jews and Poles look like
subhumans. Although it may not be their explicit
intention, numerous institutional personnel have
similar jobs now.

Isn't it ironic that we are fearful—as well we should be
—of risking the possibility that patients may be
abused, inadvertently, in programs that are designed
to help them while, with seeming abandon, we
deliberately abuse these same patients in programs
that are designed to punish.
We prohibit operant procedures for the same patients
we throw into solitary confinement.
We are afraid to abuse to help, but not to abuse to
punish.
What is the relationship of means to ends?

Existentialism may be the only philosophy truly seeking
    to provide a logic to deal with institutions.
It teaches one not to pretend to care about what will
    happen next.
Its nihilism, in the face of now, and its pessimism, in
    the prospect of a better later, are exceeded only by
    its devotion to the purposelessness of everything.
With this philosophy, one may plan for an unloved
    tomorrow.

> The perspective of history may teach us that, by cruel
> deeds, the best causes become evil. Review the Holy
> Crusades, any modern war, and asylums in America.
> Then, we may learn that the pursuit of virtue is not
> always virtuous, that the means are not always in
> character with the desired ends, and that the means
> are representative of the true character of the
> pursuers and—in the final analysis—are the true
> ends.

Silence threatens.
Quiet consoles.
Silence is a mean.
Quiet is an end.

> The substance of a situation is in the means, not the
> ends. The end is what will happen and what has
> happened. The means are what is happening.

Ends

Exodus from Pandemonium
adapted from Exodus 6:2–7

His Conscience spoke to Man and said to him, "I am
    your Conscience. I appeared to Samuel Gridley
    Howe, Dorothea Dix, and Albert Deutsch, but it was
    not enough. I established my covenant with them, but
    they not with others. I yet hear the moaning of the
    weak and vulnerable—My chosen people—because

the Keepers are holding them in bondage and I have
remembered my covenant. Say, therefore to All Men:
I am your Conscience. I will free the sick, the
retarded, the mindless, the troubled from the burdens
of the Keepers and deliver them from their bondage.
With an outstretched arm I will redeem All Men
who suffer now and—if must be—through extraordinary chastisements. And I will return My chosen
people as people, as men who are part of humanity.
And, then, I will be their Conscience."

    And that there will be a day when being taken
        seriously and being regarded worthwhile require
        no other justification than being a human being.
    And when civilized men will agree that Jimmy is as
        valuable, *as a human being,* as was Helen Keller or
        Albert Einstein.

We will achieve these ends, not by criticizing others.
We will achieve our ends when a part of each of us
    takes to task that part which does nothing or does
    what it should avoid.

    Tonight, March 31, 1969, I saw *Titicut Follies.* I am
        here for a meeting of the American Orthopsychiatric
        Association where, tomorrow, I am to address the
        membership on the reorganization of mental health
        in our Commonwealth and what it has accomplished.
    What can I possibly say tomorrow as I cry here tonight?
        How can I express my grief, horror, dirtiness,
        disgust? What are men doing to each other?
    This book doesn't tell enough.
        Nothing could—not even *Titicut Follies.*

Architects, engineers, and planners have constructed
    monuments rather than livable facilities. For two
    reasons we have bought these monuments: first, it is
    only in recent times that we knew any better; second,
    we have been fearful—and rightfully so—that when
    government is ready to allocate a facility, it will be
    many a day, if ever, before additional allocations
    can be expected.
Hence, the $16,000,000 monuments. Hence, our not
    reluctant—but enthusiastic—advocacy of monu-
    mental monuments creating monumental errors.

Hence, the attainment of ends that are neither
victories nor satisfactions. We have won prizes that are
self-deceptions and self-defeating.

Those who believe that our dismay with and distrust of
Mental Health is an illness do not distinguish
paranoia from reality. Either *they* have the illness or
they must learn better.

People do not sleep because they have either too
much to do or not enough to do.
People do sleep because they have either too much to
do or not enough to do.
One should not claim to understand an act because he
is able to describe it.

Our perceptions prevent us from seeing the world as
others perceive it. In that regard, our perceptions
are reality and theirs are distortions or falsification
of reality. A consequence of that dissonance is what
is commonly and inaccurately called "a communication gap"—inaccurate because communication
usually is crystal clear. We do not have communication difficulties as often as we perceive separate
and equally valid realities. Each mind follows its
own course, obtaining from its own experiences and
neurology. In the end, each mind must follow the
beat of its own drum and must appreciate, and turn
to advantage, the different realities of the other
beats.

The objective is to make life less a scandal and more
a life.

An end for the mentally retarded is to earn, not to take.

Our end is to see the day when custodial care will be
found only in correctional institutions.
The end for civilization is to serve, not to destroy the
living.

The end is Man in
a loving environment

The end is for Man!

chapter 5

I THINK I BELIEVE

One gets involved, takes responsibility, makes decisions—some right, some wrong—and he learns. He learns of things about which he had never imagined to exist and of things about which he had been thoughtless. Probably, he does a little good and a little harm, impresses certain people and annoys others, adds to the clarification of one issue and the confusion of another. After all is experienced, that which remains in his head—that which he's gained for himself—is what he's learned, how he's changed.

What follows is my way of expressing a personal victory, small as it may be.

The creative act is therapeutic. What has been revealed to me is that therapeutic need is a major cause of creative effect.

This book was begun on January 2, 1968, the inaugural day of my tenure in state service. The book has been therapeutically important; to me, it was necessary. It had to be written.

Pathos

The reality that is itself and untarnished
is the reality of the mind,
the reality of the vision not the visual,
of the sounds of inner passions,
not of the trumpets and drums
of worldly glories.

Faith

Professing on evil may be personally therapeutic and
cleansing to the soul. Oftentimes, it obtains a great
deal of benefit for those who have been violated
against. However, in spite of whatever good such
professions provide, they become mere empty words
—hypocritical words—when the professor doesn't
commit himself directly to the eradication of the evil.

It is claimed that few "truths" are known to Man.
Are there any?
But, Man is expected to be true . . .
to his family.
to his faith.
to his country.
to his profession.
Isn't it difficult to be true to something when
you must be in doubt from where (or if)
that truth obtains?

People who engage themselves in the research of an
issue have a more humble view of the illumination
they can bring to the issue than those who are
"working at it" in the clinics, the schools or whatever.
On the other hand, I have found that the researchers
are much more optimistic than the latter group that
the issue eventually will be resolved or brought under
scientific control. It isn't, I believe, that the researchers are more humble people; many i have
known are rather arrogant. Nor do I believe that they
are *intrinsically* more optimistic concerning human
nature and the ability to modify it.
The advantage enjoyed by researchers, and difficult for
others to attain, is their ability to take distance and
form an ideological detachment from an issue, its
consequences in general, and its influence on their
personal lives. It is very difficult to be dispassionate
and disinterested in the face of certain issues—even
for the very best researchers. However, both their
training and the way they must go about their

business makes such objectivism possible, if not
certain, for them where it is almost impossible for
others to achieve.
It is the objectivism that permits researchers to better
understand the hidden variables that many of us
never appreciate. It is this comprehension of the
complexity of an issue that causes the researcher to
be humble in the light of his ignorance and optimistic
and faithful to his scholarly creed and the eventual
triumph of science.

> You have conviction if
>   you know you are right
> When you do something
>   others know is wrong
> Or, when you do something
>   you know is less wrong
>   than anything else you can do.

Horror

I have been told that, in times past, families of institutionalized mentally retarded were advised to
publish obituaries for such persons. Given the *current*
circumstances in many state schools for too many
inmates there, my common sense—despair notwithstanding—does not permit me to take exception to
such advice *today.*

> From the elegant view of the sensitive
> The saving virtue of the institutionalized retarded
> Is their inability to communicate agony.

More people than buildings need renovations in our
state schools.

> If, in the logical order of affairs, philosophers inhabit
>   universities and theophists churches, then—surely
>   —thanatosophists rule institutions for the retarded.

Poor institutions are responsible for good decisions.
They completely discourage certain parents from
institutionalizing their children, some of whom
should best remain at home.

A Parable: Milling rot.

What is Utopia?
It is the remembrance of things that
never were,
And the embellishment and the improvement
of these for a future
that will never be.
What is Pandemonium?
K Building.

Thanatos, gorge yourself in the gore of K Building!

This is neither an exercise in sophistry
nor is it a non sequitur;
It is a circumstance that confuses
and misleads otherwise skilled professionals:
It should not be an unexpected condition
among severely mentally retarded residents
of state schools—
Many of whom are *both* chronic patients
and acutely ill.

Is the behavior of people similar to the behavior of
apples? Curious question, but we sometimes act as
if it were so. Even stranger is, at times I think we
should.
For example, consider a barrel of apples. What do we
do when we find a rotten apple? We remove it, not
add a healthy one to mitigate the effects of the
diseased one.
At the institution, we segregate the "rotten" people
into back wards. At the institution, we add healthy
staff to rectify the abuses perpetrated by our sick or
recalcitrant colleagues.
I think it may be helpful for us—at least once in a
while—to think of the patients as people and the staff
as apples, not vice versa as is presently the case.

Hope

Styles of Behavior

The Realist: tells it the way it is.
The Historian: tells it the way it was.
The Idealist: tells it the way it should have been.
The Humanist: tells it the way Man must make it
  become.

> Some believe that Man is innately good.
> Others believe that Man is innately bad.
> Wouldn't the human race be more
>   predictable if Man was either
>   innately good or bad—not both
>   good and bad, as he probably is?

To some colleagues, a dedication to the field of mental
  retardation is impossible.
To others, it is unthinkable.
Whatever their flaws, frailties, and professional naïveté,
  we must entrust our energies and resources with the
  remaining minority—and not dissipate these in
  courting the reluctant, however talented and poten-
  tially useful they may be to the cause.

> The door always must be open, but people must choose
>   to enter and not be chosen, they must be encouraged
>   but not forced or seduced, we must offer them a
>   philosophy and not our federal gold or promises we
>   may never keep.

For better or worse, we have only each other. Our
mission must not be to convert the disaffected
professionals. We have much more important and
fruitful responsibilities with the mentally retarded
and their families.

In every movement for human betterment, at least
three generations have been involved concurrently:
the oppressed generation, disinterested onlookers,
and leaders of the movement committed to rectify
errors of past and present.
Unfortunately, until today, our leaders have been one-
generation jaded and two-generations removed. They
have been too feeble to remember real passions
connected with the issue and they have, more
recently, remained on the sidelines when something
better might have been done.
Only today, when youth are led and lead—when youth-
fulness and involvement extend to the later years,
when middle age may be 60—is there the possibility
that leadership will emerge from the ranks of the
afflicted, not from the afflicting or the condescending.

The hippie has a point!
He looks you right in the eye
and through your head.
He doesn't answer your, "How are
you?" unless he believes you
care about how he is.

It isn't the bureaucracy of our democracy that offends
the young. They believe our unforgivable sin was the
creation of a "gerontocracy," a government by and
for old men.

Law

I have read the chiseled rocks of all ages, proclaiming,
at the courthouse entrance, that a commonwealth
must have a government of laws, not of men. I can't

agree. Our government may be of laws *for* men or,
better yet, *of* men *with* laws, but in the ultimate
dimension, *of* men *not* laws.

> With the law, too many civil servants settle for the
> comfort of atomistic literalness and find it their, and
> our, prison—not a vehicle to freedom. I, as one,
> would rather have a cabala. A mystical interpretation
> of the law has the virtue of unpredictability and,
> hence, there is a chance for good to obtain. A literal
> understanding offers but little opportunity to move
> ahead, to affirm positively. Its seemingly singular
> ambition is to deny, to reject, to stay within the
> letter—never understanding the word and the idea,
> which are man's only special gifts.

Order and truth are not always compatible bedfellows.
Law is not morality.
Intelligence is not thoughtfulness.
The able do more than know.
The evil do more than believe.
And the good must do more than curse them.

> If a state repeals the death penalty for acts which were
> previously capital crimes, the attorney general
> should require it to desist from assigning its death-
> in-life penalty—sentence to a back ward—for
> "mental" crimes.

Oftentimes, the punishment of wrongdoing is, itself,
   wrongdoing.
Consequently, there are situations when wrongdoing *is*
   punishment and punishment *is* wrongdoing.
That is, it is impossible to distinguish one from the
   other.

> The Rouse v. Cameron decision, written by Chief Judge
> David Bazelon for the majority of the United States
> Court of Appeals for the District of Columbia, the
> Nason v. the Superintendent of Bridgewater State
> Hospital decision in Massachusetts, the Whitree v.
> the State of New York finding, and others certain to
> be made before publication of this book advocate
> the *legal* right of a patient in a public mental hospital
> to *adequate treatment.*

It appears as if the day will be fast upon us when our
reluctant civilization will be required to serve as our
brother's treaters.

We are beginning to appreciate, now, that morality
can't be trained satisfactorily into people; nor, so it
appears, can reason be modified easily.

Possibly, we have learned that it is almost futile to
attempt to reason unreasonableness out of people,
to deal logically with the illogical. Possibly, these
are legislative, more than moralistic, matters.

Possibly, during the years, our major advocates should
have been jurists and lawmakers rather than
theologians and philosophers.

Charity

With all due respects to George Santayana, he who
knows not the difference between charity and love (or
duty and faith) may be doomed to experience neither.

Very often, when someone gives something away
either he doesn't want it anymore or it isn't (and
never was) his to give. This is another way of saying
that there is little charity, friendliness, or sacrifice
in our giving. Rather, things are more or less like an
all-pervasive church rummage sale. People give
what they no longer need or want. Collectors solicit
from donors who, if they actually value what they
give, feel "taken" rather than giving. The buyer,
more often than not, regrets the purchase—however
great the bargain seemed.

I have difficulty saying very much about charity other
than to admit that, when the giver, I am neither sure
of nor happy with my motives and, when the recipient,
terribly uncomfortable.

Love

When one speaks out for "humane treatment"—and if
he has thought much about his choice of words—he
realizes that the "humane" refers to the humans
giving the treatment not to those receiving it. Animals,
as well as people, can—and do—receive humane or
inhumane treatment. What animals can't do is
dispense humane treatment.
The standards for "humane treatment" are: (1) it be
developed and given by human beings; and (2) it
meets humanity's wish and expectation for treatment
of man or beast.

> People who love well have difficulty understanding
> and reacting constructively to hate and,
> People who hate often have similar difficulty
> with love.
> It's the rare man who comprehends and appreciates
> one and deals well with the other.
> Such a man is necessary to help solve our problems.

A true interface requires:
    interfaith
    intertrust
    interinterest
      and
    inner intercommitment

> Concerning my friends and the things we value in our
> relationship, we mention such matters as: idealism,
> honesty, trust, *and* the novelty that each of us brings
> to the other's experience.
> This last characteristic, novelty, is little appreciated,
> less understood, and terribly important. It adds
> color, zest, anticipation, and a feeling of being alive.

The "we-they" syndrome requires the "we" be right
and "they" be wrong.
Insofar as we are concerned, that's the way it really is.

> There are two kinds of people I try to avoid:
> Those whom I must be untruthful with,
> Those who have been untruthful with me.

There doesn't appear to be a right way or a wrong way
   to interact with another human being, other than to
   know that the wrong way always involves thoughtlessness, a mechanistic approach—or ennui—that is
   determined irrespective of that human being, what he
   wants, or what he is.

Civilization

The malaise of this civilization is that truth relates so
   precariously to justice, and law not at all to order.
Our strength for the coming generations is our knowledge of this and our compassion for those who do not
   view this unhappy condition unhappily.

                    Boredom is the marasmus of the masses.

All too often, our battles in mental retardation are good
   and vigorous; unfortunately, our opponents well might
   have been our friends; unfortunately, our causes
   often are forgotten before they are realized.
Our battles are true but too many victories are
   defeats.

                    There are senators and there are congressmen. In
                       mental retardation, there are too many senators and
                       not enough congressmen. There are too many friends
                       of the mentally retarded who are willing to take
                       responsibility for *all* mentally retarded but not for
                       one mentally retarded, who have a commitment to a
                       cause but not to a person, who represent everyone
                       but not someone.

The world is changing more quickly than our comprehension of not only what a change means, but if it
   has occurred.

The outspoken personality may be one whose public
and private views are not discrepant, while the
submissive personality may be one whose public
and private views are discrepant.
There is a great deal both to admire and abhor in
either personality.

I've noticed that our society is enamored with old
buildings, old crockery, old books, almost anything
old—excepting old people.
Strange that it's chic to have regard for old furniture but
not for people older than the end table.
Is the creation of humanity so much less interesting
than that of an overstuffed Victorian love seat?

In the history of mankind, two unique races have been
excused from the legal and moral protections
afforded all others. The Jew and Negro have been
lynched and burned, partly because one was
believed to be intellectually and the other sexually
superior.
There is danger from a new source. Some claim the
mentally retarded are morally superior.

The Jews of the Nazi nightmare and the mentally
retarded, in our own time, share a common heritage.
They evoked feelings not of blind hate but of deep
repugnance, not of vengeance but of annoyance, not
of wrath but of necessity, not of subjectivity but of
objectivity, not of "you" and "I" but of "the" and
"it."

What was 1968 really like? Or 1969/1970/2000/
2,000,000? We might have begun counting these
things a thousand years later; it would now be 968.
Better yet, next year could be year one. But most
people don't appreciate the insignificance of dates.
For a few, it is the people and places that signify real
meaning. But for most, it's Columbus Day, New
Year's Day, and Memorial Day, not Columbus,
renewal, and peace.

The report of incompetence's death has been greatly
exaggerated. So too has the reputed influence
of intellectual power to hasten the interment. Quite

the contrary: the activity of the mind appears
to be almost indifferent to the accomplishment of the
person—indifferent to and independent of!

> To implement any conceptualization requires an
> incredible array of planners, technicians, clinicians,
> and willing manpower. For this, among other
> reasons, a poor conceptualizer does the work of the
> devil.

All too often, the practice bears little relationship to the
theory. At such times, we must judge whether
to change the practice or throw out the theory. To
err here is to compound our waywardness.
All too often, our personalities—irrespective of the
merits of a particular circumstance—prejudge
our course of behavior. Therefore, our personalities
must be taken very seriously during such
deliberations—for our personalities are true to the
issue even when they cause wrong decisions
to be made.

> The collar, the yoke, the posey belt and the
> straitjacket are the merchandize, the soft and
> hardware of restraint and punishment.
> The pessimistic evaluation and the negative prognosis
> may be more hurtful ideational restraints and
> punishments.

Language is the expression of civilization.

> There are two kinds of questions, one that seeks an
> answer and one that gives an answer.
> And, further, there is a third kind of question, a question
> that both seeks and gives, a question that's both
> cynical and hopeful, both not caring and eager
> for new evidence and a way to retreat from dead
> center.

> *Am I a Tautologist?*

1. Do children with low I.Q.'s read poorly or do children
who read poorly have low I.Q.'s?
2. Do non-gainers not learn or do non-learners not
gain?
3. Do good teachers have good methods and bad

teachers have bad methods, or do good methods and
bad methods depend upon good teachers and
bad teachers?
4. Is something tautological something in the
eye of the beholder?

> We sometimes forget that the word is *a* deed
> And, possibly, *the* deed.

Xenogenic Yahoo Yahoo
The word is a deed and the label is the deed. For
   example, eventually a label must be invented for
   Daniel Hugon, Richard Speck and other XYY
   "criminally insane."
Shouldn't we label them:
   Xenogenic Yahoo Yahoos?
The definition of XYY would be:
   Brutish, degraded, vicious men,
   Completely different from either of their parents.
It's so much easier to understand Richard Speck
   when we know he's a Yahoo.

> What is emotion?
> The sounds of words, not the words,
> The way one moves, not the distance he
>   has travelled,
> The look of the eye, not the vision
>   in the eye,
> The silence, not the quiet.

> Sin is to crime,
> What cruel is to hurt,
> What deliberate is to consequence,
> What societal will is to individual action, and
> What victimizer is to victim-victimizer.

Institutions, much more than individuals, are responsible
   for the earth's good and evil. Yet, when we attempt
   to comprehend and cope with good or evil,
   we persist in studying individuals and individual
   actions.
We hardly recognize institutional and group influence.

> I have observed two problems interfering with orderly
>   and fruitful developments in the *Science* and *Art*

of behavior. What seems to be more and more
common during the conduct and reporting
of a "scientific" program is the conclusion (my
interpretation) of the "scientist" that it
hardly matters what one does as long as he does it
with style.

On the other hand, the "art of teaching" and the "art of
clinical interaction" seem acceptable, to both
scientists *and* practitioners, only to the degree
that there are things scientific about these
involvements.

In life, contradictions are necessary, because life is a
contradiction.

Glory

Greatness is not the goodness of a man
But the goodness he inspires in others.

Honesty is as beautiful a technique as it is a virtue.

The Doyens

a very personal assessment

1. Moses
2. Jean Jacques Rousseau
3. Jean-Marc Gaspar Itard
4. Abraham Lincoln
5. Helen Keller
6. Albert Einstein

The Masters

1. Alfred Binet
2. Maria Montessori
3. Clifford Beers
4. Sigmund Freud
5. Mohandas Gandhi
6. Martin Luther King, Jr.

The Journeymen

1. J. E. Wallace Wallin
2. Harold Skeels
3. Margaret Neuber
4. Richard Hungerford
5. B. F. Skinner
6. Seymour Sarason

Contrary to an evergrowing belief, man doesn't live
   to die.
He dies to confirm his life, that he was different
   in life than in death, that his life had value, that never
   had he been duplicated on earth.

Being dead is not being alive, but being alive is <u>not</u>
   not being dead.

The argument that man, or a man, is a trivial speck in the
   Cosmos—ending with the cliché that he isn't
   anything in 100 years—is a specious one, least of
   all for man to contemplate. If man, any man, were a
   passing unnoticed shadow, he isn't anything now,
   in life. To believe that is to believe in nothing
   and, therefore, not to even believe in a nothing belief.
   To believe that, is to be as if you were nothing. To
   believe the opposite is to know you can't be nothing,
   while the original argument must be nothing.

One knows he has experienced something important
when he is certain he will remember—and, in fact, he
does remember—a day, a week, a moment.
Most of our moments are forgotten. Those that
remain with us for the rest of our lives either are
golden or painful, but always important.

It is regrettable that more of us who participated in this
struggle were not willing to record our places in it
and views of what occurred. Those few of us
who were not so reluctant may disdain our roles
as spokesmen. However, for better or worse,
in this revolution, the spokesmen will be
the historians.

The essential factors necessary for the reformation of
state schools for the mentally retarded relate to
three concepts: regionalization, unitization,
and humanization.
Regionalization extends the responsibilities of the
schools, preserves and enhances their multipurpose
mission and, thus, protects them from becoming
custodial centers which house and—in effect—
guarantee the continuation and preservation of back
wards.
Unitization provides a method for accountability for
clients, programs, and progress. It may be our small—
but great—effort to combat bureaucracy in
government.
Humanization! Nothing has meaning if this has no place
or understanding. Nothing can be said now if it
hasn't been said until now.

And Ethos

The pathos was the ethos,
And the ethos was the pathos,
Of this book.
I have tried to transform reality to illusion,
For to be understood, this reality must
be appreciated in the context of a greater illusion.
Until this experience, I had misrepresented the
illusion as reality, while I might have clarified
reality through illusion.

3
NEEDS
AND VALUES

chapter 1

THE JUDGE IN JUDGMENT

During my year with the Department of Mental Health, I made innumerable presentations to the central office staff, institutional personnel, parent organizations, and citizen groups—if I was asked, I went! Although I wrote continuously about the conditions I observed and the problems encountered, only three papers were made public—two of these to very small "in house" groups. Soon after I began my year with the department, it was decided that it would be good to plan a retreat, a two or three day "think tank," away from the hurry and demands of the city, a place where we could renew our common fellowship and think through together our common problems. I was asked to prepare a presentation for the group which included all of the senior central office staff from commissioner to program director, many of our state hospital and state school superintendents, regional administrators, and other high level state mental health–mental retardation personnel.

I can't recall how many early mornings and evenings were spent preparing that presentation, which is the next chapter of this volume. However, I do know that I considered that assignment of utmost importance—ranking a close second to my address to the Massachusetts legislature in 1967 ("The Dark Side of the Mirror"). There was something that I wanted, very badly, to communicate to these new colleagues, many of whom I came to respect and very much admire. I wanted to tell them that I appreciated their inhibitions and anxieties concerning the field of "mental retardation." Further, I wanted to have them understand that I did not expect them to turn away from commitments of many years and the skills they so carefully developed and nurtured. I did not expect them to abandon their work or interest with the mentally ill. I did not expect them to be any less zealous concerning their mission than I am concerning mine. However, I did want them to know how deeply some of us felt about the treatment the mentally retarded are receiving in our state schools and other programs. I did want them to know that we knew that resource allocations for mental health and mental retardation were not comparable. I did want them to understand, as plainly as possible, that, although we are in little position to threaten, the mentally retarded and their families have waited too long for "their day" and may not wait very much longer. I wanted to write a paper that rang true and had conviction and, at the same time, created an illusion—an image of *Christmas in Purgatory, Titicut Follies,* The Holocaust, and all of the evils designed by man and demons. While struggling with the writing of that paper, I was—at the same time—writing an introduction to Book II of this volume. After completing the narrative section of the "think tank" paper, it occurred to me that the introduction to *Pandemonium* would make an interesting conclusion to the presentation on mental health and its effects on mental retardation. The reactions to "Empty Revolutions Beyond the Mental" were—literally—the most unusual, gratifying, and disheartening ever experienced in a paper I presented. Even today, almost one year later, I am asked about that paper. People who were there comment about this person's reaction or that person's support or negativism. I think that the paper did communicate to some who were unaware of our feelings and beliefs. It made some friends for mental retardation. On the other hand, there may be some who will never forgive the suggestion that mental retardation might better stand alone and apart from mental health, especially if the current circumstances of our "partnership" are not greatly modified.

The chapter "Our Uncommitted Virtues" was written on a snowy night and presented the following morning to the President's Committee on Mental Retardation. The third paper that was written during the same year and presented for public reaction was *A Plan for Reformation of Services for the Mentally Retarded in Massachusetts,* publication number 1029, Massachusetts Department of Mental Health, August, 1968. Soon after I came to the department, the Commissioner of Mental Health asked each of the assistant commissioners to prepare a plan outlining the current status of programs and services under his responsibility, needs for the coming years and expectations for fiscal support, facility and program development. I worked on this plan rather continuously, presenting an early draft in the spring of 1968 and a final report in August of that year. Since that time—especially through the fall of 1968 before my return to Boston University—the plan was disseminated to every appropriate state agency and key staff. Many meetings were held in the central office with other assistant commissioners and directors. It became, in numerous ways, our working "bible." It gave us focus and direction and, although projections—based on a demographic study that we have not yet completed—may not have had the fine-grain precision we may achieve some day, the plan did provide us with a degree of cohesion and coordinated purposefulness that was absent prior to its development.

This book is an attempt to deal with some constructive measures for preventing or eliminating or mitigating human abuse. The following chapters deal with the influence of policies concerning mental health on the development of services for the mentally retarded, the influence of training on performance, and the larger issue concerning the law, manpower and human resources for mental retardation services, and public opinion and reaction to society's commitment to the conservation of human values and needs. It concludes with a summation of what appears to have been accomplished and where our journeys are yet to take us. As a proper setting for the introduction to this book on needs and values, I have edited the aforementioned *Reformation Plan* for presentation here. Although it deals specifically with the Commonwealth of Massachusetts, I believe that the sections on economics and incidence will be pertinent to other parts of our country. Further, the section on needs may, similarly, be valuable to planners elsewhere in that it attempts to coalesce such diverse factors as economics, incidence, current problems, social theory, and political realities. The last chapter "Judging the Priesthood and the Priest" will attempt to assess our activities and progress during this past year in light of the *Reformation Plan* and in light of our values and needs.

The Economics of Residential Care

Currently, about 7,000 children and adults are residents in our five state schools and two vocational training centers for the mentally retarded. The Commonwealth charges $7.70 a day for this care, which is approximately the daily maintenance expenditure. In a report of the President's Committee on Mental Retardation, it was shown that the per resident daily cost in the United States in 1967 was $7.60, just ten cents less than the resident cost in Massachusetts. National statistics for the year 1966 indicated that Massachusetts received a rank of 31 out of 50 states in relation to its daily maintenance expenditure of $6.69 in institutions for the mentally retarded. (See Butterfield's "Basic Facts About Public Residential Facilities for the Mentally Retarded," in Kugel & Wolfensberger, *Changing Patterns in Residential Services for the Mentally Retarded,* 1969.)

Our relative standing *vis-à-vis* a commitment to state-supported residential programs for the mentally retarded does not speak well of a state that is far more affluent than many other states that spend more.

Table I: Daily Maintenance Expenditure, 1966

State*	Daily Maintenance Cost per Resident	Rank
Alaska	$22.38	1
Kansas	12.18	2
New Mexico	12.11	3
California	11.41	4
Rhode Island	10.64	5
Wisconsin	10.63	6
Connecticut	8.82	7
West Virginia	8.78	8
Maine	8.66	9
Colorado	8.55	10
Kentucky	8.44	11
Hawaii	8.31	12
Louisiana	8.23	13
Michigan	8.07	14
Oklahoma	8.05	15
Iowa	7.97	16
Maryland	7.72	17
Illinois	7.54	18
Georgia	7.47	19
Indiana	7.42	20
Washington	7.36	21
Florida	7.32	22
Delaware	7.17	23
Idaho	7.13	24
New Jersey	7.13	25
Pennsylvania	7.09	26
Arkansas	7.07	27
Oregon	7.02	28
New York	6.94	29
North Carolina	6.92	30
Massachusetts	6.69	31
District of Columbia	6.58	32
Wyoming	6.50	33
Missouri	6.36	34
Minnesota	5.95	35
Tennessee	5.92	36
Utah	5.86	37
Vermont	5.76	38
New Hampshire	5.60	39
Arizona	5.38	40
Ohio	5.08	41
Montana	5.00	42
Texas	4.88	43
Virginia	4.71	44
North Dakota	4.39	45
Alabama	4.04	46
South Carolina	3.90	47
Nebraska	3.58	48
South Dakota	3.17	49
Mississippi	2.30	50

* Nevada not included; District of Columbia referred to as a "state."

Differences among institutions, and even within institutions, highlight glaring inequities in treatment for certain individuals and raise the question of the unfair distribution of the Commonwealth treasure. For example, in fiscal year 1969, $3,100 was expended for each resident in the Belchertown State School, while $3,600 was expended for each resident in the Fernald State School. With the development of the Hathorne State School, the Rutland Heights Vocational Training Center, and the John T. Berry Vocational Training Center, differences are even more striking. Further, the comparison of expenditures for state school programs for the mentally retarded with the state hospital programs for the mentally ill demonstrates clearly that the mentally retarded have been, and continue to be, a very neglected group. For example, the 2,300 residents at one of our state schools (W. E. Fernald) are cared for by approximately 1,000 employees, while 1,300 residents at a particular state hospital (Boston) are cared for by approximately 1,200 employees.

However, our greatest inequity is demonstrated by prevailing conditions for the large number of residents who are in so-called "back wards."[1] For example, we investigated the daily per patient expenditure in four dormitories at the Walter E. Fernald State School. The overall daily expenditure for the school is $7.92 per resident. However, the daily expenditure for the residents of North Building (a so-called back ward) is $4.27; at West Building (another back ward) the expenditure is $4.23; but at Green Blind Unit it is $8.85; and at Farrell Hall $12.66. The expenditure for one group of residents is almost three times the expenditure for another. It should be mentioned that the back ward group of residents, as a group, is much more severely retarded. They present many more behavior problems and are more difficult to manage and train than the former group. Those residents of North Building, where we spend $4.27 per person daily, are severely retarded adults who are, for the most part, ambulatory, incontinent, assaultive, denuded

---

1 Back wards are characterized by: a) overcrowdedness, disrepair of older buildings, as well as by the excessive use of locks and heavy metal doors, and by the enormity of buildings and numbers of patients assigned to dormitories; b) day rooms or recreation rooms, characterized by overpowering odor, where patients often appear nude or dressed in institutional garb, where there is a lack of purposeful activity, communication or any interaction, and where there is, in each day room, an attendant or two, whose main function seems to be to "stand around," and on occasion, hose down the floor "driving" excretions into a sewer conveniently located in the center of the room; c) infant dormitories where cribs are placed side by side, head to head, and very young children, one and two years old, often lie in cribs without interactions, without any adult, without playthings, without any apparent stimulation; d) solitary confinement cells, or what is officially referred to as "therapeutic isolation," usually located in the basements of large dormitory buildings, sometimes located on an upper floor, off to the side and away from the casual or official visitor's scrutiny, which are generally tiny rooms, approximately seven feet by seven feet, shielded from the outside by a heavy metal door having either a fine strong screen or metal bars for observation of the individual, some having mattresses, others blankets, still others, bare floors, and few having either a bed, a washstand, or a toilet.

and non-verbal. They live in a multi-level dormitory built before the turn of the century. There are rarely more than three attendants on duty at any one time. The residents of Farrell Hall, where we spend $12.66 per person daily, are young children. They are the fortunate recipients of a better than average program, in a modern dormitory with a staff ratio that exceeds the national average and meets the standards of the American Association of Mental Deficiency.

It is not my intention to request the transfer of staff from Farrell Hall to mitigate current difficulties in North Building or West Building. What is needed immediately is the: *quadrupling of per capita expenditures for all residents in our back wards in order to provide these individuals with basic human care* and, thus, rectify permanently the disgrace of our back wards and the shame of our Commonwealth. As I have said earlier in this volume, it is my deep conviction that any society—our society—is judged most harshly by that which it should be most ashamed of—that which demonstrates its inhumane treatment of humans—and that judgment is the most accurate reflection of the society's sickness. This sickness has the power to flood out whatever good we are doing. Witness the example of Germany during the 1930's and 1940's. Most of us do not remember the scientific achievements of Hitler's Germany.[2] History has judged that society by Buchenwald and Dachau, not by the Germanic ethos of scientific achievement, industrial excellence, or world power. Witness the judgments some have made on the character of the white southerner. It isn't his gentleness or good manners or friendliness that distinguishes our Southern brother in the eyes of many; it is his attitude toward, and treatment of, the Negro. Witness the attitude many Massachusetts citizens have toward our state schools for the mentally retarded. It isn't our excellent Hospital Improvement Programs, research contributions, or community clinics that distinguish us. To our misfortune, among laymen and professionals in Massachusetts and elsewhere, we are often known only for our back wards and our inhumane treatment of the severely retarded.

Approximately 20% of the retarded in our state schools are in so-called back wards. We must *immediately* quadruple our expenditures for these residents before any real progress can be made in upgrading standards for all residents in institutions and, for that matter, before any real progress can be made toward implementing a full community program for the mentally retarded living at home. At the present time, we are expending approximately $4.25 daily for each of 1,200 back ward residents. This $5,100 total daily expenditure must be increased to a total daily expenditure of $21,600, or $18.00 per resident.

---

2 Possibly, scientists at our great universities recall, or still speak about these great contributions. The average citizen is unaware of, or cares little about such matters. Similarly, the parent of a child in a state school for the mentally retarded is not particularly interested in our scientific university affiliated programs at that school. She is, naturally, more deeply concerned with programs available to her child.

*It is recommended that an immediate appropriation of six million
dollars be allocated for this desperately needed upgrading of programs
for the severely retarded in our state schools.*

The Incidence of Mental Retardation: The Real Problem

From many sources, we hear that 3% of our total population are
mentally retarded. Some reports go as far as to claim a 5% incidence
and it may be reported, with a degree of justification, that psychometric
retardation affects 16% of the population. Most estimates indicate that
5½ million Americans, or approximately 3%, are mentally retarded.
After four years of intensive involvement in a carefully developed and
executed demographic study of the incidence of retardation (still not
completed) I am persuaded that we are dealing with no more than 1%
of the total population, and possibly no more than 3/4 of 1% of the total
population, who *at any one time* need (or are known to have needed)
special services because of their mental retardation. That is to say,
although it is quite true that at least 3% of our population are psycho-
metrically retarded, no more than 1% of our population are in need of
special services because they are mentally retarded. During the past
four years, we have been trying to locate and provide programs for all
those mentally retarded residing in two contiguous counties in southeastern Connecticut. These counties have a total population of 320,000.
As a result of searching for retarded individuals residing in these
counties, who are attending or have attended special classes for the
mentally retarded, in state or private residential facilities for the
mentally retarded, in day care or other community facilities, at home
and in need of services, in prisons, in mental hospitals,[3] or in other
state, community, or voluntary agency programs, we located 2,500
known mentally retarded. Of these, 912 are active cases in need of
regional center services, 240 of whom are in regional center residence.
Based on this uncompleted study, which we believe is one of the more

---

[3] In the United States, there are 37,440 patients estimated in mental hospitals with a
primary diagnosis of mental retardation. A census is not currently available on the
number of patients with a secondary diagnosis of mental retardation and a primary
diagnosis of mental illness. Based on the above figure, in proportion with the 1966
total number of residents in mental hospitals in the United States, we estimate that
Massachusetts has approximately 1,428 patients in mental hospitals with a primary
diagnosis of mental retardation.

	U.S.	*Mass.*
Number of Residents in mental hospitals	452,329	17,253
Number of Residents with primary diagnosis of mental retardation in mental hospitals	37,440	*estimated* 1,428

carefully conducted demographic surveys available to the field of mental retardation, it is our tentative estimate that:

1. At any one time, no more than 1% of the total population are known to be mentally retarded.
2. ½ of that 1% are either in public school special classes for the mentally retarded or do not need any special services *at the present time.*
3. ½ of that 1% of the total population need special services other than those which the public schools can provide.
4. $\frac{1}{10}$ of 1% of the total population need residential care.

Based on the above, it is our considered estimate that the following data pertain specifically to the Commonwealth. Further, the accuracy of these data is supported by the known incidence of special class populations and institutional populations in the United States (see Table II):[4]

1. There are 55,000 identified mentally retarded in the Commonwealth of Massachusetts.
2. There are 13,000 children in special classes for the mentally retarded in the Commonwealth of Massachusetts. (These data are in agreement with the national statistics reporting approximately 50 million children through 12th grade in our public schools in the United States. One half million, or 1%, are in special classes for the mentally retarded.) The 13,000 children in our special classes represent approximately 1.3% of the total Massachusetts' school population. Based on national statistics, where mandatory legislation for special classes has been passed, 1.3% of the public school population attend the special classes (our Commonwealth meets, exactly, the national average here). However, we estimate that, to provide a special class program for all mentally retarded who need these services, Massachusetts' public schools should plan for 1.5% of the total school population.
3. There are approximately 7,000 residents in Massachusetts state schools for the mentally retarded. (This total represents a population somewhat higher than $\frac{1}{10}$ of 1% of the population of Massachusetts.) There are approximately 200,000 residents in state schools for the retarded in the United States, also approximately $\frac{1}{10}$ of 1% of the national population.[5]
4. There are approximately 4,600 individuals in pre-school programs, day care centers, sheltered workshops, or vocational training programs operated by state, municipal, or voluntary agencies in Massachusetts.

---

[4] The population of Massachusetts is approximately 5,300,000. Estimates, prepared by Program Planning and Research of the Executive Office of Administration and Finance, project that in 1975, the state population will be 5,600,000—an increase of 6.4%. With regard to long range planning, we should take cognizance of the increases in population. However, these increases do not appear to affect substantially either the priorities or the needs that we predict for the Commonwealth.

[5] We learned recently that there has been a marked annual reduction in Massachusetts' live births since 1961. This reduction in births, no doubt, will result in a reduction of children under 10 years of age having mental retardation associated with gross brain damage and physical handicaps. Projections for the needs for inpatient facilities for young children with this type of retardation should take into consideration the likelihood of a somewhat lessened demand for services by this type of child.

Table II: Incidence of Mental Retardation

Based on Massachusetts Population of 5½ Million

Category	Percent of total population in categories	Estimated number presently in categories in Massachusetts	Estimated number of individuals in categories after completion of all phases of the program
Percent of the total population needing special services due to their mental retardation	1% of entire Massachusetts population	55,000*	55,000
Individuals in need of special classes in public schools at any one time	1.5% of school population	13,000	15,000
Individuals in need of no services other than special classes during school years	50% of entire Mentally Retarded population	27,500	27,500
Individuals in need of residential care, at any given time, with alternative programs available	.1% of total population	7,000	5,500
Individuals requiring other services			
Clinical nursery school classes	5% of the Mentally Retarded population	1,000	2,500
Day care classes	5% of the Mentally Retarded population	150	2,500
Vocational training and sheltered workshops	10% of the Mentally Retarded population	450	5,500
Community recreation	20% of the Mentally Retarded population	3,000	11,000
Individuals in need of minimal to moderate supportive services some time in life: diagnostic, recreational, physical therapy, speech therapy, family counseling, short term residential care	50% of the known Mentally Retarded need this at some time	Probably most to some degree; few to the desired extent	27,500

* All estimates at completion of program rounded off to the nearest 500.

5. It is estimated that:
   a. With a viable, full range of community programs, our residential popula-
      tion can be reduced to 5,500.
   b. To achieve (a), community programs must be expanded to include:
      (1) 2,200 additional children in clinical nursery school classes
      (2) 2,300 additional children in day care classes
      (3) 3,200 additional individuals in vocational training centers
      (4) 1,850 additional individuals in sheltered workshops
      (5) 8,000 additional individuals in community programs
   c. Of the known mentally retarded, 50% or 27,500 need the following mini-
      mal to moderate supportive services at some time in life: diagnostic,
      recreational, physical therapy, speech therapy, family counseling, or
      short term residential care.[6]

*It is recommended that, with deliberate speed and thoughtfulness,
the Commonwealth of Massachusetts develop community mental retardation programs for all of the above citizens not now receiving
necessary care, training, education, or treatment.*

The Need: Unfolding of A Truly Regional Program

What is a comprehensive regional program for the mentally retarded?
Our best judgment maintains that such a program must be committed
to the following staff and service characteristics:

A. Staff

1. The Program should reflect the fact that mental retardation involves many
   different fields and personnel, i.e., it is not the responsibility of any one professional field. The administration and organization of programs should be
   given to individuals not on the basis of field or title, but rather on the basis
   of their leadership qualities, innovative ideas, commitment, and community
   involvement, as these meet the functional needs of the mentally retarded.
2. The training of professional and non-professional personnel should be an
   essential part of a comprehensive program and should be organized and
   conducted in a way so as to maximize overlapping experiences among the
   different personnel in training, i.e., to avoid training programs which do not
   emphasize communalities among fields. The training programs should be
   weighted in favor of sustained on-the-job, supervised experiences, with lesser
   weight given to lectures or readings.
3. A comprehensive program should take into consideration that neither now,
   nor in the foreseeable future, can enough high quality professionals be
   trained to man existing or proposed programs. Consequently, one of the
   major goals of the program is to locate and develop latent talent in the

---

[6] Although we can not claim high order accuracy for all the above estimates, these
being extrapolated from previously mentioned studies, the above estimates will give
the planner a way of proceeding most sensibly in light of currently available data.

community—regardless of where in the community it is—so that more and better proposed services can indeed be rendered.
4. To achieve maximum returns with existing manpower, state personnel should be available for assignments within all the programs of a given region. To facilitate this policy, new regulations or statutes may be required.

B. Service

1. The Program should seriously seek to help existing agencies meet their obligations better and to a larger extent, i.e., the program should deliberately avoid taking over existing ones or facilitating acceptance of the view that there is an agency to which all problems are referred.
2. There is explicit recognition that in the past, the larger the size of a residential facility the poorer the services within the facility, the less there is of community awareness and responsibility, and the greater the likelihood that more and bigger facilities will be built.
3. The Program rests on the recognition that a sizeable proportion of those currently in residential facilities could have been kept within the community, at far less psychological and financial cost, if appropriate services had been available.
4. Where residential facilities are needed, serious attempts should be made: a) to rehabilitate or renovate existing small housing units which can accommodate a dozen or so residents, b) to secure these units in the neighborhood from which the residents come. This characteristic, it should be noted, describes what has been successfully done in other countries.
5. Services should not be characterized by a single focus on the mentally retarded individual, but rather reflect that "the case is the family." There should be information and counseling services, the aims of which are to help parents and normal siblings gain a better knowledge and understanding of the problems, both present and future, with which they will deal. In any instance, programs should be developed *with* families and not for them. Whenever possible, families should help families, i.e., service should not be conceived of or defined in terms only of what professionals can do.

It is our best judgment that the implementation of a truly comprehensive regional program will require the following:

I. 1968–1970

A. *The Immediate Eradication of Back Wards:*
It is recommended that a quadrupling of expenditure be appropriated for all residents in our back wards in order to provide these individuals with basic human care.
B. *Improvement and Enrichment of Institutions:*
It is recommended that a minimum of expenditure of $15.00 be appropriated for the daily per capita cost of caring for and treating each resident of a regional center. The most recent American Association of Mental Deficiency survey indicated that we must, at a minimum, double the staff at our state schools for the mentally retarded.
C. *The Regionalization and Reduction in Size of our State Schools (1968–1978):*
It is recommended that by 1978, the Belchertown State School, the Dever State School, the Fernald State School and the Wrentham State School, each

reduce its resident population to 500, a total of 2,000 for the four state schools. For these schools to become regional centers, they must expect to serve four community-based individuals for each person in residence. Therefore, no new construction should be approved for these schools except for the following two explicit reasons: the development of education and therapy facilities and the development of experimental models for enhancing residential care. In light of our goal to substantially reduce the residential populations of these centers, no dormitory construction should be approved, *under any circumstances,* that would merely duplicate current dormitory facilities or programs. In addition, we need to explore the use of currently vacant beds in state mental hospitals and public health hospitals. (See Tables III, IV, and V.)

Our state schools must be transformed into comprehensive regional facilities that will, in addition, serve as high level diagnostic and research centers for large regions, and, further, as back up residential centers for the smaller regional programs. We can estimate the types of individuals presented for admission to residential centers by studying current information available on age and level of retardation at admission to our state schools. (See Table VI.)

II. 1968–1976: Community-Based Programs

During the next eight year period, as mandated in Section 18 of Chapter 19, amended, by the Commonwealth Acts of 1966, the Division of Mental Retardation will concentrate its efforts on developing short-term and moderate term diagnostic and emergency residential programs for the mentally retarded in: the Lowell Comprehensive Mental Health Center, the Fall River Comprehensive Mental Health Center, the Government Comprehensive Mental Health Center, the Tufts University Comprehensive Mental Health Center, the South Shore Comprehensive

**Table III: Percent of Current Capacity in relation to
Bed Capacity in Public Health Hospitals**

Hospitals	Bed Capacity	Census 6/30	Beds Available	Percent of Capacity
Lakeville	240	174	66	72.5%
Shattuck	350	247	103	70.5%
Mass. Hospital Schools	258	112	146	43.4%
Pondville	110	81	29	73.6%
Rutland Heights	184	161	23	86.4%
Tewksbury	1633	1091	542	66.7%
Weston	141	103	38	73.0%
Totals	2916	1969	947	

**Table IV: Percent of Current Capacity in relation to
Bed Capacity in Mental Hospitals**

Hospitals	Bed Capacity	Census	Beds Available	Percent of Capacity
Mass. Mental	186	154	32	82.7%
Boston State	1534	1281	253	83.5%
Danvers	2167	1883	284	86.8%
Foxborough	913	1058	—	115.2%
Gardner	1208	1053	155	86.3%
Grafton	1366	1168	198	85.5%
Medfield	1032	932	100	90.3%
Met. State	1912	1506	406	78.7%
Northampton	2006	1928	78	96.1%
Taunton	1502	1358	144	80.4%
Westborough	1857	1463	394	78.7%
Worcester	2424	1004	1420	41.4%
Totals	18112	14788	3464	

**Table V: Percent of Capacity in relation to Bed Capacity in
State Schools for the Mentally Retarded**

State Schools	Census 10/31/67	Rated Bed Capacity	Percent of Capacity
Belchertown	1427	987	144.6%
Dever	1787	1716	104.13%
Fernald	2083	2040	102.1%
Wrentham	1726	1343	128.5%
Hathorne*	69	116	59.5%
North Reading**	47	50	94.%
Rutland Heights***	17	24	70.8%

  * Hathorne opened March 6, 1967.
 ** North Reading opened October 18, 1965.
*** Rutland Heights opened June 19, 1967 (capacity will increase to 50 after proper installation of fire escapes).

**Table VI: Estimated Age and Level of Mentally Retarded
Individuals at the Time of Admission to State Schools**

| Level | Ages | | |
	0–7 Pre-School	7–21 School	21 and Adult
Mild	1%	3%	6%
Moderate	10%	15%	15%
Severe	30%	15%	5%

Table VII: Waiting Lists for Massachusetts State Schools for the Mentally Retarded

| Regions | ACTIVE WAITING LISTS FOR STATE SCHOOLS | | | | | Total number of applicants from each region |
	Fernald	Belchertown	Dever	Hathorne	Wrentham	
Fernald	143		71			214
Belchertown	13	40	35			88
Dever	12		67		7	86
Hathorne	80		42	59		181
Wrentham	51		26		134	211
Total of applicants for each state school	299	40	241	59	141	781

| Regions | URGENT WAITING LISTS FOR STATE SCHOOLS | | | | | Total number of applicants from each region |
	Fernald	Belchertown	Dever	Hathorne	Wrentham	
Fernald	28		6			34
Belchertown		3	2			5
Dever					3	3
Hathorne	4		4			8
Wrentham	3		9		9	21
Total of applicants for each state school	35	3	21	0	12	71

As indicated, applicants residing in one region often request admission to schools in another region. We are working energetically with the waiting list populations to re-assign all applicants to the school designated for their specified region.

Mental Health Center, and the Massachusetts Comprehensive Mental Health Center, totaling approximately 200 residential stations at any one time. This important facet of our program must be developed if we are to achieve a state-wide program that is available to all residents without the encumbrances of harassing waiting-lists and debilitating frustrations.

It will be noted that in spite of the development of 12 additional regional centers, 2 vocational training centers, plus a collaborative program with comprehensive mental health–mental retardation centers, we are calling for a total reduction in resident population from approximately 7,000 to 5,500. Further, we are assured that we can not only reduce our resident population by 1,500, but at the same time eradicate completely the oppressive waiting-lists now confronting us. (See Table VII.) However, to permit this prediction to obtain, each regional center must accept responsibility for the development of programs for four community-based individuals for each regional center resident. For example, a regional center that has responsibility for 200 residents must give service to 800 community-based clients. Further, to permit this prediction to obtain, eventually all programs sponsored by the Department of Mental Health must be coordinated by the regional mental retardation administrators. Lastly, the regional center must be central in providing services while, at the same time, it must not view itself or be viewed as the sole provider of services.

In order to permit the development of an array of programs that provide each retarded individual and his family with a continuum of services from onset of need until habilitation, the following community-based services will eventually be needed:

1. A total of 250 clinical nursery classes for 2,500 children
2. A total of 275 full day care classes for 2,500 children
3. A total of 37 vocational training centers for 3,500 young adults and adults
4. A total of 37 sheltered workshops for 2,000 young adults and adults[7]
5. A total of 37 community recreation programs for 11,000 children and adults

Lastly, the combined efforts of all the regional center programs in providing family counseling, diagnostic and evaluation services, day camping, therapy and other educational and training programs, must provide for a total of 27,500 community-based individuals, of which the above enumerated 21,500 will be a part.

It is recommended that an omnibus law be enacted to mandate the education, training, habilitation, or therapy, for all school age children who are excluded or exempted from public school.

The *immediate* (1968–1970) financial responsibility to the Commonwealth for community-based programs, insofar as mentally retarded children are concerned, would be (see Table VIII):

1. An additional 1,000 children in clinical nursery school classes $1,000,000
2. An additional 600 children in day care classes 900,000
3. An additional 1,000 individuals in vocational training centers 750,000
4. An additional 600 individuals in sheltered workshops 450,000
5. An additional 3,600 individuals in community recreation programs 1,000,000

---

[7] 3 and 4 can be combined in communities that so desire.

Table VIII: Community-Based Programs

Categories of Community-Based Services	Estimated number of individuals presently in categories in Massachusetts	Projected number of individuals in Community-Based Services 1968–1970	Projected number of individuals in Community-Based Services 1976–1983	Estimated number of individuals at the completion of Community-Based Services*
Clinical Nursery Schools	1,000	1,000	500	2,500
Day-Care	150	600	1,750	2,500
Vocational Training Centers	300	1,000	2,200	3,500
Sheltered Workshops	150	600	1,250	2,000
Community Recreation Programs	3,000	3,600	4,400	11,000
Totals of individuals in each column	4,600	6,800	9,100	21,500

* Estimated number of individuals in the program at completion rounded off to the nearest 500.

III. 1968–1976: The Addition and Completion of Regional Centers

A. During the four year period 1968–1972, the Boston, Worcester, Springfield, and Pittsfield regional centers should be added to the Hathorne Regional Center, providing a total of approximately 1,200 residential stations. Each of these centers, for which our Commonwealth legislature has given initial approval for land procurement and preliminary architectural planning, will maintain no more than 250 residential stations and will serve 800 to 1,000 community-based participants. Each residential cottage will house a maximum of 32 individuals. Encouragement will be given to those regions who wish to develop residential programs outside of the geographic boundaries of the regional center. For example, the Division of Mental Retardation will view favorably the development of small residential units serving specialized purposes and located in various sections of the community, within easy commuting distance to population centers and industrial areas. We envision the development of group care homes, providing for 8 to 10 individuals who can work in the community, but need the supervision that a group home can offer. We envision the development of halfway houses for those individuals who are leaving the large regional center and who are at an intermediate point before full return to independent living in the community. We envision

the development of small residential units for individuals with special needs, such as those who require a great deal of medical attention or who are aged or infirmed. At the risk of redundance, we will encourage the development of residential programs, supervised by the regional center, but geographically outside the center itself. In fact, we would encourage the development of a regional center that does not have one bed located on the grounds of the center itself.
B. During the years 1970–1974, regional centers should be developed in Boston, the Framingham Area, Franklin County, and on Cape Cod, providing a total of 900 residential stations.
C. During the years 1972–1976, regional centers should be developed in the Cambridge Area, Haverhill Area, Fitchburg Area, and Newton-Wellesley Area, providing a total of 900 residential stations.

IV. 1974–1976

During these two years, two additional vocational training centers should be developed to add to our John T. Berry and Rutland Heights facilities, providing a total of 350 residential stations. These centers should be established in Berkshire County and southeastern Massachusetts. As with the John T. Berry and Rutland Heights Vocational Training Centers, the new facilities will permit mentally retarded adults who live in sparsely settled regions to enjoy the opportunity for vocational training and yet maintain close contacts with families and communities during week-ends at home. Other vocational training programs, in more populous areas, may be on a day basis and will not require residential facilities.

V. Staffing

It is recommended that, as new regional centers are developed, a minimum cadre of ten administrative and supervisory personnel be employed during the planning, construction, and early implementation stages of each new regional center. The remainder of the full complement of staff for the centers will be drawn from the existing state school facilities as they reduce their residential populations. The double per capita expenditure for each resident, due mainly to increased staff, would permit them to supply personnel for the center while they continue the development and enlargement of their community programs.

VI. 1976–1983

The completion of the regional plan: The eventual completion of a truly regional program requires that services for community-based individuals be provided in full. The initial eight years already discussed (1968–1976) will see the development of the Regional Centers as well as the establishment of programs to meet the immediate needs for community-based services. In the seven years following this initial

Table IX: Chronology for Implementation of the Comprehensive Regional Program

Requirements for implementation of comprehensive regional program	1968	1969	1970	1971	1972	1973	1974	1975	1976	1977	1978	1979 ----1984
I (a) Immediate eradication of back wards		▓	▓									
I (b) Improvement and enrichment of institutions		▓	▓									
II Immediate community programs		▓	▓									
III Construction of 12 regional centers	▓	▓	▓	▓	▓	▓	▓	▓	▓			
IV Construction of 2 vocational training centers							▓	▓	▓			
V Employment of 10 administrative and supervisory level personnel for each new regional and vocational center	▓	▓	▓	▓	▓	▓	▓	▓	▓			
VI Completion of community-based programs									▓	▓	▓	▓

stage, the community-based programs for which the Commonwealth has responsibility would be completed, with provisions for:

1. Another 500 children in nursery schools	$ 500,000
2. Another 1,750 children in full day care	2,625,000
3. Another 2,200 individuals in vocational training centers for young adults and adults	1,650,000
4. Another 1,250 individuals in sheltered workshops	937,500
5. Another 4,400 individuals in community recreation	880,000
TOTAL	$6,592,500

In summary, we visualize the unfolding of the regional program as having two phases: the first of which takes place during the next eight years, in which the Regional Centers will be built and the immediate responsibility for community-based services will be met by the Commonwealth; the second phase will cover the seven subsequent years (1976–1983) and will see the completion of the community-based services. (See Table IX.)

Predicted Long-range Financial Commitment

What will this program cost? The following expenditures will be in addition to current Department of Mental Health allocations for programs for the mentally retarded and should provide for:

I. 1968–1970

A. Immediate eradication of back wards involving the habilitation of 1,200 residents in desperate circumstances	$ 6,000,000[8]
B. Improvement and enrichment of institutions (an increase of $7.00 per daily capita expenditure for 4,300 patients)	11,000,000

II. 1968–1970

Immediate development of community services for 6,800 mentally retarded individuals	4,100,000

III. 1968–1976

The construction of 12 regional centers each providing 200–250 residential stations	72,000,000

IV. 1974–1976

The construction of two vocational training centers, each providing approximately 175 residential stations	6,000,000

---

[8] Funding estimates rounded off to the nearest one hundred thousand.

V. 1968–1976

The employment of ten administrative and supervisory level personnel for each new regional and vocational center   1,400,000

VI. 1976–1983

The completion of community-based programs providing services
for an additional 9,100 mentally retarded individuals   6,700,000
                                                    TOTAL $107,200,000
                                        (See Table X.)

Table X: Predicted Long-range Financial Commitment

Millions*

| | 0 | 10 | 20 | 30 | 40 | 50 | 60 | 70 | 80 |

I (a) Immediate eradication of back wards

I (b) Improvement and enrichment of institutions

II Community programs

III Construction of 12 regional centers

IV Construction of 2 vocational training centers

V Employment of 10 administrative and supervisory level personnel

VI Community-based programs

*all funding estimates rounded off to the nearest hundred thousand

Issues to be Studied

1. *The principle of free choice as related to residential care must be examined. How can the Commonwealth of Massachusetts encourage a beneficial competition between private and public facilities and permit a family to select the setting of its choice for its retarded member?*
2. *We need improved screening of waiting lists and evaluation of clients.*
3. *We must better utilize Medicaid and Medicare programs for eligible residents of regional centers.*
4. *We must better utilize available unused public or private modern chronic hospitals, monasteries, and mental hospitals.*
5. *We should establish grant-in-aid programs in communities to develop sheltered workshops, group homes and day care facilities.*
6. *We should better utilize quality private nursing homes.*
7. *We need better utilization of foster home care programs.*
8. *We should develop more effective recruitment techniques.*
9. *We should develop high level professional training programs as well as training programs for heretofore untrained, unskilled workers.*
10. *We should establish collaboration with university and research training centers.*
11. *We should establish a truly collaborative effort with community mental health programs.*

The Reformation

A reformation of residential and community programs for the mentally retarded in Massachusetts must be the number one priority of all who feel deeply that all men are human beings and all human beings are valuable. There is a sickness in our Commonwealth, as there is in many other parts of our country. The plan presented here is, in my most considered judgment, a viable method to rectify the errors and abuses that resulted from a century of indifference and callousness to a segment of society that is the most maligned and neglected in the history of this civilization.

chapter 2

EMPTY REVOLUTIONS BEYOND THE MENTAL

**An Address to members of the
Massachusetts Department of Mental Health[1]**

Our so-called revolution now being waged on behalf of the mentally retarded is an empty revolution as were those of its progenitors. It is an inert revolution, a formless revolution, an irrational revolution, and— that which is least justifiable and most irrational—it is a hoax. The fire of its purpose is in its oratory, not its action. This oratorical crusade, this still-mutiny will—if we permit it—cause a reformation to sameness. If we permit it, the revolution will entrench what is; we will have revolted to what we were, and are, rather than to what we should become. We will have won the battle for the mentally retarded but the spoils of our victory will be ashes. For ashes are what we fought for, nothing more, and these we had from the beginning, nothing else.

Our no-change revolution in mental retardation is a random revolution, a random journey where the magnitude and direction of each step—of any progress—are determined by chance. And, contrary to other forces for change, its leaders are the caretakers of the oppressed, not those who are themselves oppressed, some with conviction for their cause, some without conviction. I wish I could speak differently today. I wish I could say that "our time has come." I wish I could advise those who have waited so long for so little that, now that great progress has been achieved on behalf of the mentally ill, those who have fought that valiant struggle will devote their talents and energies and resources to the least of the least, the mentally retarded. I

---

[1] The reader wishing to recreate the full text and "atmosphere" of this address may find it helpful to conclude with "Reformation in Pandemonium" (Chapter 1 of Book II), since this—in a slightly altered format—formed the final section of the original address.

want to believe that, in our day, things will be different for the mentally retarded, but my disillusion is deep. The evidence supporting it is like an ideational anchor holding fast in the mire of our history. And, although that history has taught us to crawl when we were not permitted to walk, to be grateful for small gains as we experienced chaos around us, it has also demonstrated the futility of compromise that is resignation, of modesty that is cowardice, of change that is deception, and of responsibility that is irresponsibility. As the world is changing, as the lot of mankind becomes less arduous in our civilization, the condition of the mentally retarded remains what it was in our fathers' time, which is what it was in their fathers' time. And as each seeks to establish his innocence for this condition, each knows the degree of his responsibility—one, because he did little when he should have done a great deal and another because he did too much of what should not have been attempted.

In other forums and formats, in innumerable confrontations, I have presented evidence for everything said here. However, the evidence hasn't been very helpful. That is, it hasn't done very much good. I was troubled about this until I realized that it isn't evidence that you need because you know—almost as well as I do—that I speak the truth. The evidence is all about us. However, for those who really don't know, who need evidence, review the public record. Review and compare the annual budgets for state mental hospitals and state schools for the retarded. Review and compare our community programs for the mentally ill and the mentally retarded. Review and compare the empty beds in our mental hospitals and the human warehouses in our schools for the retarded. Survey the indifference of our medical schools, schools of social work and nursing, and their learned societies, toward the mentally retarded and form comparisons with their involvements with the mentally ill. No new evidence will be presented here. It is fruitless and I see no need for it. The need for such data is long passed. My mission here is to ask you who represent "Mental Health"—ask you, not tell you, because you are in control—to welcome us as full and equal partners for human welfare or give us our freedom to defend and prosecute for our defenseless and persecuted brothers as you are so successfully defending others in as great need, but fortunately, receiving more of their due.

Our two fields—mental health and mental retardation—have always had a dichotomy of nomenclature as well as objectives, services, and share of the public treasure. The classic differentiation between mental illness and mental retardation is found in the meanings of our traditional terms "dementia" and "amentia," one signifying a loss of mentality and the other that mentality was never present. Beyond that relatively simple discrimination, however, are all the implications and inferences that give true understanding of these terms. Mental illness, a sickness, where there is hope, possible cure, is the concern of the physician and the therapist. Mental retardation is a condition which is traditionally without hope, without cure, with little more than the drudgery of day-to-day habit training and the ameliorative effects of prosthesis. It is not an accident that with each rendering of the term "mental illness," the corollary "mental health" is either echoed or assumed. It is not an act of forgetfulness or impreciseness that we have no such corollary for "mental retardation." We have no associations for mental adequacy. The chronicity of our charge defeats any optimistic objectives we have for it and almost guarantees the total uninterestedness of those trained to heal. Consequently, in the light of logic, it is not surprising that organized medicine, social work, nursing, and even government have not shown the same interest and concern for the mentally retarded that they have for the mentally ill. Nor can I say to you that mental retardation is, to a large degree, preventable or, to an undetermined degree, curable. I believe that we are now finding ways of preventing mental retardation and we will find procedures to cure this affliction. However, I would have to reach far beyond the evidence currently available to make such guarantees to you. Neither will I claim any special significance for my personal belief that what was just said concerning the possibilities for prevention and cure for mental retardation can be said—with equal justification—for the mentally ill. That is, my evaluation of the available research and my personal experiences lead me to conclude that mental retardation is no less amenable to prevention and cure than is mental illness. However, the ethos of mental health is one of faithfulness and optimism.

In many ways, our cause has been served by its affiliation—largely unwanted on both sides—with the field of mental health. The term "mental" denoted to the world that the deficiency was in the mind, not the soul or the spirit. Whatever communality we share protects us somewhat from the banalities and stupidities of those who would have us correlate retardation with evil or with the vengeance of Jehovah. Further, it is probable that the "mental" preceding retardation, and our keeping company with the field of mental health, have helped us to recruit mental health workers, some of whom may not have viewed their affiliations with us as last resorts or testimony to their own failures and incompetencies for employment in their "true" field. But, "beyond the mental" our jointure has been fruitless and, consequently, the revolution in mental retardation has been empty.

For too many decades we have received a disproportionately insufficient share of the mental health treasure. Further, the allocation for mental retardation is made less useful by the encumbrances and "strings" that always appear to accompany it, "strings" that may be appropriate for the alleviation of mental illness but, insofar as mental retardation is concerned, are untenable. We are told, on the one hand, that administrators of public institutions for the mentally retarded must be physicians, at least, and, in the best of all possible worlds, psychiatrists. On the other hand, the medical profession—collectively and in innumerable individual demonstrations—makes it abundantly clear that no self-respecting physician should ever accept a position in a state school for the mentally retarded. The results of this ludicrous contrivance are predictable. We do have administrative shortages in our schools for the mentally retarded; we do have too many foreign physicians, medical failures, and others who are ill themselves—mixed in a profoundly complicated juxtaposition with a minority of the most ennobling and dedicated humanists who are consciously sacrificing wealth and prestige to serve this cause for reasons I can't fully comprehend but for which I am thankful. Add two questions to this problem and then ponder the difficulties created for us, albeit unwittingly, by the field of mental health: In that utopia of all worlds, are physicians most qualified to administer residential facilities for the mentally retarded? In that utopia of all worlds, what is the relative importance of medicine as contrasted with other professions in caring for and treating the mentally retarded?

I don't claim definitive answers to the above questions although, obviously, I have my own biased notions concerning what those answers would be if a book of all truth and wisdom was available to us. I do claim that a terrible injustice is being perpetrated in the name of comprehensive mental health–mental retardation planning. In other years there were other names proffered in the guise of progress and unity, probably well intentioned, but leading inevitably to dereliction in our responsibilities to the mentally retarded. Nor, as I envision the future from the clouded jaundice of today, will things be different in our children's time. The shibboleths may change, the irrationalizations will be modified or redefined, but if we continue our current course the plight of the mentally retarded will remain invariant from now until then—however long from this time that "then" will be.

Human beings may invent and define words such as "mental retardation" and "progress" but the subtlety and·meaning of these usually escape our full comprehension. These incredibly complex and superior minds that shape language are, ironically, not equal to utilizing this unique human product in the intended way. We have created a language but are trapped by our own brilliant invention.

There are two human struggles which together parallel the history of efforts to include the mentally retarded within the family of mankind and to give him all the benefits of such inclusion. The coldness, disaffection, that organized medicine, psychology, social work, and even nursing demonstrate toward the geriatric patient is virtually isomorphic with their attitude toward the mentally retarded person, and for substantially similar reasons. Secondly, the alienation a person such as I feels as one apart from the mental health movement is strikingly similar to the alienation that blacks are said to feel as people apart from society. And what I hope will be done about this problem parallels what they hope will be done about the structure of society.

We are asking you to cease thinking of our cause, or any human concern, as a hopeless one that's doomed to failure before it has had a chance to be. We are asking you to integrate us, to make us truly a part of you and you truly a part of us, or to set us free, to separate your mission from ours. We are not certain how well we can exist apart from you; we do know that our situation is now intolerable and will not change as long as our concerns are secondary ones and as long as we are ministered to with the left hand, if at all. As I have stated at the beginning, I will not catalogue for you the almost inexhaustible and unremitting lists of grievances that can be documented concerning the unavailable, inappropriate, abusive, scandalous treatment a family of a mentally retarded child may expect when they place their child in a state residential facility. Nor will I present the abundant documentation clarifying, for all but those who do not wish to see, that there are no alternatives for the mentally retarded other than institutionalization or, if the child is both lucky and capable, public school special classes. For those who are not eligible for the public schools or are no longer children, the choices are few indeed—if they exist at all in most communities—other than institutionalization which itself, because of the unavailability of community programs and the subsequently large waiting lists for residential placement, is most often not available as a choice.

In recent years, those of you who call yourselves mental health workers have appeared to be seeking a rapprochement with the field of mental retardation. Yet, so it seems to me, and I have participated in attempts toward reconciliation, you have been rebuffed and hurt by the unwillingness of those in the field of mental retardation to trust you or welcome your support as other than a mixed blessing. It is true! We have been distrustful, possibly with good reason. As with black-white relationships, for untold years you have denigrated our purpose and have caused the term "mental deficiency" and all of its successors to become pejorative terms. Now, for your own purposes—be they guilt, rescue fantasy, the lure of federal gold, or genuine humanitarian concern and realization of a horrible neglect—you come to save us, bringing your science and your prestige and your power, yet knowing so pitifully little about either whom you will help now or the condition that gave rise to his problems. Those of us who have struggled alone have learned that our ignorance is great concerning the nature and conditions of mental retardation. Those of you who have not given thought to this problem, because you have not given thought to this problem, know far less, yet behave with a certainty that derives from naïveté and a raw opportunism that the superficial and unsophisticated are addicted to. If your true purpose is to join with us in the common struggle for the mentally ill and the mentally retarded, then you must come to be taught as well as to teach, you must come to serve as well as to be served, and you must be humble in a confrontation with uncertainty and complexity. Unfortunately, you must expect abuse from those of your colleagues who have been defamed and those parents whose problems have been ignored. For there is a suspicion among many professionals and parents concerned with the mentally retarded that will not easily permit such offers of friendship and coalescence of values that may come from workers in mental health. If your motives are genuine, you will not permit our rejection to discourage you. You will understand this and allow for it. You will understand that we don't want to be apart from the field of mental health. In fact, we realize that progress for the mentally retarded will never be truly achieved until we have achieved progress for all of the afflicted and burdened and those whom society now derogates.

If it is the true desire of the field of mental health to join as one with the field of mental retardation, mental health—being the more favored and more advanced—will have to treat sympathetically a condition they are, at least, partially responsible for. For want of a name, as no name for this now exists, I call this condition "Oligophrenic Racism." By "Oligophrenic Racism," I mean the attitude expressed by many in my field that the mental health profession should set us free to struggle for ourselves, to find our own way and not be shackled by the restraints that you have placed upon us and the roadblocks you have constructed between our current condition and our envisioned destiny. However, if your purpose is genuine, if you can withstand some initial frigidity and caution in response to your warmth and good will, you will find that we truly want to join you and, in fact, we need you as you need us. On the other hand, if the field of mental health does not view the field of mental retardation as part of a common endeavor, then you *must* permit us to disassociate ourselves from you and join forces with other groups or "go it alone" as we have in the past, but, now, without the weight of your resistance diluting our efforts and progress.

Before our revolutions proceed further, new decisions concerning these burdensome questions should be considered.

chapter 3

OUR UNCOMMITTED VIRTUES[1]

In general, one can hardly claim that there has been unusual progress, during his lifetime, in residential care programs for the retarded. Certainly, there is scant evidence for this contention. It is true that federal and state legislation now permit progress and enhance its possibility—when, heretofore, government was just another roadblock in a global scheme of indifference, unawareness, and "priorityitis" for *other* programs. It is true that we now have more scientific terminology, greater sources for program funding, and some new buildings. It is certainly true—much to our harassment and discomfort at times—that we are now involved in a great deal of activity in behalf of the mentally retarded and their families.

However, I have observed that we change terminology more often than we cause children to change. We confuse activity with progress and we equate money and buildings with improvement. I have observed that—insofar as residential programs are concerned—little, *of consequence,* has changed. Nor have we changed. However, there is one alteration: we have not changed *differently* from the way we have not changed before. We know that things should be different and we have some plausible ideas on how to rearrange for a better world. But, virtue is not in what we know or say but in what we do. And, progress is not in what we plan (or hope) for but in where we are now, and in what road we have taken, and in where we have been.

I sit in my office during the commuter rush hour, preparing this

---

[1] An earlier draft of this chapter, substantively unchanged here, was presented to the President's Committee on Mental Retardation, Boston University, November 16, 1967. Parts of it were published in *PCMR Message,* April 1968, p. 3.

report. The city is in the grips of a terrible early storm. And as I look out of the snow-caked window, gazing onto Storrow Drive, I see endless streams of cars, completely stopped in a city that is paralyzed. The resources of Boston have not been squandered or plundered in the hours between our "normal style" and this storm. The cars are as powerful as ever and the drivers as competent. However, we were not prepared to use our full talents and services in dealing with this problem. More cars—or even snowplows on Storrow Drive—would only worsen the problem. It is probable that all the concentrated talent and resources of our city could not now unsnarl this holocaust any more quickly than the analgesic and healing effects of time and nature rectifying that for which they were responsible. It seems to me that, tonight at least, our programs in mental retardation—in general—and those specifically relating to our residential centers resemble the effects of this storm. These programs are great, powerful, super-colossal affairs. They are also ponderous, unstable, and often mis-guided. To make them bigger and more powerful without changing their central values, purposes, and expectations is to create even more trivial—and worse—even more dangerous programs.

A survey reported in August, 1967, by the Department of Health, Edu-cation, and Welfare disclosed a per capita daily expenditure then of $6.71 per patient under treatment in public institutions for the mentally retarded in this country—higher today but, regrettably, far from suffi-cient.

Without doubt, an enormous new building program is necessary if we are to alleviate the desperate circumstances of most state facilities. The President's Committee on Mental Retardation reported in June, 1967, that three-quarters of all of our institutionalized retarded live in buildings fifty years old or more. It is quite clear that before we build new structures we must destroy old ones and we must do both with great speed and efficiency.

However, before we build new buildings we must design new pro-grams or revive old ones that were too advanced for their times. As we destroy old structures, we must lay to rest those philosophies and programs that no longer serve us well. If we are unable to form a coalescence between our bricks and money, on the one hand, and our philosophies and practices, on the other, I know that the small residen-tial centers planned for our future will differ from current "human warehouses" only in size and, for awhile, in smell—but not in the per capita harm they will promote unwittingly and the wasted lives they will not be able to salvage.

To other panels and in other formats, I have made countless recom-mendations concerning ways to improve our institutional and com-munity programs for the retarded. All of us here have discussed and even acted on ways to "open up" our state schools, to bring life to their dormant programs, and to involve our universities and professional disciplines in a problem in which we feel few people, other than ourselves, are interested. I, and you, have made these recommendations under two implicit beliefs—which, unfortunately, are erroneous. We have planned and plotted and passed legislation and received a greater share of the public treasure *assuming* that, with each new program: (1) professional personnel would be available to staff these facilities and activities; and (2) fiscal and material resources are the weakest links in a chain of conditions that, admittedly, is a catalogue of all the styles and sizes of defective links.

Unfortunately, data on graduates from professional schools of education, medicine, nursing, psychology, and social work categorically deny the assumption that professional personnel, in sufficient numbers, are—or will be—available to adequately staff our current programs, much less our projected much more elaborate ones. Unfortunately for us, in our despair with the past, and in our near-disillusionment with the future, we will not be able to substitute money for talent, buildings for convictions and legislation for *conceptions of human potential* which—in the final analysis—determine how people develop and change.

My suggestion is, first, to consider seriously the concept that non-professional personnel can be recruited and trained for assignments currently involving professional or quasi-professional staff. Secondly, everything I have learned about human behavior and potential for change—everything I know about the concepts of intelligence, and its educability, and personality, and its plasticity—lead to my conclusion that *love* (or what some call dedication or motivation) overcomes what appear to be insurmountable barriers, and *faith* in one's methods and beliefs is a far better predictor of the program outcome than the peculiarities of the methods and beliefs themselves.

There are few truly evil or mendacious people. There are few people without some saving virtues. There are *many* among us who have virtues that are yet to unfold and there are still others who have virtues that are yet to be committed. If we are ever to behave toward the mentally retarded as we prefer to believe we feel toward them, we must discover new sources of human energy to commit to our cause and we must develop new programs to prepare ourselves to view optimistically the potentials man has for changing and, further, to view this belief in terms of our own development as well as for *all* other people.

chapter 4

THE PROCESS OF LEARNING: LOVE'S CONQUEST— FAITH'S VICTORY

There are two truths: life and mortality. Intervening is our process for learning (or changing) which, from the beginning to the end, is man's effort to fathom his being. This struggle to understand has its reward. It causes one to confront the relevancies of life's essential concepts: love for your brother and faith in his ultimate good.

All that remains of the process are the tactics of our design for survival and advancement. Anthropologists sometimes term these tactics "mores." In this enterprising, highly literate, and relatively impersonal western society, we plan mores or educational programs for transmitting and strengthening our accumulated cultural heritage. As a teacher, my concern has been with various pedagogical choices at my disposal. These choices involve such broad longitudinal problems as the depth and extent of my own professional preparation, and numerous specific issues as they relate to what I teach and how I teach.

Each man gropes toward a personal analysis of his conceptual ascendency. Teachers go about this business for much the same reasons most people do. They confront the same truths and essential concepts as others. They merely express themselves differently. For most teachers, process is in the method selected and the material presented. For the scientist, process is in reason and replication. For the poet, process is in his passion for the sound of the word. For any of the aforementioned, and others, who are humanists, process must be in the extent and depth of one's involvement with other human beings. I believe the latter process has the power to flood out the effects of other processes. The humanist tradition of love and faith in our eventual capacity to create good transcends the main effects of such precious modern essentials as science and technology, education and training, legislation, material resources, and comprehensive planning.

Obviously—I hope it is obvious—I do not advocate a return to alchemy or witchcraft, a moratorium on universal education, any declaration of nonsupport of programs for human welfare, or a halt to cooperative development. I am recommending a reordering of our primary considerations for obtaining those ideals rational men have espoused since the beginning of civilization. This reordering has led me to conclusions that may appear, to some, astonishing and, to others, bizarre. For example, my logic contends that we have placed far too much value and trust in the unshakable necessity for professional preparation and standards for such activities involving health and welfare, child care, and education.

Through the years, I have periodically observed denouncements of the state of professional respectability and pride. Most of us have heard (I have been overheard!) the furious rebuttals of teachers when asked to expend effort as clerks, lunch attendants, crossing guards, recreation aids, janitors, or toilet adjutants. It is little different in other professions, for example, medicine. Doctors who are responsible for the health of residents in state institutions for the mentally retarded are loath to serve as educators, social workers, or child care attendants. And, so it appears that, in the professions concerned with human welfare, society has exacted an unbearable price for the status and rewards it provides this privileged class. With the right hand, it doles out public honors and the vestments and finery of the pampered educated man. However, with the left hand, it deals us a cruel, never expected, but inevitable blow. It rubs our pride and skills in the affairs and duties of the great unenlightened, undereducated, ordinary man, the nonprofessional—worse still—the semiskilled nonprofessional.

What questions must we ask to, first, begin to understand the wisdom of our professional involvements and, secondly, begin to cope with a process for learning on a level which contributes to *our* learning? I'll start with the following:

1. What are the essentials for acquiring new skills, changing attitudes, or deepening understandings?
2. If education were at an ideational crossroad, which it may well be, should the teacher learn to accept, and use competently, the tools of the clerk and the custodian or should the clerk learn the trade of the teacher? Or, should things remain, more or less, as they are, with disgruntled and frustrated teachers who are professionally exclusive but not exclusively professional?
3. How efficiently are the material and human resources of our public treasure contributing to the creation and support of viable and meaningful learning settings?

One may ask *how* people acquire new skills or change attitudes. However, the ponderability of *how* lies in our introspective meanderings for we can't "see" learning, as this occurs in our heads. Therefore, with whatever science there is at our command, this question is imponderable. Suppose we ask *why* people acquire new skills or change attitudes. This, too, provides a degree of scientific uncertainty that may not be acceptable to those who adhere to the experimental tradition; e.g. the interrelationship of covert needs and overt motives is little more understood today—although far more widely accepted as a fruitful dimension for hypothetical testing and theory building—than at that time prior to Freud's birth. Then, suppose we ask, "What are some of the consistently observable conditions present some time during the process of learning?" Although a formidable question, this can be discussed profitably. Moreover, this kind of question breaks from the trivial, unproductive, tautological investigations social scientists are wont to pursue. For example, a perusal of the literature on the use of sub-professionals or quasi-professionals in education, health services or welfare will reveal a concentration on such issues as: Should we employ sub-professionals? How can these individuals achieve upward mobility during their careers? What types of training programs are needed for these neophyte social welfare assistants?

In several obvious, certainly pragmatic, ways, the above are not completely unimportant questions. Notwithstanding, they are the "wrong" questions if we are interested in developing the fullest utilization of our human resources. For, if we are, we should investigate the nature and conditions of learning. When we study the effects of employing trainees to, eventually, serve as classroom assistants, we must confront the question, "Under what conditions—if any—can these people learn to behave as effective classroom assistants?" The response to that question will confirm or deny whatever evidence we have concerning whether we should employ these individuals, whether they should be promoted at some stage of their training and experience, and what training programs are most suitable for them.

Under what conditions do people—children, their teachers, their teachers' teachers—learn? People learn or change (these are, to me, synonymous terms) when they: (1) need to change, (2) aspire to change, and (3) are optimistic about the possibility that they will change. Further, *all* individuals should be assumed to be capable of learning and those who are not learning should be viewed in terms of both their own needs and aspirations as well as the program settings they are involved in. Stated another way, I believe it is far more necessary to seek better ways to convince people of their need to learn and the probability that they will learn than to seek better curricula and methods to promote their learning. I believe that, in the ultimate analysis, we will find that our professional preparation or our curricula or our methods cannot be viewed distinct from those individuals we seek to serve. Further, although the process of learning involves the aforementioned, the core of any such process is the degree to which we are convinced that the individual can learn and he is convinced that he both can and should learn. Fundamentally, whatever its superficial characteristics and manifestations are, *interaction* and *faith* are the inherent qualities of this process.

The burgeoning training programs operating with support from our various anti-poverty agencies are mixed blessings. They give the impression of fair tests of the hypothesis that previously-unacceptable people can be prepared during very short training periods to assume responsibilities typically held by professional or otherwise very skilled individuals. These programs run the gamut from the training of nurse's aides and medical technicians to social work assistants and teaching personnel in the headstart preschools. Quite surprisingly, and quite contrary to principles of scientific methodology, reports I have received demonstrate the effectiveness of such programs beyond the realm of chance; surprisingly, because the hypothesis is being tested with those least likely to provide a fair test. In fact, utilizing such populations offers less a test of the hypothesis that the unskilled can learn to perform on skilled or quasi-professional levels, than a test of the hypothesis that the uneducable can be educated. The first hypothesis assumes the existence of a basic strength of purpose and ability that needs support and nurturement to enable one's potential to be achieved. The second hypothesis assumes that strength of purpose and ability can be encouraged in adults who never previously demonstrated such qualities. That is, intellectual and social skills are plastic; they can be incremented by practice and training. A truly fair test of the hypothesis that the untrained nonprofessional can be trained to assume X amount and kind of responsibility, now reserved for professional workers, will require enlisting subjects who are currently functioning as competent and responsible—albeit nonprofessional—human beings. Quite the opposite kinds of people have been selected for such studies. The overwhelmingly major thrust of these projects has been to employ the unemployable—many who have never been employable and others who now have some chronic disabilities. Hence, my surprise at the success of such programs and my enthusiasm and wonderment concerning the possibilities of utilizing the untrained in much more demanding situations if they are not screened into programs because they are: aged, illiterate, physically handicapped, alcoholic, mentally retarded, or impoverished. I applaud the rehabilitation of all of the above and wish that those programs not only continue but expand. However, additional projects are necessary if we are to explore the parameters of human competency. That is, if we take seriously the need to develop new kinds of professional and semi-professional workers in the fields of human welfare we must attract and compete for individuals who, in global terms, perform adequately but do not have the formal higher education currently necessary for these assignments. I believe that these kinds of individuals can be trained to serve as first-rate teaching assistants (who teach children), social work aides (who evaluate and help families), nurse's aides (who provide good care to patients) and, obviously, excellent clerks, matrons, mimeographers, projectionists, and child care attendants. If we had sufficient numbers of these individuals, teachers and doctors and social workers may be permitted the freedom to practice their highly developed professional skills and to supervise and continue the in-service preparation of their less intensively educated colleagues. It is even possible that we shall discover that some of these trainees can be selected, eventually, for regular teaching or nursing or social work positions—in certain settings and under certain conditions of supervision and continuing in-service education.

Given adequate support for the above kinds of programs, it is entirely possible that we will eventually solve the crushing and demoralizing problem all health and education agencies now face: the incredible shortage of teachers, doctors, social workers, nurses, and various specialized therapists. Certainly, a review of data concerning graduates in the above disciplines reveals that it is hopeless—in fact, a denial of external reality—to expect sufficient increases of these personnel to change this bleak situation during our lifetimes. In fact, the reverse is true. As our population increases alarmingly, and as new services and programs are sponsored, competition for professionally prepared workers becomes keener and, consequently, shortages will exacerbate. In the coming generations, the expected roadblock to improved and expanded health and education services will not be induced by material insufficiency but by the sheer unavailability of human resources.

The above leads inevitably to an accounting of our efficiency in conserving and placing in best use our common treasure of trained personnel. I believe that our record has been incredibly poor. Further, only through the grace of our extraordinary natural and hard-won affluence have we been able to survive complete and catastrophic breakdowns of our systems of free public education and other health and welfare activities. It is probable that no other nation could operate so inefficiently and thoughtlessly in these areas and continue to provide the quality and continuum of programs that are available in this country. However, what results here is not only wasteful and inefficient but unequal and discriminatory. We have the greatest universities and diploma mills, the most inspiring public school systems and those that are scandalous, the world's most powerful scientific mobilization toward the prevention and treatment of mental retardation and mental illness and, for certain of these groups, the absolutely poorest care found anywhere on the face of the earth. One factor contributing to this awful variability is our squanderous use of professional talent and, ironically, our blind faith in this talent. All too many times, I have heard that certain untrained teachers or untrained social workers actually perform such jobs equally as well as trained personnel. This is probably true, not because training is unimportant but more likely because the training does not prepare one for the multitude of tasks that the professional is required to attend to, tasks that have little, if anything, to do with either his training or the historic tradition of his profession. Certainly, many reasonably intelligent laymen can compete equally with social workers in most social work settings.

Social workers often have more responsibilities that require anything-but-social-work skills than those that demand such talents. Why, then, should it be shocking to learn that a congenial business school graduate or home economist is as effective as the graduate of a social work school? Some social workers spend a good deal more of their time and energy in budget planning (both for their central offices and for indigent families) and in home management than they do in case-work and group counseling. Similar examples can be given in the fields of education, medicine, psychology, and nursing.

It is apparent that we should no longer tolerate this abuse of what consumed years of effort and thousands of dollars to produce a highly trained professional. Our current practices are self-defeating for they, in effect, guarantee both the continuation of our shortages and the training of first rate people for incompetence; i.e. we are not permitting our professional groups to practice the skills they were taught, and we are requiring them to perform in areas where they have no formal preparation and only chance competence. We should urge our policy makers to ensure much more conscientiously: that our doctors practice medicine, not business administration as heads of institutions; that our best teachers are not forced, for economic reasons, to become journey-men administrators; that our nurses once again minister to patients; and that our social workers become social workers. For this to happen, we will need a cadre of assistants to perform many tasks now believed to be the inviolate provinces of card-carrying professionals. We will need lateral as well as upward mobility options for vocational growth and advancement. We will, at the same time, have to take more seri-ously—and less seriously—the importance of professional preparation: more seriously, in that we must use to much better advantage the specialized talents of the highly trained professional; less seriously, in that we must concede that not all roads to the helping vocations lead from the University.

Essentially, I have postulated that, for most people, interaction skills and a faith in humanity can be trained. For some, these skills appear to be inherent for they are present with or without training. For others, it seems almost impossible to train for these functions. It is the responsi-bility of those who prepare and employ workers for the fields of human welfare to seek out and place those who have these skills, to encourage those who can attain them, and to counsel into other endeavors those who cannot. Until such time when we will employ, without prejudice, capable workers whose competencies were not formally developed and, until such time, when we will refuse to sustain the activities of those who have proceeded through formal training but remain incompetent, we will continue to neglect huge reservoirs of human talent and dedication that might have been channeled to our causes and, unfortunately, we will continue to support those whose only claim for such consideration is our refusal to admit our earlier errors in selecting and attempting to prepare them for tasks in the area concerned.

Training is the method society employs to change an individual who did not or could not change through his own resources. It is not that I deprecate formal training. On the contrary, I prize both the value and power of a formal approach to engender change in people. I am upset not by our enthusiasm for standards but by our certainty that there are only a few well-defined tracks that must be negotiated to obtain required standards. I am upset that we have distorted the objective of our training program by treating it as the evaluation of that program and, thus, in the process, we have precluded any possibility that one can obtain the objective through means other than *that* program.

In a way, I have been saying that, at least for us in the fields of human welfare, formal preparation must not be a goal, but a method to inculcate certain desired skills and insights. The goal relates to what we do, not to what paths we have traveled to permit us to do what we do. When this distinction is better understood we will have made progress in our recruitment of manpower and utilization of all human resources.

All human beings have the capacity to learn. The process of learning depends for its success on the interaction of the learner and the teacher and the faith each has in the strength of that enterprise. We are dealing, then, with human qualities and traits that oftentimes defy the effects of formal training and, certainly, when all things are equal, contribute mightily to what has been learned and how significant that learning is. I cannot comprehend that any factors involving professional preparation, curricula, methods, or facilities are more central than interaction (or love) and faith to the concept of learning and how learning proceeds.

chapter 5

THE LAW

With the widespread publicity given to the Sirhan Sirhan case, the "Boston Strangler"–DeSalvo case, and the group of "XYY chromosomes" suspected murderers, it was inevitable that more and more lay and professional attention would be turned to the law, protection and safeguards for society, and the welfare and treatment of individuals who are judged mentally incompetent. Added to the aforementioned notorious cases, are those—while not nearly as well known to the general public—that may come, eventually, to have more profound and long lasting effects on mental health and mental retardation programs and practices in the United States. Those cases, ranging from the pioneering Rouse v. Cameron case to one of the most recent, Whitree v. the State of New York, affirm the court's opinion that a patient can secure release from a mental hospital by proving he is receiving no treatment or he is receiving inadequate treatment. Further, he may press a successful suit if he proves that he was wrongfully confined in the state hospital. Consequently, in recent months, a great deal has been written about the so-called "Right to Treatment" cases as well as other legal aspects of mental health and mental retardation. For those readers interested in careful study of these problems, a good beginning may be Curran's article in the *American Journal of Public Health,* November, 1968, and the February 1969 issue of *Psychology Today,* which is devoted entirely to the law and how, and under what conditions, it works for you and against you.

Although the above-mentioned problems are very important and little studied, the focus of this chapter will be on a different—but related—set of problems. Each legislative season, federal and state legislators are flooded—literally—with bills or proposals for bills. Added to the virtual impossibility of studying each bill in detail and determining its merits and liabilities is the task of looking at an even greater array of regulations that are promulgated each year as a consequence of legislation and, in effect, become as powerful as laws in that they carry the strength and authority of whatever laws they were developed under. Then, added to the sheer impossibility for the most dedicated legislator of reviewing all bills submitted to him—or even those bills that come to his committees—is the equally monumental task confronting local communities who are asked to comply with new laws and regulations, sometimes before they have had opportunities to study and comprehend—much less implement—some laws and regulations already on their books. It appears desirable that, at this time, we consider the development of a model to assess legislation concerning the mentally retarded—or any other group of handicapped or, for that matter, of any individuals with special needs.

The Measurement of Public Ethics Relating to the Mentally Retarded

What is the relationship between laws, regulations, and practices, on the one hand, and our best information and knowledge, on the other? How may we narrow whatever discrepancy exists between laws and those conditions that give rise to laws (e.g. pressures, political expediency, confusion) and whatever carefully accumulated body of information and knowledge exists? For example, what is the relationship between laws affecting public school exclusion or exemption, mandatory education for the handicapped, sterilization, and PKU prevention and treatment *and* our best information, insights, and professional practices? It is possible that if a method can be developed to measure public ethics relating to the handicapped or—if you will—to measure the relative merits of legislation proposed for the handicapped, more thoughtful and beneficial laws will be passed and, consequently, the lot of the handicapped will be improved. Such a model, implemented impartially to legislated proposals, may do a great deal to help legislators prepare their "homework" and vote more intelligently and thoughtfully than in the past.

To prepare for the development of such a model, I have asked the following questions and applied them to selected pieces of proposed legislation that have come across my desk during the past two or three years:

1. Does the legislation protect the rights of each man?
2. Must the legislation be passed to preserve the general welfare of the community?
3. Does the legislation benefit, explicitly, the individual in whose behalf it is submitted?

4. Does the legislation benefit, explicitly, the community in whose behalf it is submitted?
5. Does the legislation hold promise for the future benefit of the individual?
6. Does the legislation hold promise for the future benefit of the community?

Obtaining from the above set of questions, listed in my assignment of order of importance, is the following model or, to be more accurate, the following draft of a model or of some hypotheses concerning the development of a model.

A Preliminary Model to Assess Legislation Concerning the Mentally Retarded

Based on my experiences, research, and the research of others, the following preliminary model is proposed for the assessment of legislation and regulations relating to the mentally retarded. The model requires a substantive knowledge of the issues before decisions may be made concerning the relative merits of certain pieces of legislation or regulations. It requires the careful research of each piece of legislation, focusing on certain factors that will be outlined subsequently in this chapter. However, once such a search is completed, it may be, then, much less difficult to assess legislation, and such legislation may be assessed much more accurately *vis-à-vis* its potential benefit to the individual and to mankind. The model is based on two levels of legislative action: Level I, where mandatory action is required; Level II, where action is permissive:

1. Level I: Mandatory Action Required
   If the legislation (or regulation) is intended to prevent, reduce, or overcome a threat to the physical, moral, and/or social welfare of the communty while it guarantees equal protection of the ethical and legal rights and privileges of each person, *then* legislation must be supported.
   If the legislation (or regulation) acts to deprive any man of his inalienable guarantee of equal treatment under the law or acts to deprive him of whatever ethical and legal rights and privileges enjoyed by free men in our society, *then* legislation must be rejected.

2. Level II: Permissive Action Criteria
   Therefore, all other legislation may be endorsed *if:* (a) the action does not do violence to the Judeo-Christian democratic heritage of our people and (b) if it is clear that this action will not precipitate or encourage a deterioration of community welfare. The following are suggested criteria to rank proposed legislation that: (a) is not included under mandatory Level I (for direction of action is categorically plain here) and (b) passes above requirements for permissive action. These criteria include:
   (a) Legislation is intended to benefit explicitly those individuals with whom it is centrally concerned. This criterion is usually mandatory for endorsing proposed legislation. Further, it is often sufficient for such endorsement.

(b) Legislation is intended to benefit explicitly the community, in addition to or as distinguished from those for whom the action will most affect. This criterion is not mandatory and will seldom be sufficient rationale for endorsement of proposed legislation.

(c) Legislation is intended to benefit indirectly those individuals with whom it is centrally concerned. Meeting this criterion is desirable but rarely sufficient for supporting proposed legislation.

(d) Legislation is intended to benefit indirectly the community, in addition to or as distinguished from those whom the action will most affect. Meeting this criterion is desirable but rarely sufficient for supporting proposed legislation.

Discussion

The model assumes that sufficient information relating to proposed legislation can be gathered and analyzed and, utilizing appropriate criteria, judgments may be reached concerning the importance and worthiness of the proposed legislation. The model recommends that positive action should be taken if the proposed legislation protects the rights of each man as it preserves the general welfare of the community. Conversely, the proposed legislation should be rejected if it does not protect the rights of each man or threatens the general welfare of the community. Insofar as proposed legislation that does not require mandatory action—i.e., it is neither a threat to particular individuals nor a threat to the community—several criteria are suggested to test the importance of the proposed legislation and the benefits that would accrue to society. On this permissive level, if the proposed legislation promises to guarantee the rights of each individual and does not threaten the general welfare of the community it should receive a specific priority ranking. Proposed legislation that seeks to provide direct benefit for individuals should receive high priority ranking. Proposed legislation that does not directly benefit the individual but benefits the general community should receive medium priority ranking. Lastly, proposed legislation that only indirectly benefits or promises possible future benefit to either the individual or the community should receive medium to low priority ranking.

In efforts to refine this preliminary model for assessing legislation, I applied the above criteria for mandatory and permissive action to various types of legislation and regulations that either interest or concern me. That is, in a very general kind of way, I tested the preliminary model against certain widely accepted laws and practices. In one state, where children are regularly excluded or exempted from public school, I evaluated their laws and regulations pertaining to such actions. As their current legislation acts to deprive an individual of his right to equal treatment under the laws and regulations relative to education, I concluded that current legislation must be rescinded and new legislation enacted that guarantees protection of an individual's right to schooling and due process before either exclusion or exemption from such schooling. On the other hand, when applying the research available on the efficacy of special classes for the mentally retarded—both educable and trainable—to current mandatory legislation that has been enacted in most states since World War II, it was concluded that such legislation enjoys but a modest ranking. That is, the evidence does not support mandatory legislation for special classes for the mentally retarded. These classes, from the evidence available, are not necessary to prevent, reduce, or overcome a threat to the physical, moral, or social welfare of the community or of the individual. On the other hand, there is sufficient evidence to pass legislation so that such classes become optional with the community. Stated another way, there is no compelling evidence to either mandate the inclusion *or* exclusion of special classes in our public schools.

In the same manner as above, I have applied laws relating to sterilization, teacher certification, mandatory school attendance, minimum hours for daily school attendance, early childhood education laws, and laws and regulations as they affect care and treatment in the institutions to the above preliminary model. The model has proven helpful to me and, I believe, will be helpful to legislators and others responsible for judging the relative value of proposed legislation.

A Final Remark

I have felt, for many years, that merely passing more legislation is not necessarily beneficial to mankind or helpful to particular individuals—even those for whom the legislation is intended. Oftentimes, legislation is passed for capricious reasons, sometimes for political reasons, sometimes from ignorance, and sometimes after thoughtfulness and intelligent deliberation. Obviously, the preliminary model proposed here can be no more effective in aiding such deliberations than the kinds of information and insights that are gathered and brought to bear on the decision-making process. The value of this model may lie in the focus it provides for the assessment of legislation, the priorities for such assessment that we may eventually agree upon, and a formula and quantitative methodology to rank legislation in a much more precise way than heretofore. To date, I have developed a prototype formula and quantification system. It is hoped that, some day, it will be sufficiently refined and usable as to provide guidance to those responsible for passing and implementing legislation and regulations relating to the handicapped. Until such time as a more refined methodology becomes available, it is recommended that the preliminary model presented here be utilized for making general assessments of the relative value of legislation concerning the mentally retarded.

chapter 6
LETTERS[1]

This chapter explores some of the ways in which we might increase public awareness concerning the plight of the institutionalized retarded. After all we have seen and after so much has been said, one wonders what new tragedies must occur, what new injustices must be transformed, what new threats must be made before society responds. I am concerned both with what motivates people to react to what is distasteful to them in their environment and also what conditions prevent them from involving themselves and taking direct action about such situations.

Quite recently, a small nation state in Africa declared its independence. The eight million people of Biafra, with very meager physical resources, attempted to secede from Nigeria. The estimates of the numbers of Biafrans who died in this struggle for freedom vary, but all run into millions. And of those millions, millions were women and children, systematically, knowingly, starved.

We remember a nation that, during our lifetime, allowed the murder of thirteen million people, six million of them Jews. While these atrocities were occurring, many countries looked on, either not believing that such things were happening, or not caring enough to do anything about

1 Miss Roxann Joseph, administrative assistant to the author during his tenure with the Massachusetts Department of Mental Health, contributed greatly to the development of this chapter. She helped to sort and classify the hundreds of letters and joined with other volunteers in answering every one. In addition, she was a partner in constructing the theoretical position taken here and in the subsequent analysis of the letters. Lastly, the author wishes to express his gratitude to Miss Pamela Weeks who completed the earliest analysis of the letters, which was of considerable help during our later formulations.

them. What more would have had to occur in order to mobilize citizens to react?

Our own nation is presently faced with many serious problems—our involvement with the war in Viet Nam and our internal disruptions on the streets and in the schools. A small minority of people respond to social and political unrest by burning draft cards, marching on the Capitol, rioting in the streets, or simply "dropping out" of society. How many more riots must occur, stores burn or lives be taken before our own country provides enough jobs and food and equal opportunities for those presently in desperate need? How many more young people will adopt the "hippie philosophy" as a better way of life before the rest of us realize that things aren't as they should be?

Hypotheses

One might think that these crises would evoke concern. Since this is clearly not the case, it may be in our interest to develop hypotheses in order to better study public reactions to the kinds of human issues discussed here. It is hypothesized that, under certain conditions, individuals show sympathetic concern and, under other conditions, they choose to be insensitive to the ills surrounding them. The following hypotheses may be helpful in our attempts to comprehend these conditions and the variety of reactions they give rise to:

1. *It is hypothesized that an individual will react to a condition if he fears that it might affect him directly.* For example, one might immediately build and equip a bomb shelter if he felt, personally, the threat of nuclear war. Or, a person might be inoculated against smallpox if an epidemic was imminent. A person might even purchase a gun if he felt his family or property were in jeopardy.

2. *It is hypothesized that an individual will react to a condition if it has already affected him directly.* In other words, a shopkeeper would keep his cash register nearly empty if he had experienced several robberies. Or, a husband and wife might seek genetic counseling if they already had one retarded child.

3. *It is hypothesized that an individual will react to a condition if he feels that certain relevant and pertinent information has been distorted or withheld from him.* An angry citizen might openly criticize the war in Viet Nam if he felt that government reports were deliberately misleading the public. An employee might decide to resign if he felt his employer was concealing unfair business practices.

4. *It is hypothesized that an individual will react to a condition if his concept of human ideals is challenged.* A dog lover might react with repulsion to the tribal culinary custom that regards dogs as edible. A mother may react with horror to the abandoning of a small infant.

While the above hypotheses may apply to the reactions of some people, there are alternative hypotheses relative to other people who choose not to respond to identical or similar situations.

5. *It is hypothesized that an individual will not react to a situation that he has been conditioned to accept.* To protest against long hair on males (dirty or not) might have initiated change in years past; today, this sight is so common, even in schools, that such protest may not result in much more than a polarization of unresolvable differences. Years ago, demands to legal authorities requiring penalties for marijuana users and suppliers often led to legal action; today, it appears that action is taken less and less frequently, and fewer complaints are made in proportion to the number of users. At the turn of the century, violent protest against the use of solitary confinement cells in mental hospitals might have made living conditions there more bearable; today, there are budgetary requests for more cells.

6. *It is hypothesized that an individual will not react to a condition if he feels he can do nothing to rectify it.* A doctor might choose not to attempt to help a cancer patient if he believes that the illness is terminal and unbearably painful.

7. *It is hypothesized that an individual will not react to a condition if he fears personal involvement.* We often hear or read about brutal street beatings witnessed by an inactive, horrified audience. There are also instances when an individual possesses pertinent evidence about a crime (e.g., one involving the Cosa Nostra) but refuses to offer this evidence to the authorities for fear of being personally harmed. There are people witnessing automobile accidents who choose not to report the incident or take the time to involve themselves in ensuing legal action. We might also know of politicians who are blatantly aware of dishonest government dealings, but make no charges that might jeopardize their own positions.

8. *It is hypothesized that an individual will not react to a condition if he is unaware of the relevant circumstances.* Obviously, although there are people who may be truly ignorant of a situation, we feel that they represent a much smaller group than those who are not so ignorant but prefer to pretend they are.

The above hypotheses and examples reflect my concern with the kinds of public responses to some of our most crucial current problems. A number of the crises confronting us have already been mentioned—the war, domestic problems, political and social unrest. However, in my opinion, one of the most tragic and ignored dilemmas facing our nation today is the existence of man's callousness to man, as exemplified by living conditions in the back wards of our institutions for the mentally retarded.

I estimate that there are, today, 40,000 mentally retarded individuals residing in our so-called back wards. The question is: how can public interest be aroused, so that the horrifying conditions in which so many of these people exist can be improved.

Public Response

When the "Tragedy and Hope of Retarded Children" appeared in October, 1967, in *Look,* no one involved with the publication anticipated the overwhelming response. Hundreds of letters from all parts of the country poured into *Look,* into my office, and into that of Fred Finn, superintendent of The Seaside Regional Center. According to *Look's* "Mail Report" for the year, the article received the fifth largest number of responding letters. If letters directly to the author were included, the article was first. The kinds of responses aroused require examination. The letters received will be analyzed in terms of the writers' backgrounds, their probable motives, and the proposed hypotheses discussed earlier.

Relative to the backgrounds of the writers, they are categorized into four distinct groups:

1. People having no connection with mental retardation, i.e. neither concerned professionals nor parents.
2. Professional workers in the field of mental retardation.
3. People who plan to study or are presently studying in the field of special education.
4. Parents or close friends and relatives of retarded children.

There were several themes pervading the contents of the letters that overlapped all of the above categories. These appear to be related to the various emotions aroused (irrespective of backgrounds) by the article.

Anger was expressed in many letters in a variety of forms—anger at the institutions for allowing such conditions to exist, followed by requests for the names of the institutions described so that proper action might be taken. Demands for action ran the gamut from burning the institutions to writing the superintendents, governors and congressmen of the states involved. There were also expressions of anger at governmental red tape, at the difficulty of obtaining any immediate legislative action, and at the current misuse and waste of public funds; anger at this country that fought with determination against Nazi Germany and yet allows conditions similar to those in German concentration camps to exist within its own borders; and puzzlement at parents of these children who allow them to exist in such circumstances.

In addition to anger, one senses a feeling of inadequacy in coping with the situation. These questions are asked repeatedly: *If the parents cannot, or do not care enough to, change these conditions, how can I? How can one person influence government officials enough to get something done?*

Expressions of pity and compassion were frequent. These emotions were aroused by the observation that children, so vulnerable and, consequently, so protected in most circumstances, could be allowed to suffer such torture. Reference was made on many occasions to the little boy behind the locked door saying "Touch me, play with me."

In dealing with a sample of all correspondence received, 194 letters were analyzed. With regard to geographic distribution, the country was arbitrarily divided into five sections:

North and Middle East	88
South East	29
Middle West	38
South West	33
North West	2
Foreign	4

The states from which more than ten letters were received were:

California	17
Connecticut	11
Illinois	13
Massachusetts	17
New Jersey	12
New York	27
Pennsylvania	14
Texas	12

In all, letters were received from thirty-two states. There were also several letters from servicemen stationed abroad and from Canadians.

Referring to the aforementioned four categories of writers, our analysis reveals the following:

1. Letters from People Having No Connection with Mental Retardation.

This group of letters was by far the largest. A total of 108 letters was received from such individuals, or more than one half of all the letters analyzed. When reading these letters, the most impressive occurrence is the repeated question—"What can I do to help?" This was asked in 80 of the 108 letters. People offered their old toys and clothes, their money to buy new beds, their time to scrub walls or play with the children, and their voices to speak for the rights of these children.

Another statement found in slightly more than one-third of the letters is that previously the writer did not know that such conditions existed. Many people were aghast that, in this era of missiles and computers, some people still live in the "middle ages." But the great majority of these people were not satisfied to say, "We're sorry, we didn't know." They did say, "Now that we do know, tell us what to do about it." Letters of this type, expressing ignorance but not apathy, comprise about one-third of all letters received in this category.

The remaining two-thirds stated that they suspected, or knew, that institutionalized children and adults were not receiving adequate care. However, this was something so far removed from their everyday lives that it could conveniently be ignored or denied. After having read the article, they could no longer remain passive. Again, the majority asked for guidance in doing something to help change these conditions.

There were clearly more letters written by females than males, 85 letters received from the former and 23 from the latter. However, many of the women said they were writing on behalf of their husbands and entire families.

It was not possible to determine the exact ages of all the letter writers although, many times, a close approximation was made when occupation or current activities were stated. For example, of the 23 males, 4 were servicemen, 4 students, and the remainder (15) business-men of undeterminable occupation.

In the 55 letters from mothers of typical children, one finds the same kind of sentence repeatedly: "But for the grace of God, these children could be mine; let me help them." The strength of the maternal instinct seems quite powerful. These women feel themselves responsible as mothers, not only for their own children, but for all children. The 22 letters from teenagers all expressed concern and willingness to help. The remaining 8 letters were from women who do not mention their occupations or backgrounds. Their letters express much the same sentiments as do the others.

It is of interest to note the concrete suggestions offered by these people and the action previously taken by many. These letters are not only saying, "We are ashamed." Most letters demonstrate considerable thoughtfulness and, in a number of cases, a good deal of effort. Nine people, in addition to writing to me, have written similar letters to their governors, their senators, the President's Committee on Mental Re-tardation, and state departments of mental health. I received an invita-tion to speak to a rotary club, two letters suggesting television shows, and two letters from newspapermen who plan to write their own articles on the same subject.[1] Numerous people requested reprints of the article for circulation in their communities or among government offi-cials. Two letters urged me to appeal to teenagers. The large response from teenagers indicated that they do care and they do want to get involved. A woman, originally from Australia, wrote that, because of the

---

[1] In addition, many, many invitations came via telephone, telegram, and personal visit to speak before groups and appear on television and radio programs.

laws concerning employment of non-citizens, she cannot obtain work in an institution for the retarded. Finally, a woman wrote that her governor claimed that such conditions could not exist in his state's institutions even though, that same week, an exposé of conditions in one of those institutions had appeared in a major newspaper. What good does it do, she asked, to bring these conditions to the attention of senators and governors when they can, and do, say, "Not here, not us."

2. Letters from Professionals in the Field of Mental Retardation.[2]

This group, although the next largest in quantity, seems small when compared to the previous one. A total of 37 out of the 194 letters were received from various professionals. The professions represented were: special education teachers (11); college professors of education (4); institution directors and personnel (5); staff of state and federal departments of mental health, officials of associations for retarded children and boards of education (6). Two letters were received from people seeking help in founding private schools for the retarded. Letters also came from a school social worker, an administrator of a school for exceptional children, and a rehabilitation worker. One-third of all those letters came from personal friends expressing their endorsement and approval of the article.

Six of the special class teachers and two of the institution directors described the work in which they are engaged and asked for any advice that might improve their personal situations. One special class teacher expressed the importance of recruitment of prospective special class teachers.

The letters written by professional workers in mental retardation gave me a strong impression that these are people (and there are many more) deeply dedicated to improving the lives of the retarded.

3. Letters from People Who Plan to Study or Who Are Studying to Become Special Education Teachers.

There were 16 letters in this category, the majority from females. Primarily, these letters requested advice on how and where to pursue the field of special education. Seven letters were from high school students, all of whom want to teach exceptional children. Two of these attribute their interest to the fact that they have retarded siblings.

The remaining 10 letters were from older people, who are now teach-

---

[2] Several hundred letters—mostly from professionals, governors, congressmen and officials of voluntary agencies—were (and continue to be) sent to us in response to our book, *Christmas in Purgatory*. Incredibly, we have not received letters that could be considered critical of either the book or the *Look* article. Whatever criticism we found was very modest, quite rare, and, essentially, indirect and "second-hand."

ing or studying special education. One gentleman had been a teacher of the mentally retarded in an institution and wanted information about further graduate study. Three women requested the same kind of information. The remaining letters asked for guidance concerning graduate courses they might pursue while teaching.

And most impressive, in my opinion, were the fourth category:

4. Letters from Parents or Close Friends and Relatives of Retarded Children.

Letters in this category totaled 36, again, the majority from women. Of this group, 26 were from parents of retarded children, 9 from brothers, sisters and grandparents, and 1 from a woman who wants to become a "mother" of a retarded child. She grew very fond of a little boy while working in an institution and now wants to adopt him.

The children of ten of the parents are institutionalized. These letters were the most poignant received. Many of them described vividly conditions in state and private institutions, conditions as distressing as those discussed in the *Look* article. These parents are at a complete loss insofar as what they should or should not do. They do not know which way to turn. One child had been placed in several of the "finest schools for the retarded." But these schools employ "therapeutic isolation cells" and other punitive practices similar to those mentioned in the article. All of these parents asked advice about placement, many of them about the possibility of placement at the Seaside Regional Center, mentioned in the article.

Eleven letters were received from parents whose retarded children were, or now are, attending special classes. These ones were much more encouraging than the others. All of these parents seemed satisfied and very pleased with their child's progress in school. One mother described her 21-year-old daughter who had attended special classes all her school life. She now drives a car, votes, and is self-supporting. All of these parents offered their help in changing institutional conditions. They know that retarded children need not live useless lives.

The remainder of the letters in this group were from friends or relatives of retarded children. All of them expressed appreciation for bringing the tragedy of retarded children to the public's attention, and all offered their support and help in transforming this tragedy into hope.

I have attempted to describe, as objectively as possible, the letters received in response to my article. Before drawing any conclusions about the letter writers' degree of commitment to the problem, it may be of benefit to add a few facts that may assist the reader in drawing his own conclusions.

We asked *Look* and Fred Finn of The Seaside for data on responses to the article that they received. *Look* replied:

> While we cannot give you the exact figures (this is against policy), we can tell you that the article was a very heavy puller—perhaps the best puller of any article we have ever carried on mental health. The previous related article, "Bobby Joins His World"—dealing with brain-damaged children—drew a great deal of mail, but less than "The Tragedy and Hope of Retarded Children."

Fred Finn sent us copies of all the letters that he received to that time, totaling 119. The large majority of these were from parents seeking placement for their retarded children.

In reading all letters received (313), I found not one that was critical of the *Look* article in any way. Some denied that conditions described in the article exist in "their" institutions, but none disputed the seriousness of this situation nation-wide.

One cannot question the depth of commitment to the cause of retarded children of the individuals whose letters are included in the last two categories: i.e. letters from Professionals, Future Professionals, and Relatives of Retarded Children. These are people who have chosen (or been chosen for) the education and care of the retarded child for their life's work. Insofar as this study is concerned, those people whose lives are relatively unaffected by mental retardation are of major significance. That is, the bulk of America must be reached somehow, those with whom we have scarcely made fleeting contact.

Previously, I enumerated some of the emotions expressed in the letters. The letters from unrelated laymen are especially full of anger, compassion, and doubt—doubt that an inexperienced nonprofessional can do very much to alleviate the suffering of retarded children. I answered all of these letters and, in so doing, attempted to discourage this feeling of inadequacy and to channel these emotions in a positive direction—in the direction of active participation as volunteer workers in institutions and in local programs sponsored by associations for retarded children, or in the direction of active agitation through any number of feasible outlets.

The responses to these suggestions have been quite reassuring. As of this writing, more than thirty people have written a second or third time saying that they have visited institutions, have begun doing volunteer work with retarded children, or have written to governors, congressmen, and departments of mental health.

It seems hopeful to me that, in this year of war and racial hatred, people appear to feel moral obligations to involve themselves in these issues. Many of us no longer condone our *own* apathy; for too long we have merely derogated the apathy of others. Viet Nam is far away and, for some, not a justifiable cause. The racial issue is, for some, too deeply personal—festering unhealed wounds—for any rapid or direct action. But the suffering of innocent children is a social evil to which practically every human being can respond.

It is impossible to count the children that have benefitted from re-actions to "The Tragedy and Hope of Retarded Children." There is no way of measuring—much less understanding—the amount of suffering that has been lessened. However, two things appear certain. Today, there is no one who can guarantee that every child in residential care is receiving adequate treatment. Unfortunately, we cannot be assured that tomorrow will be different. What, then, do I believe? Too many people are being sacrificed needlessly for a better tomorrow, that may not be better because, if for no other reason, when one person is sacrificed everyone involved is sacrificed or lost. We might reduce that sacrifice if we understand better the power of lay activity and use more efficiently the talents of lay volunteers.

Illustrative Letters

The following letters are illustrative of all the correspondence received. They were selected for inclusion to represent geographic areas, back-grounds of the writers, and the hypotheses considered earlier. They are categorized according to the aforementioned hypotheses.

Hypothesis I: It is hypothesized that an individual will react to a condition if he fears that it might affect him directly.

Long Island, N.Y.

Dear Dr. Blatt,
I have just finished your article in *Look*. I am heart sick. But for the grace of God one or all of my four children could have been born re-tarded. I am just a homemaker but I would very much like to help—How may I do so?

Sincerely,
Mrs. _____ D_____.

Roslyn Heights, Long Island, N.Y.
October 20, 1967

The Honorable Senator Robert F. Kennedy
Senate Office Building
Washington, D.C.

My dear Senator:
Some months ago you showed concern for retarded children. I see now, more than ever, that your concern was justified. In the current issue of *Look Magazine* (10–31–67), Dr. Burton Blatt writes, but I cannot be-

lieve, about helpless, retarded "material" in institutions throughout the United States. I cannot begin to paraphrase Dr. Blatt's compassionate, sensitive description of existing conditions in these, *our* institutions.

Dr. Blatt has the facilities of *Look Magazine* at his disposal, yet I doubt that he is permitted to write all that is in his heart—but I can. I can tell you that we have billions for a war that doesn't make sense, billions for foreign aid, and billions for pork barrel projects, but precious little for anguished children that cannot speak out. They are "guarded" by people who are devoid of compassion. What manner of being is it that has the capacity to make his life's work a keeper of these children?

Senator, read Dr. Blatt's report. Do something—you have the power— do something now! My wife and I stand ready to help you. There, but for the grace of God, go any one of your children or mine.

Sincerely,
Mr. and Mrs. J. A. F_____.

Copies to: The President
              The Honorable Governor Nelson A. Rockefeller
              The Honorable Senator Jacob K. Javits
              Honorable Lester L. Wolff, Representative in Congress
              Dr. Burton Blatt
              Charles Mangel, *Look* Senior Editor

Hypothesis II: It is hypothesized that an individual will react to a condition if it has already affected him directly.

_____, Maryland
October 17, 1967

Dear Dr. Blatt:

Just had to write you this morning after reading your article about the retarded in *Look* magazine. Have thought of so many things I want to say to you. I may possibly write you another letter later.

You most certainly would have to be the parent of a retarded child to have such insight and to describe so graphically the plight of these pitiful people. If I were as brilliant as you I would have written the article word for word. We do have a 25 year old retarded son in _____, _____ State Institution for the Retarded. You described so well the barren life those people live. I suppose my son is in one of the better cottages (I've seen worse there) but it is so far from ideal. I agree with you; the care, comfort, their very lives depend on the attendants. We cannot make attendants love those children (only parents love a retarded child) but it does seem likely that the attendants could be supervised so closely that they would have to pay some attention to the children.

_____ gave the attendants a raise this past year so I understand the salary isn't too bad. But the turnover in personnel is terrific. Lately, I sent three letters, one to the Governor of _____, about the lack of help at _____. Within a week I saw more help there—capable looking people, a couple of the new ones were actually standing in the room (where they sit all day on benches) with the children. I was so thrilled, I hurried home and wrote a thank you letter to the superintendent of the institution for putting more help in that cottage. He was grateful for my compliment and promised to circulate my letter among the employees. Yesterday, a week after seeing the new employees in the room with the patients, the picture was different. I stood at the locked door ringing the buzzer several times and could look through the screen straight back, viewing two sitting rooms, occupancy over 100 male patients—there wasn't an attendant in sight. One badly crippled boy whom I befriended flailed and beat on a door which leads to the bedrooms (the office is way past that bedroom). The boy was trying to tell them that I was at the door. Finally an attendant unlocked the bedroom door and came out. Then another attendant made the scene. I asked why they were in there locked in and the patients were alone. What would the patients have done if there had been an accident? (Some do throw chairs, twist arms, etc.) The attendant explained they have to keep that door locked or the boys would mess up the beds. I told them the children are more important than the beds. I went to the Administration Office of this cottage and repeated my fears. The supervisor was away—I spoke to 4 other employees. One remarked, "if there had been something wrong with the patients, they would have made a different noise." I'm not insinuating my letter to the Governor had anything to do with the new help I saw there. It was just a coincidence.

Honestly, I believe the new employees were in the room with the children, touching them, speaking to them, paying attention to them because the employees *were new*. Perhaps now they see how the old timers do it, and fall right in the routine. Please Dr. Blatt and please God do not let anything I have said here cause unhappiness of an attendant anywhere. Even a bad attendant is better than none . . . apparently they are hard to keep.

If we care too much about our children, complain, etc., we are referred to as crazy and emotionally disturbed. I'm sure we are disturbed. To see a warm, sweet, patient, loving, innocent human being just existing, rather than living the good life, disturbs me greatly. It takes the joy out of my life. How can I enjoy the blessings I have . . . if those people have to live like that?

Please write more articles, please use your mind and knowledge to help the retarded. Only people like you can do it. I feel so absolutely helpless, so inadequate, and I want so much to help.

Sincerely,

Mrs. _____ G_____.

P.S. Could you or would you please tell me how to help in the most effective way? I do write letters.

Long Beach, N.Y.

Dear Dr. Blatt,

I read your article on retarded children in *Look Magazine,* October 31 issue. I have a retarded boy age 18 years. He is at _____ _____ School for Retarded. I do not like his treatment there, as he comes home with all kinds of bruises, cuts, stitches, black eyes—you name it, he has it. I am very disgusted when I take him home. He does not want to go back and it upsets me very much. We wrote for a transfer in February, 1965, to the new school in _____, The _____ School for Retarded. We were to hear in 1966 but nothing has come out of it yet.

I would like to know a little more about this Seaside, on the shore of Long Island Sound. I tried to get a phone number of the place, but couldn't, there was no listing of it. I am a mother of 9 children and it happens to be my oldest that is retarded. The other 8 children are all well, thank God, and are all very good to their brother when I take him home for the summer and all holidays. He is happy at home but gets out of hand after being home awhile. Please try to help me and let me know any information you can. Thanking you in advance.

Mrs. _____ B_____.

University City, Mo.
October 18, 1967

Dr. Burton Blatt
Chairman Department of Special Education
Boston, Mass.

Dear Sir:

I have just read your article in *Look Magazine.* It is one of the most heartbreaking articles I have ever read.

I am the mother of a retarded boy 18 years old. I can't conceive how people can be so inhumane, as those you wrote about.

Here in St. Louis County we have one of the best educational systems for our retarded and other handicapped children. Our teachers are so dedicated to our children.

When my husband was killed in an hunting accident 3 years ago, I didn't know what I would have done without my son's teacher. I did not know how to explain to him so he would understand, but they did.

We may not have the best of institutions here, so far as facilities are concerned, but the children are cared for by personnel who care.

I hope your most enlightening article will come to the attention of our federal as well as those state officials who can do something about those horrible conditions. It will also have to be we parents, as well.

Thank you for your investigation and your article.

Sincerely,
Mrs. K_____ S_____.

_____, N.J.
October 24, 1967

Dear Dr. Blatt,

Your article in *Look Magazine* certainly was published with perfect timing.

My husband and I have just come back from touring one of our state institutions in _____ _____. We found much the same situations there only not quite as bad as the ones you saw. We too found many of the children lying on the floor idle, others tied in chairs, fifty beds crammed next to each other, playrooms void of toys, books, curtains and other childrens' decorative items. We visited the school on Sunday so we didn't see any school program or play program going but we were told that those children who can participate do, but the majority do not attend and they are just breathing lumps of flesh. Thank God we didn't see any confinement cells or "therapeutic isolation" cells. The nurse attendants seemed pleasant but as far as we could see offered nothing to the children.

Our son is 14 years old and has been in public school classes since he was 6. He talks beautifully, reads, spells, does simple arithmetic problems and functions higher than his I.Q. of 50. As a result of this he has been in both trainable and educable classes. Besides being brain damaged and mentally retarded, he is also physically handicapped. He cannot walk, and his hand coordination is poor. He can take care of some of his personal care but must be helped with toilet needs even though he is toilet trained.

We have been advised by a very fine neuro-pediatrician in N.Y. to place _____ for his benefit as well as ours. He feels _____ will always need custodial care and will never be able to function independently. We don't know where to place him. Most schools for the retarded do not accept the physically handicapped.

Our state, because of _____'s problem, has come to realize their responsibility and in our newest state school promise to have a cottage for this kind of child.

In the meantime we are faced with the problem of where and what to do to help _____. If you have any suggestions we would be most happy to hear from you. Seaside Regional sounds marvellous. I hope New Jersey and other states can come up with similar facilities for these children.

Hoping to hear from you soon.

Sincerely,

Mrs. _____ E_____.

_____, Pennsylvania
October 23, 1967

Dear Dr. Blatt,

I was very happy to read your article in *Look Magazine* this month, not that I was happy that these conditions exist, but the fact that someone finally has the guts to let the people know what goes on behind the closed doors of these so called, "Lovely Homes For The Retarded." My name, sir, is _____ _____ and I have had and am still having a problem of getting someone to believe me on what is happening at the _____ _____ School For Exceptional Children, which is located in _____, _____. I would like to explain my problem to you, sir, and possibly, you could advise me what to do. I have a child who was born with cerebral palsy and he cannot walk. He has limited use of his arms, and he can speak to a certain degree to us, his family, who understands him. At the age of four years old, we sent him to the _____ School, which is under the jurisdiction of the Easter Seal Society, and is located on _____ _____. At this school, _____, our son, was given all types of therapy, and a little schooling. He was permitted to attend this school for two years, and then he was transferred to the _____ School, which is located in the _____ section of Pittsburgh. At this school, through the continued use of therapy and leg braces, he started to ride a tricycle, and take a few steps with help from the staff and crutches—at this time he was six years old. He was at this school also under the Easter Seal Society. He then was transferred to the _____ _____ School in the _____ section of Pittsburgh. At this time _____ was learning to feed himself, and he was getting schooling.

In general, he was doing wonderful. The above named schools were only day schools and _____ would return home every night. This leads to the troubles I started to have. My wife developed a troublesome back from lifting _____ to and from the wheel chair, as I worked the swing shift at a steel plant, and was not able to be home all the time when the child had to be taken to the bathroom or to bed. I then was forced to go through a lot of red tape, to have my son put on the waiting list, until there was an opening in a state school. He was supposed to be placed in the _____ _____ School in _____, Pennsylvania, but until there was an opening, he was to be placed in a secondary school. This school is the _____ _____ School which I mentioned above. We took our son to this school in February, 1964, and upon entering the school we were met by a Mr. _____, who was supposed to be the therapist for this school. He told my wife and I, at the elevator, that day, that our son was not bad at all, and that he would make him walk in no time at all. We were so happy, my wife cried all the way home that day. We later found out that Mr. _____ was not a therapist, but he was a gardener and caretaker for the school. At this school, the braces were taken off of our son, he was put in a wheel chair, and there he stayed from the time he awoke until the time he went to bed. As of now this child has regressed to a point that is unbelievable. He cannot even straighten out his legs anymore. We were permitted to bring him home every week-end while he was there, and not a week-end passed that he didn't have something wrong done to his body that didn't require mending from my wife or a doctor in a hospital. He has had stitches put in his face, his arms and neck were ripped and gouged. The latest incident was when he laid in that school for three days with a ruptured appendix before he was rushed to a hospital, unconscious, and where he was in critical condition for two weeks, while peritonitis was being fought. The only reason that he didn't die was that he was in a wheel chair and not active, and the poison localized itself.

After our son was in well enough shape to be released from the hospital, we brought him home to build his body back up again, as he was in very poor physical condition. Two days after we had our son home, _____ _____ School called our home and demanded that we return our son to the school immediately. I told them that they had tried to kill my son for the last time and until I can get someone to look into the situation at that school, I was not going to return him. I then got in touch with juvenile court, as they were the ones that had _____ placed in the school in the first place. I was informed by juvenile court that if I was not pleased with the situation at the _____ _____ School, to take my son out, even after I explained that my wife was unable to lift the boy. I was told by a Miss _____, at juvenile court, that my wife's health was of no concern to them. This then is a person's ultimatum—let your son be abused in the school, or take him out. We brought our son home and saw blood running down the back of his neck. After asking the supervisor what happened, we were told that the man who cuts the hair of the children at the school had some teeth missing from the clippers that were used to cut their hair. I would like to get a similar pair of clippers and cut the supervisor's hair with them and see how he would respond. These things, and a number of other things exist at this school Dr. Blatt, and I am truly afraid of the retaliatory measures that may be used against my son if I return him to the school, yet I have no choice because of my wife's back condition. After talking to the people at juvenile court, and after their telling me that I dreamed these things up, that these things never happen at these schools, I referred your article to them for reading. Please excuse my typing, sir, as I am a one finger typing person.

Thank you,

_____ _____.

Santa Barbara, Cal.
Oct. 30, 1967

Dear Dr. Blatt:

This is to thank you for your hard-hitting article appearing in the October 31 issue of *Look,* entitled "The Tragedy and Hope of Retarded Children."

The conscience of materialistic America has been so long in cold storage, it will take many more hot blasts like yours to warm it even to room temperature. So please keep writing!

Our precious daughter (Down's Syndrome, mongolism) is now 21, a delight and joy to all who know her. She reads, writes, dances, swims, drives a car, votes. . . . She has always lived at home with her family and attended special classes in the public schools.

Families who face this challenge together grow stronger, more united, and learn to help others in facing up to the burden of a retarded child. Society should help, not hinder our endeavors in behalf of these innocent human sufferers.

Gratefully yours,
Mrs. N. R. R_____.

_____ _____, Pa.
October 22, 1967

Dear Dr. Blatt:

Last Sunday night, sick at heart after returning our young son to a psychiatric hospital following his regular weekend visit home, we wished we had the time to write an article on conditions in mental hospitals and schools for the retarded. Monday we read your own excellent and much needed exposé in the October 31 *Look* magazine.

You write of the state schools. Our experience has been with the private, those known to be the best. Our son is now 13 years old, a very hyperactive, disturbed, autistic type of child. He is considered severely retarded on the basis of a verbal I.Q. test, moderately retarded on a non-verbal I.Q. Whatever the label, he is certainly highly trainable when not disturbed, and completely self-sufficient in caring for his personal needs. Even at thirteen he is trying to speak more but cannot articulate. Frustration at not being able to communicate has caused much of his disturbance through-out the years. We never had a clear diagnosis, but Dr. _____, at Johns Hopkins, felt he was brain damaged.

When our son was five we were faced with the decision to place him in a residential school. Our own health was failing and our two older children were being adversely affected. After some investigation we decided on _____ _____, N.J. We never considered our own Penn. State Schools. _____'s overcrowded conditions were infamous. During his eight years at _____, our child had a steady stream of houseparents. Some were good, most were terrible, all were overworked and underpaid. None stayed more than a year, most only a few months. Two years ago the top personnel began leaving, disgusted with the administration's unwillingness to support progress. Some good new professionals were hired, but they too have now left.

Our son, and some other children, reflected this turmoil in their own disturbance. They became difficult to manage and the "help" didn't try to give them the security they so badly needed. On the orders of the staff M.D., an old man who considers such children hopeless and who told us to resign ourselves to the fact that _____ would have to be locked up for the rest of his life, and with the consent of the psychiatrist, _____ was locked in an isolation room for ten days. No one would show us this room, but we were told that it had nothing but a bare mattress on the floor. No toys because they said he would only destroy them. No window to look out of, just a high pane of glass in the door for the nurse to look in. Being treated like an animal, he acted like one. There was no toilet for him to use and no way to tell anyone, so he used the floor and smeared his feces. He ripped his clothes to shreds in anger, frustration and boredom. There were a few kindly souls who occasionally let him out of his cell, but we doubt if it was for long. We were not even told the school was having trouble with _____. When we finally found out on our regular visit that he was locked up, we took him home.

At this time a new psychologist and director of cottage life decided to start an operant conditioning cottage for the disturbed boys and asked us for another try with _____. It was highly successful for five months. The boys were like different children, _____ especially responded well and showed practically no signs of disturbance. But the director of the school decided to abandon this project. The houseparents quit, the psychologist quit, and the director of cottage life began looking for another position. New houseparents came who had no interest what-so-ever in the children. Without our knowledge, they began locking _____ in his bedroom. The disturbance returned worse than ever before. He tore his clothes, bit his arms and in sudden flashes would bite others or throw his dishes. Again he was locked in the isolation room in the infirmary. This time we were notified and withdrew him from the school immediately.

We arranged for an emergency admission at a small, private, adult psychiatric hospital, which is used by _____ _____ Schools for their disturbed children. It is no place for a child, or adult either for that matter. They have no program of any sort, and our son is the only child there. However, after six weeks he did become somewhat stabilized through the use of medication and fairly kind treatment. We applied to _____ Institute and they agreed to accept him on the condition that we withdraw him immediately if he does not fit into their program. We are waiting for his admission there in another few weeks. Incidentally, we applied to but were refused by some small private schools and by _____ Schools. _____ and _____ do not want to be bothered with the really disturbed child. We didn't even try _____ because we were told by various professionals that they have their back rooms too, and our child would surely be in one of them,—this for about $10,000 a year, which we cannot afford.

Our son has been at the psychiatric hospital for five months now. It costs us $200 a week. Six weeks ago we began to notice the old signs of disturbance returning. Every Saturday when we brought him home we had to buy a whole new wardrobe. His clothes were torn to shreds, a feat which could only be accomplished in long periods of time with no supervision. The kindly and able nurse in charge of the afternoon shift tipped us off that the 7am–3pm shift was locking _____ in the "strongroom." The old horror all over again. The psychiatrist admitted it was true, that there was no excuse for it, and blamed the old "help problem."

I need not describe our anguish. We decided to hire a private nurse to care for _____ on the offending shift. She is a wonder of a woman, and again the disturbance is subsiding. This is now costing us almost $400 a week! We bring _____ home for all day Saturday and Sunday. And still we wait for his admission to _____, knowing that he may not succeed in their program.

We have finally resolved ourselves to applying for state placement, and _____ is helping us get on this five to six year waiting list. The state school for our region is unfortunately _____. The social worker there admitted that a boy like _____ would be in a locked ward with no program. They are overcrowded and understaffed. She suggested the state school at Ebensburg, near Johnstown, which now caters to the hyperactive, retarded child, and will accept children from throughout the state. Have you any knowledge of conditions at this school? Is Pennhurst one of the state schools you describe? And what is your opinion of Elwyn?

We are also continuing to look at private schools, since we must have somewhere to turn immediately if _____ doesn't keep him. Keystone Training & Rehabilitation Residence, a very new school in Scranton, sounds promising. They all have waiting lists, however.

Could you suggest a good placement for our son? Unfortunately we are not residents of Connecticut, though my husband is tempted to quit his job with the National Park Service, which he likes so much, and establish residence there. At the age of fifty this is hardly feasible. The small state of Connecticut may soon be faced with a deluge of retarded children whose parents are more mobile than we.

We thank you for taking the time to read our long tale, and would appreciate any helpful advice you could give us.

Yours truly,
Mr. and Mrs. _____ G_____.

_____, Washington
October 19, 1967

Dear Dr. Blatt,

I have just finished reading your marvelous, yet very disturbing article, "The Tragedy and Hope of Retarded Children." This story reached deep in my heart as I am an ex-attendant of _____ State School. Although you mentioned no "names," I am positive that you were referring to this institution in many paragraphs. For eleven months, I saw exactly what you are trying to put across in this article; of course, I could supply you with enough information to write a continuing chapter on "The Care and Treatment of Retarded Children." Unfortunately, the majority of the public refuse to believe that such conditions exist in this day and age.

To get directly to the purpose of this letter, my husband and I are in need of some educated advice and opinions.

While I was working in this institution, I became very attached to a six year old Mongoloid. We were granted permission by the school and his parents to take him home on week ends and special occasions. He adjusted rapidly, was very happy and was learning to speak clearly. It was necessary for us to return to _____ in June. Since that time we have been very concerned about him.

Is it possible to adopt a retarded child with the permission of the parents???? This is what we would like to do but would be satisfied if we could convince the parents that he should be transferred to a Washington school, enabling us to bring him home occasionally. I do not know if his parents left him in New York when they moved to San Diego because they felt that the only place he can be transferred to is the home of his parents. Is there a way it can be done with the consent of the parents?

Do you have any opinions or facts on a child adjusting to this type of situation? We are a young couple, unable to have children of our own and have no desire to adopt another child. We realize that _____ would in all probability have to be placed in a school in a few years if he were to live past his teen years. We are prepared for this but want to give him a good home as long as possible.

I have written to his parents concerning this but I expect a negative answer as I don't think that they are aware of the existing conditions or they feel that he is "better off" there. If we have some information concerning the possibilities of adoption we can continue to try convincing his parents.

Any information you can send us would be greatly appreciated, including your personal opinions and the names of anyone you might know who could be of some help to us.

Thanking you in advance for a quick and reassuring reply, we remain,

Sincerely yours,

Mr. and Mrs. _____ E_____.

_____ _____, Minn.

Dear Dr. Blatt:

Your article in *Look Magazine* is testimony that there are those who care. I hope that man's inhumanity to man can be stopped. This mad profit in misery, society creating monsters for the sake of profit. What else can you call it where poor white and poor black are taught to hate and even to destroy another for the sake of their daily bread. Nothing will ever justify what has been and is yet true today of our system.

I have seen children crammed in steel cages. I have seen the results. The strong ones win their freedom one way or another, to become the anti-social class—the criminal class—the ideal cradle to the grave victim of the welfare state. To believe in the philosophy of kindness is one thing. To enforce it another. Too few people really care, too few know the truth; even worse, few want to know the truth—they are afraid of the freedom that goes with truth. True man loves scandal, yet he wants little to do with truth.

I spent five years in a steel cage—a pie tin a day kicked under a cell block door—I know what you say is truth. Yet how can you get the public to care, much less act on it. I am fortunate. I will not live for what passes as democracy—I showed my willingness to die for it—I reap a harvest of benefits. I am fortunate, I chose war as a way of lifting myself above that which was laid out for me in life. How terrible the less fortunate and helpless among us do not have this way out.

Never before has America needed angry men to speak out. I would be first to encourage you to rant, to rave, to do whatever must be done to end this madness called society. I can't rant, I can't rave, you have the status, the prestige, and the power that gives you the means to do so. No one wants to hear from the victim of society. Perhaps that is why we hide our shame in the worse places we can design for our fellow man; create a hell on earth and the strong and able of mind and body will ignore and stay as far away as they can.

I have known of people who have visited relatives in the kind of places you describe. They only visited them once. The evidence of beating and abuse was enough to keep them away for all time. They were people caught up in fear of the powers that be. How can we send so many men of high ideals to Washington and still tolerate such conditions I will never know. We build churches to console us; we are not so evil after all. We don't trouble ourselves to build them in the shadows of the hells we build for others.

Some months ago, a superintendent of a school told me he was going to write a book, just as soon as he retired and it was safe to do so. A school designed to discriminate against the Indian—to keep and educate the Indian in his place. We don't just have these problems with our mentally retarded and ill. We have a rash of these problems in every phase of life that helpless people are caught up in. Any wonder mankind is on the verge of self-destruction? At times it almost seems just—at least as just as we force others to suffer.

I have pounded at Washington for years. We must end this living of wasted lives—dying senseless, often violent deaths. America's living dead must be helped. We can no longer control the things society is creating. The day will come when the evils we compromise with will compromise us. But I am nothing in the general scheme of things. The powers that be have to be convinced. How I would like to take some of the power to be on a tour, place a few of their loved ones in conditions that exist—one look might be enough.

How do we enforce the power of kindness? We can't even enforce law and order. We are reaping what we have sowed. How can we make justice-hungry men show compassion to those less fortunate than themselves. Find the answer to this question and things will have to get better. Riots (we call them open protests) by people reacting to the treatment they have been victims of—victims of a society that doesn't want to hear from them.

We have hospitals here in Minnesota overflowing with people. Thank God they are designed to help the people, not make animals of them. Perhaps some day man will stop this insane idea of building bigger and better jails and even worse to cram the helpless and hopeless in. It is your fight sir; you have the power to dare to speak out. It takes power to expose the truth. It takes courage to go on exposing it until something is done. I hope you can see your way to keep the fight going—it will be a fight.

We start with laws that say it is a crime to be poor. This law we can enforce. I will never forget how when I came back to the states, I was taken into a kangaroo court and accused of the crime of being poor. I was ignorant. I didn't even know there were employment offices, or that a person could look in the paper for a job. I worked 120 days at slave labor, creating parks for those who knew the better things of life. Needless to say when I got out, I ran as fast as I could and went back to war, to battle, to fighting over nameless hills. It was better than being an ignorant helpless being, at the mercy of a kangaroo court that enforced the law against being poor. How much worse for those who have no war to escape to.

Society brands people like myself as mad. It is easier than facing truth. It makes it easier for the powers that be to convince themselves that perhaps we aren't so bad after all. I think you know how terrible the price in wasted lives we pay for this idea. Any wonder the poor black and poor white wage war in the streets? They are destroying a society that has condemned them for being poor and helpless. I believe they will win. The terrible part is not in winning, but the extremes they are being forced to go to to win.

It is strange that when I say I too can go back to the slums and build an army, the powers that be are kind. We can't give all our helpless the same weapon. We must some of us take up the means and do what can be done for them. Ignorance and law are strange bed partners. For some reason the marriage of the two has been consumated. What you write about is the ends that justify the means or wedding of ignorance and law. It remains the same evil any way we look at it.

Fight it, sir. Fight, fight, fight. Look about you, count the needs. None answer the calls of the helpless or hear their pleas—and it will be a fight. Society can stand setbacks. If their ends are what we have, better to destroy the present society and start over. Look about you. Everyone is in on the act. Why not something good for a change? Hope and more hope—this is your power.

Respectfully,

F_____ S_____.

_____, Kentucky
October 20, 1967

Dear Dr. Blatt:

Thank you very much for the article "The Tragedy and Hope of Retarded Children" which appeared in *Look.* I too want people to know the dreadful conditions which the retarded must endure. I too want people to know that these children can be helped. There is hope when someone cares.

I am a student nurse at the University of Kentucky. During our unit on Psychiatric Nursing, our class visited _____ _____ for mentally retarded children (adults are also hospitalized). The buildings are old and dirty and dismal. Most of those who care for the children are attendants rather than nurses. The day rooms smell, and excrement can be seen on the children's clothing and shoes. Attendants can at least keep the place clean! Some children are exhibited (not to the public) because they are such interesting cases. Attendants are not careful what they say around the children. For example, one attendant told us that a particular child had already outlived her life expectancy. She said this by the child's bedside, and we had been told earlier that the child could understand what was being said to her. There is much more, but you have seen it many times.

At this hospital an attempt is made to educate some of the children. This is good. Some attendants and nurses do care what happens to the children, but they do not have the facilities they need or enough help.

Recently my state spent two million dollars for a beautiful horse farm.

This farm will be used experimentally for animals and crops in connection with the other experimental farms owned by the University of Kentucky. I do not understand how this money could be spent on such luxury for animals when human beings, children, must live in those horrid conditions.

But what can I do? I am only one student with very little influence and with very few to hear me.

Sincerely,

S_____ S_____.

Hypothesis III: It is hypothesized that an individual will react to a condition if he feels that certain relevant and pertinent information has been distorted or withheld from him.

St. Louis, Missouri
November 3, 1967

Dear Dr. Blatt,

I have just finished reading your article published in *Look* magazine and never have I had an article both horrify and anger me such as this.

This letter is being written while I still feel the heartache and absolute despair that these thousands of children must feel. It is also my fear that if these lines aren't written now I might feel disturbed for several days and then slip back into the blessed ignorance, or is it indifference, that most of us enjoy on this subject.

I pride myself as having control of my emotions, but every time I remember the lines and pictures describing the conditions under which these flesh and blood creatures of God exist—not live—I feel as though I could weep.

Your article, needless to say, was excellently written and, as it was meant to be, most disturbing.

The question is, Dr. Blatt, exactly what can a non-professional like myself really do about these deplorable conditions. I mean what direct action is actually possible? There is no way for me to be certain that these unbelievable back wards do not exist in my state's institution, but the thought that they well may terrifies me.

It would be a comforting thought to know that your article reached and affected professional people as it did me; whether it did or not the fact remains that I, as an ordinary, concerned citizen, would like to know what I might do to somehow help remedy the appalling plight of these children.

Most sincerely yours,
Mrs. C_____ H_____.

St. Louis, Mo.

Dear Dr. Burton Blatt:

I am writing in regards to the article that I just read in the *Look Magazine*, pertaining to retarded children. As a mother of two normal children, I was very ignorant about what happens to the care of some of these children, to think that this kind of treatment, or torture I should say, can exist in our so called modern times.

The purpose of this letter is to ask what can I do to help, even if it means to go into these institutions just to clean, so help me I'll do it.

Sincerely yours,

Mrs. J. W. B_____.

Hypothesis IV: It is hypothesized that an individual will react to condition if his concept of human ideals is challenged.

Bay Shore, N.Y.
October 25, 1967

Dear Dr. Blatt,

I am writing this letter to you, because of peoples' interest in your article "The Tragedy and Hope of Retarded Children," that appeared in the October 31, 1967 issue of *Look Magazine.*

I would like you to know, there has been an overwhelming reaction among my friends and neighbors about this article. I believe you have stirred people's anger enough to act on this matter.

We have sent many lists of names and addresses to the editor of *Look* magazine (Mr. Arthur).

Allow me to take this opportunity to speak for myself, friends and neighbors, to thank you, for your dedicated work on this grave situation. We are trying to do our share to see your task has not been in vain.

Let us hope that your great work and our small contribution, will help make life more bearable for these poor children.

Sincerely,

Mrs. A_____ S_____.

Dear, Sir

I read your article about
The Tragedy and Hope Of
Retarded Children. I feel
sorry for them. I cry
everytime I read it. You are
right , the world is hell
for them. They are treated
like animals, not even that.
Lucky there are men that
still help.Please help them.

Name—T_____ H_____, Jr.
How old—9 years old
City—Ormond Beach
State—Fla.

Conclusion

I was made aware of some of the possible effects of mass media from responses to my article. It is not possible to determine what sensitivities were most offended, what motivations were stirred, what it was that prompted each reaction. The reader may have his own conclusions after examining our analysis of the letters in light of the proposed hypotheses. Rather than being concerned with focal points of cause and effect, I prefer to react to the total impact of the article. It seems reassuring and encouraging to me that people did feel the need or desire to respond, and that emotions were aroused: anger, gratitude, dedication, sorrow. I was impressed with the variety of backgrounds of people reacting. While I have no reasonable estimate of how many people read the article and chose not to respond, I do feel that those who did represented enough of a cross-section to justify my encouragement with the article and its influence.

The article has long since been read, maybe not as easily digested by all. I feel that it "reached" some of the "right" people. Some of the effects were good. In predicting what the future holds for the retarded, I can only hope that, by such efforts, man's inhumanity to man might gradually be reformed into man's love and expectation of man, and that the small voice of the retarded and their advocates might eventually be heard more meaningfully than in the past. Someday, the mentally retarded will cease to exist as the least of the least.

chapter 7

JUDGING THE PRIESTHOOD
BY THE PRIEST

Usually, in last chapters of books, the author attempts to restate his problem and summarize the various ways he examined and dealt with it. For many reasons—partly because this is a volume of three books, not one—I am unable to summarize adequately, in a concluding chapter, the major ground we attempted to cover. With the exception of two chapters, all of my writing for this volume began in January of 1968 and ended soon after my return to Boston University in January of 1969. Afterwards, months were devoted to rewriting some parts, deleting others, sharing sections of the manuscript with colleagues and friends, seeking opinions about one thing or another, adding a chapter that was not planned for but—now—must be added, and writing this last chapter. During my early conceptualizations, it was thought that the volume should conclude with an analysis of the accomplishments of the past year. However, I have now come to the conclusion that such analyses will have to be provided by other individuals if they are ever to be made. Further, I have little doubt that others are better equipped to judge this "priest," just as he believed himself to be capable of—and even responsible for—judging other "priests" and their "priesthoods." Therefore, this chapter is not intended to either summarize the contents of this volume or judge our affairs during the past year. All the chapter can hope to do is restate a few of the more important lessons we learned or re-confirmed, and also mention some of the things we think were accomplished. We will begin with those perceived accomplishments. However, it should be emphasized again that such judgments are better made by those who have the luxury of taking distance and more dispassionate views of problems and intended solutions.

What We Think We Did

On March 31, 1969, I saw, finally, the film, *Titicut Follies.* I was in New York City for a meeting of the American Orthopsychiatric Association. Through the kindness of several people who had access to the film and were responsible for its showing to the Association membership, I was privileged to see it at a private screening held for two or three people who were preparing for public discussion of the film to be held two or three days later. I wish to state publicly—for whatever it may be worth—that I believe that Frederick Wiseman is a cinematic genius and that this film, *Titicut Follies,* will live in history alongside such documents as Dorothea Dix's Address to the Massachusetts Legislature, the original work of Clifford Beers, and the contributions of such men as Albert Deutsch, Emil Kraepelin, and Upton Sinclair. I say this publicly because, now that I have seen the film, I realize that many more of us could have—and should have—made public statements two years ago, when the film was first shown. Very few citizens of Massachusetts have seen the film because the Massachusetts Judiciary declared it illegal for the film to be shown in our Commonwealth. For those readers who do not know about this film, permit me to summarize hastily by mentioning that Mr. Wiseman was given permission by the superintendent and staff of the Bridgewater State Hospital for the Criminally Insane to film life at the hospital. As George Albee discusses it in his chapter, *Titicut Follies* is the documentary resulting from Wiseman's experiences. After the first public showing of the movie, and especially because it received *both* severe denunciation and lavish praise—controversy and bitter recriminations swirled around Mr. Wiseman and the *Follies,* to the extent that the substantive issues he raised so brilliantly have been almost totally disregarded, submerged in contrast with the issues concerning whether the film should or should not have been produced. This is all by way of saying that reactions to Mr. Wiseman's film were many times more often focused on the merits or demerits of the film, the right to its existence as a film, and its artistic integrity than on the merits or demerits of Bridgewater as an institution, its right to exist as an institution, or its integrity as an institution—artistic or otherwise. The film brought about an analysis of the character, motivations, and moral judgments of Mr. Wiseman. Very little has been said about such matters as they concern superintendents, psychiatrists, legislators, civic groups, the courts, and you and I and all of us who permit such institutions to exist. I, too, have been caught up in the *Titicut Follies* controversy and in discussing the wrong issues. About a year ago, Robert Coles, the brilliant Harvard psychiatrist who has been speaking out on matters concerning mental health, poverty, and education, reviewed *Titicut Follies* in the *New Republic.* As one might have predicted, he compared *Titicut Follies* with *Christmas in Purgatory,* especially the reaction of the Massachusetts legislature to each. Dr. Coles made this comparison because of the storm surrounding *Titicut Follies* and either no reaction or some very positive response from the same legislators to *Christmas in Purgatory.* Coles concluded that, in fact, my descriptions of hospitals in several states ". . . make *Titicut Follies* seem like a whitewash job." Because of several of Dr. Coles' statements which were not completely accurate (e.g. he wrote that we did our study with mental patients), I sent a letter to the editor of the *New Republic,* which was published subsequently. Unfortunately, although I believe the "record" was corrected in my letter and, further, I mentioned a few things about royalties and profit-making and handling confidential material, I performed as the others did in their reactions to *Titicut Follies.* The important judgment about that film, the important morality that should be discussed and debated, the important issues that have been set before us, the important human needs and values that the film illustrates are related to the things that are happening (and why they are happening) at Bridgewater State Hospital and not to the idiosyncratic world of Frederick Wiseman—however beautiful or mendacious his life and world are.

I think one of the things we were able to accomplish this past year was to understand better—and help others to understand better—the difference between individual behavior and public accountability. In that regard, I don't give a damn about Frederick Wiseman or his manners and morals. If his film is an accurate portrayal of life at Bridgewater—which I have every reason to believe it is—then our energies and efforts should be dedicated to the reformation of Bridgewater, not Mr. Wiseman. If his soul is damaged or defective, I am certain that civilization can entrust its repair to whatever resources Mr. Wiseman can bring to this need. There is still a home, a church, a self to deal with one's moral and spiritual character. Organized civilization and its resources must concern itself with the issues in the film, not with the mind or the heart of the film maker. As I mentioned in an earlier chapter, Vonnegut once said that people are exactly what they pretend to be. Therefore, each of us must be terribly careful about what we pretend to be. Wiseman is a remarkable man and it is hoped that others have learned with us why and how such people become remarkable.

As was discussed in the chapter, "The Judge in Judgment," a plan was developed to reduce substantially the residential populations of each Massachusetts state school and develop a network of regional community and residential services for every mentally retarded individual and his family in need of special programs and facilities. Obtaining from that plan and our attempts to implement it were guidelines for construction, guidelines for program and facility priorities, capital and operating needs predicted to the next 15 years, and manpower needs for the same period. The plan not only provided us with goals to strive for but, because of their logic and corroborating evidence, these goals also provided considerable support for immediate program development and approval. In September, 1968, we opened our first seven classes for school age children who were either excluded or exempted from public school participation. These classes, supported with a grant from the Massachusetts Department of Education, are the first publicly sponsored day care classes for the mentally retarded in our Commonwealth. This new program is, I believe, one of the most important forward steps taken on behalf of the mentally retarded in Massachusetts, comparable to the 1957 legislation authorizing the establishment of preschool classes for the mentally retarded which now enroll 1,000 children.

As new programs for the retarded developed, such as the aforementioned day care classes, as we expanded substantially our preschool clinical nurseries and day and residential vocational training facilities, our large state institutions developed goals and implementation plans to reduce their residential populations, on the one hand, and to develop community-based activities, on the other hand. As a result, the past year witnessed a rather sizeable increase of community-sponsored programs by the Department of Mental Health and its affiliated agencies and, at the same time, a comparable decrease in the residential populations of, at least, three of our state schools. One regional center, constructed two years previously as a small state school, is—today—approaching our concept of what a regional center must stand for and what it must accomplish. It will be the progenitor of, eventually, a dozen or more regional centers strategically developed in every section of the Commonwealth and, upon fulfillment of our plan, this network of facilities and services will enable anyone in need of care or treatment or education to receive such opportunities when he needs them and for as long a period of time as he needs them. Possibly, our development together of a conception of responsibility for events such as those that transpired at Bridgewater or at our state schools, and our willingness to be held accountable and hold others accountable for the regrettable conditions described in this book, was our most significant accomplishment, if we accomplished anything. This need to assign responsibility and accountability led, directly, to our plan for reformation of services for the mentally retarded in Massachusetts. Eventually, we expect the plan to be fully implemented—or implemented in ways that are now beyond our ability to comprehend and conceptualize—and we expect the reformation or revolution for the mentally retarded to be concluded successfully.

What We Think We Learned

As I mentioned in Book II of this volume, during the recent controversy concerning the annual slaughter of 50,000 harp-seal pups in the Maritime Provinces, one Canadian official commented, "If we could find a way to make pup seals look like alligators, our problems would be over." I learned and confirmed and reconfirmed again the wisdom of that Canadian's remark. We behave to others—people and animals—in ways which reflect clearly our conception of them as people or as animals. Further, as society makes judgments about groups of people— judgments that may be related to race, religion, economic level, physical or mental characteristics, or what have you—certain of these groups are treated with special positive consideration and others with special derogation or abuse. It is for the sake of this latter kind of group, those individuals who are treated with special derogation or abuse, that this book became necessary for me to write. It was the purpose of this book to examine a group of individuals, the mentally retarded, who have been abused by historical precedent and as public policy for many, many generations. As was mentioned in the preface to this volume, our focus was on mental retardation, but the issue is much broader: human abuse and public policy. There is no doubt in my mind that other books have been and will be written—and this book could have been written—about the legal, sanctioned, and, even, advocated abuse of other groups in our society. Ironically, and hopefully, however well society approves of and disguises its offenses against segments of humanity, that society is judged by those actions; it is judged—as a society—most harshly by that of which it is most ashamed; and that judgment is the most accurate reflection of that society's sickness and the possibility that it will ever achieve greatness.·

We have learned that, although assessing blame—or, if you will, responsibility and accountability—for the conditions described in this volume may be important, even necessary, our true mission is not to assign blame or establish responsibility. Nor is our true mission to determine whether or not the conditions described in this volume need to exist—because of the nature of the mentally retarded or those who treat them. Our true mission is to guarantee to every human being the right to be treated as a human being and our true mission is to eradicate, forever, the evils of back wards, the philosophies that breed them, and the conception that those evils resulted from the condition called "mental retardation" rather than from the condition called "civilization."

By our observations of Jimmy—added to all we have learned from the lives of Victor (the Wild Boy of Aveyron), Helen Keller, and so many others—we were reinforced again and again in our conviction that intelligence, that all human development, is plastic and is a function of practice and training and motivation and stimulation, as well as it is a function of neurology and chromosomes and genes.

Lastly, to reiterate what was taught to me many years ago by a great lady and has since been confirmed innumerable times, I believe that there is a design of things and that the design for each of us holds nothing but good. This concept has its severest test in the back wards. However, it is also true that Jimmy spent all but a short portion of his life in the back wards, and his life may show the way to a better design for all of us.

appendix

THE DARK SIDE
OF THE MIRROR[1]

An Address to the Legislature of Massachusetts

(1967)

In 1949 I started a teaching career and serious study with the mentally retarded. In the subsequent years, I learned some valuable lessons concerning this human condition. Notably, from the inspiration and clinical acumen of three great teachers and one institutional administrator, I began to understand and appreciate several major concepts concerning behavior, concepts that have been verified repeatedly during interactions with those generous children and families who welcomed my intrusions into their lives. I learned, or do not disbelieve, that:

1. Man, traditionally, underestimates his potentials for changing or, to use a more common term, for learning.

---

[1] On May 2, 1967, the Massachusetts Legislature adjourned its formal deliberations at noon and reconvened at one of our four State Schools for the mentally retarded in order to pursue a thorough discussion and on-scene observation of the more serious problems confronting these settings. It was their purpose to achieve a deliberate focus on our State institutions in the hope that we might find the resources and talent to solve or ameliorate current problems and, also, prevent these from occurring in the future. The writer was invited to deliver the Keynote Address to this Legislature, as well as to the professional administrative staffs of the institution and the State Department of Mental Health, and the officers of the parent association identified with that institution. This entire project received the full endorsement and participation of all of the aforementioned groups. In light of the writer's belief that the conditions and issues he is concerned with here have national rather than local relevance and have general rather than specific interest, he edited his paper of that occasion for presentation to the membership of the American Association on Mental Deficiency at its Annual Meeting at Denver, Colorado, on May 20, 1967, and publication in their journal, *Mental Retardation,* October, 1968.

2. Man's pessimism concerning the conditions of change becomes a self-fulfilling prophecy. We don't learn when we become convinced that we can't or when we become convinced that we shouldn't.

3. Given proper conditions, it can be demonstrated that intelligence is a function of practice and training. That we have not been able to guarantee such behavioral modification is, I believe, less a defect of our theory than it is of our practice.

4. I believe in a design of things, I believe there is some spiritual workmanship about. And, I believe, the design for all of us holds nothing but good.

But there is a dark side of every mirror, a side beyond inspection because it is without thought. And while the optimism and pride—the light—of our lives is for the gains made in civil rights, for our achievements in mental health, for the concept of the Declaration of Independence and the Constitution, surely a dark side in the evolution of our civilization in this mid-20th Century must be reserved for the deep unremitting, unrewarding lives of drudgery and pain we inflict upon our institutionalized brothers who are called severely mentally retarded.

As some of you may know, I have recently completed a study of children and adults in state institutions for the mentally retarded (*Christmas in Purgatory: A Photographic Essay on Mental Retardation*). It was my purpose to describe in words and pictures the treatment of the retarded in these institutions, point out some of the more serious imperfections of their programs, and suggest ways to prevent or ameliorate problems. I expected that men of good will from all walks of life and all professions would then sit down at the planning table and seek viable solutions to the issues uncovered. It is not necessary here to discuss my findings, my recommendations, or the flood of extraordinarily encouraging mail and calls I received in response to this study. However, it may be instructive to mention that some of the reactions to the project were negative. I was subjected to mild direct hectoring and a good deal of indirect and second hand pejorative assaults. I had undertaken the study of institutions and written the truth, as plainly and as simply as I saw it. As some of you may know, there is little reward in exposing the ugliness (or beauty) of certain truths. It can be a dangerous business.

The view I am about to share with you today is no less real to me than our photographic essay—in spite of its impressionism, its vagueness, its distorted textures and freely associated construction. This is the stuff of which nightmares are made and, if you will permit me, I will share mine with you. I have been to many state institutions for the mentally retarded, before and subsequent to the just-mentioned study. It is fitting that we concern ourselves today with one local state school. I accede to this reasonable decision. On the other hand, my remarks have a much more general applicability.

I have been to the depths, believing all the time that I would awaken, as I always had before, from this most terrifying of all nightmares. And, as I always had before, I did awaken—to the mawkish horror and degradation of N. and W. Buildings. I have walked beside their soiled waters where, floating gently by their dayroom shores, were the human flotsam and jetsam, the wasted and unfulfilled programs, hopes and plans of countless generations of discouraged failures who were once known in these buildings as patients, attendants, and professional staff. I have filled my nostrils and inflated my lungs in N. Building until every pore of my body felt the nauseating zing of 70 years of cankered rot that will continue to generate *ad infinitum* until the seams of N.'s construction burst at the top and at the bottom and at its sides, until its cup of human refuse and despair runs over and drowns us all or causes us to realize, in time, what grief we perpetrate there. I have sat in its dayroom, surrounded by desperately lonely patients huddled together in their nakedness of body and spirit, defenseless against the elements, defenseless against assaults to their persons, to their souls, and to their consciousness. I have seen a hand reach out for human contact—if not for ennobling friendship—only to see it struck down by the fear and confusion of its intended recipient, as he was struck down by the fear and confusion of another recipient, as he was struck down, as he was struck down—*ad nauseum.*

If these remarks this day communicate any of my deepest thoughts and hopes it should become very clear that I do not believe we can correct the blight of an N. Building and the plight of its residents with a new set of curtains, or a new paint job, or modern plumbing, or increased attendant staff there, or new words and slogans. In the past, to one degree or another, all of these shibboleths and gestures were implemented and found wanting. All were enveloped by the mire of that totally oppressive environment. We do not suffer so much the lack of structural architects and interior designers as we do the absence of ideational architects and moral interventionists.

It is not that the amenities and courtesies are not appreciated. They are, for they demonstrate that, essentially, the conditions at N. Building are *not* due to evil people. They are *not* due to more incompetent or mendacious people than one finds in any large socio-political organization, such as are found in your legislature and in my university. Nor are these conditions due only to insufficient capital budgets and ludicrous per capita operating costs. Obviously, a more appropriate financial structure, a more tangible and pervasive method to encourage the considerable number of dedicated and enlightened individuals who are employed at the school, and better ways to cashier those that are incompetent, will reduce many of the problems you observe here and will make life habitable for those whose lives are now intolerable.

However, significant change, meaningful change, change all of us can be truly proud of, change that will result in objectively superior residential treatment—not subjectively relative improvement—will not obtain until we alter our conceptions of human potential and our methodologies implementing those conceptions. In addition to a far greater share of the public treasure; in addition to more competent, more numerous and more available staff; in addition to much smaller living and training units, we must develop more optimistic convictions concerning the abilities and potentials of those we call mentally retarded, however severe that retardation may be. The prophecy of incompetency and vegetation associated with the mentally retarded is self-fulfilling. Equally self-fulfilling can be the prophecy of competency and achievement.

I have irrefutable evidence, from 18 years of clinical experience in the field of mental retardation, that NO RESIDENT needs to live in a denuded state, needs to be a head banger, or needs to be locked in solitary confinement. I have irrefutable evidence that practically every resident can be taught to eat meals independently, can be taught to live among his fellows without being of danger to himself or others and without the use of physical restraints. I have irrefutable evidence that *all* building odors can be eliminated without the need for even more powerfully repugnant chemical treatments or electronic gadgetry that masks the sources of these odors but does not eliminate the causes: filth and neglect. I have very substantive evidence that intelligence is educable, that is, people can change—learn—and that this concept applies both to the retarded and those who minister to their needs. It applies to us too. We can change in our conception of human potential and, thus, we can promote change in others. The lives of Anne Sullivan and Helen Keller speak volumes about this concept, as do the lives of Jean Itard and Victor, the Wild Boy of Aveyron.

It is my hope that our governor, our legislature, and commissioners who have faith in these immodest claims will encourage us to develop a network of small community-centered residential facilities, interrelated with a total community program of pre-service and in-service training and research, collaborating with our best universities where students in medicine, nursing, social work, education, and psychology may be employed during the course of their training, and may devote to our common need and common good their idealism, service, and professional skills. From such endeavors, we will develop new pathways and new models and new and vigorous ideas and ideals to better comprehend and confront that complex devastation, mental retardation. Without such approaches, we will continue to fund new curtains and paint jobs and, once or twice in a century, we will demolish old buildings. Without such approaches, we will continue to divert overwhelming problems with flimsy thoughtless plans. We will continue to fertilize huge deserts with watering cans. Without such approaches, for every N. Building we demolish we will participate in the procreation of a new—

equally large—residency which will be little more than the portrait of N. Building as a child.

This address need not be necessary to convince you of the imperative need to—*at least*—destroy forever the physical structures and the symbolic disease represented by N. and W. Buildings at our State school. Some men dedicate their lives to build edifices. Before *we* can build, we must first dedicate ourselves to systematic annihilation. That these buildings continue to exist is either a massive indictment of our collective intelligence and relatedness or a colossal testament to human inertia or our incompetence. All that would be necessary to convince you that the danger point was reached many generations ago, that the point of no return—the time for physical and conceptual demolition—was passed before the oldest in this assembly was born . . . all that would be necessary would be to lead you now to these buildings.

"The triumph of evil requires only that good men do nothing." Good men do something; do not turn away from these blights we call N. and W.! Do not rest until you can guarantee to all of our citizens that these buildings, wherever they exist in our Commonwealth, no longer serve the gods of pain, sorrow, and chronic hopelessness. And do not rest until, across the land, the hundreds of these buildings—and the philosophies they breed—are laid to their unholy eternal damnation.

A little child we knew and loved was buried a few days ago and my wife and I, in shocked awe, pondered the senselessness of a life taken almost before it was lived. However, Michael did live and, as all of us must, he died. Although his life was too brief, Michael lived a good' life. We rejoiced in his life and now mourn his death. But, the funerals for those in N. and W. Buildings come not with death but in life. For them, it is life that is the terrible avenger; it is life that we mourn. And as we are part of this grand design, we mourn for ourselves and for our helplessness.

Believe that you are more than your brother's keeper. Believe that, while on this earth, you are his savior and he is yours.

SELECTED, ANNOTATED BIBLIOGRAPHY ON ABUSE OF HUMANS[1]

Legal Governmental Abuse

Alvarez, A. Concentration camps. *Atlantic,* 1962, *210,* 62–72.
Discusses the relevance of concentration camps to modern society.

The Case of Daniel McNaghtess. May 26–June 19, 1843. Nutley, New Jersey: Roche Laboratories, Reprint, 1966.
Established rules which for generations governed criminal law with respect to insanity. First legal definition of "criminal madness."

Central Commission for Investigation of German Crimes in Poland. *German crimes in Poland.* Vol. I. Warsaw: Author, 1946.
Results of investigations into extermination, concentration, and labor camps during World War II in Poland. Compares German crimes and Soviet power in Poland.

Eitinger, L. *Concentration camp survivors in Norway and Israel.* Oslo, Norway: Universitetforlaget; London: Allen and Unwin, 1964.
Author, a Norwegian psychiatrist, systematically examines former concentration camp inmates in both Norway and Israel in an effort to evaluate psychological effects that may be attributed to concentration camp experiences.

Farb, P. The American Indian: a portrait in limbo. *Saturday Review,* 1968, *11* (*41*), 26–29.
Describes the history of the treatment of the American Indian, his present condition on the reservation, "poverty-stricken islands, surrounded by an ocean of American bounty." Problems of housing, unemployment, health, education, and deprivation of their own culture are considered.

[1] The author is grateful to Misses Karen Arentzen, Carol Bennison, and Mary Higgins who contributed considerably to the preparation of this selected bibliography. We prepared it in the hope that it may encourage others to continue their interest and deepen their understanding of this problem.

Grebink, J., Penn, N., Sindberg, R., & Stover, D. Some considerations for future mental health legislation. *Mental Hygiene*, 1969, *53* (*1*), 11–13.
Discusses individuals currently labeled "criminals" or "mentaly ill." Recommends system of reviews before depriving the individual of his rights.

Hoess, R. *Commandant of Auschwitz: the autobiography of Rudolf Hoess.* New York: The World Publishing Company, 1959.
Contains story of a member of the SS working in Dachau and Auschwitz; written in prison while Hoess awaited his Nuremberg trial.

Jacobs, P. *Prelude to riot: a view of urban America from the bottom.* New York: Random House, 1967.
Discusses relationships between government and minority poor (primarily black poor) in Los Angeles, and how these relationships led to hatred, bitterness, riots, and various injustices. Author maintains that government reinforces the degrading situation.

Leighton, A. H. *The governing of men.* Princeton, New Jersey: Princeton University Press, 1945.
Problems of a Japanese Relocation Camp are discussed. Author talks about the history of camp, its organization, and the conditions it bred.

Meyer, D. Lawyers in a mental hospital: the New York experiment. *Mental Hygiene*, 1969, *53* (*1*), 14–16.
Discusses lawyers in mental hospitals, their influence, and effects.

Metcalf, G. A century of no progress? *The Reporter*, 1967, *37*, 31–32.
Traces the enforcement of open housing. Author discusses the case pending in the Supreme Court of Jones versus Mayer, which tests this issue.

Okubo, M. *Citizen 13660.* New York: Columbia University Press, 1946.
Contains a young girl's illustrated account of life in a Japanese Relocation Center in the United States during World War II.

Penn, N., Roberts, A. & Sindberg, R. The dilemma of involuntary commitment: suggestions for a measurable alternative. *Mental Hygiene*, 1969, *53* (*1*), 4–10.
Discusses statutory definitions of mental illness and mental retardation. Recommends need for more objective definitions and observations of behavior. Discusses provisional placement in institutions in times of crisis.

Poliakov, L. *Harvest of hate: the Nazi program for the destruction of the Jews of Europe.* Philadelphia: The Jewish Publication Society of America, 1954.
Offers a documentary and psychological record of the extermination of six million European Jews by the Nazis in World War II.

President's Commission on Migratory Labor. *Migratory labor in American agriculture.* Washington, D.C.: U.S. Government Printing Office, 1951.
Presents the government view of the labor problem and its recommendations in 1951. Report discusses: illegal entrance of foreign labor, wage problems, housing, health, welfare, safety, education, child labor, and employee-employer relations.

Prucha, F. P. *American Indian policy in the formative years.* Cambridge, Massachusetts: Harvard University Press, 1962.
Presents and discusses the acts and laws involved in United States Indian policy between the years 1790–1834. An epilogue describes current condition of American Indians.

Ryan, P. E. *Migration and social welfare.* New York: Russell Sage Foundation, 1940.

Discusses lack of social provisions for migrant workers, and the implications of conflict between the local community and the migrant.

Schalk, A. Return to Auschwitz. *Commonweal,* 1965, *82,* 498–501.
Provides a look at Auschwitz today, and a comparison of Polish and German attitudes towards it.

Simrell, E. History of legal and medical roles in narcotic abuse in the United States. *Public Health Reports,* 1968, *83* (7), 587–593.
Discusses narcotic abuse as a medical-social problem and looks at international, federal, state and local action to combat narcotic abuse.

Steiner, J. F. *Treblinka.* New York: Simon and Schuster, 1967.
Reconstructs life under the Gestapo and life in Treblinka. The attitudes and feelings of the victims during the planning of an uprising are dramatically portrayed.

Szalet, L. *Experiment "E": a report from an extermination laboratory.* New York: Didier Publishers, 1945.
Provides a personal story of life in Sachsenhausen, a Nazi concentration camp.

Szasz, Thomas S. The insanity plea and the insanity verdict. *Temple Law Quarterly,* 1967, *40* (3–4), 271–282.
Describes how a successful plea of insanity in a court of law can involve an "imprisonment" more severe for the "acquitted" than for the guilty.

U.S. Senate Committee on the Judiciary. *Constitutional rights of the American Indian.* (Hearings before the Subcommittee on Constitutional Rights, August 29, 30, 31, September 1, 1961.) Washington, D.C.: U.S. Government Printing Office, 1962.
Presents the testimony of witnesses before this committee on current conditions for American Indians.

U.S. Senate Committee on the Judiciary. *Constitutional rights of the American Indian: summary report of hearings and investigations by the subcommittee on constitutional rights.* Washington, D.C.: U.S. Government Printing Office, 1966.
Committee presents its conclusions and recommendations concerning the American Indian, relative to proposed legislation.

Sanctioned and Unsanctioned Experimental Abuse

Appleton, W. Legal problems in psychiatric drug prescription. *American Journal of Psychiatry,* 1968, *124,* 7.
The author submitted a number of relevant questions resulting from growing concern among psychiatrists about risks in prescribing drugs.

Ethical aspects of experimentation with human subjects. *Daedalus,* Spring 1969, *98* (2).
Sixteen papers resulting from meetings of an interdisciplinary American Academy of Arts and Sciences' Working Party. Ethical issues involved in current and future experimental work are analyzed and guidelines suggested for the medical profession. Gives some examples of unethical practices on patients, mentally-retarded children, etc. Sourcebook for references to case histories and studies of subject.

Lear, J. Do we need new rules for experiments on people? *Saturday Review,* 1966, *49* (6), 61–70.

Article discusses various experiments and research on humans, including Dr. Jose M. R. Delgado's work on physical control of the brain, and David Krech's statement on controlling memory. Particular attention is given to the cancer research of Drs. Southam and Mandel at the Jewish Chronic Disease Hospital in Brooklyn, for which they were placed on probation by the New York Board of Regents for one year. Author stresses the need for responsibility in human experiments.

Pappworth, M. H. *Human guinea pigs.* Boston: Beacon Press, 1967.
Report on legal and ethical issues concerning American and British medical experimentations. Describes specific studies and offers recommendations for regulating experimentations and reducing abusive practices.

Wolfensberger, W. Ethical issues in research with human subjects. *Science,* 1967, *155 (3758)*, 47–51.
Article emphasizes the need for providing a rationale for a general code of conduct in human experimentation, and offers suggestions on guidelines for ethical conduct. Consideration is given to necessary types of consent and research risks.

World Medical Association. Position statement code of ethics on human experimentation. (Adapted from the Helsinki Declaration of the World Medical Association.) *American Journal of Orthopsychiatry,* 1968, *38 (4)*, 589–590.
Article contains the AOA adaptation of the code of the World Medical Association.

Abuse: Public Issues

Addison, P. H. Legal aspects of sterilization and contraception. *The Medico-Legal Journal,* 1967, *35 (4)*.
Report from the British Medical Defense Union, and their opinion on sterilization: ". . . sterilization was not unlawful, whether performed on therapeutic or eugenic grounds or for any other reason, provided there was full and valid consent to the operation by the patient concerned."

Church of England, National Assembly Board for Social Responsibility. *Decisions about life and death: a problem in modern medicine.* Westminster: Author, 1966.
Theological discussion on euthanasia.

Epstein, C. J. Social aspects of medical genetics. *Medical Annals of District of Columbia,* 1967, *36 (4)*.
Discusses genetic manipulations of human beings.

Fletcher, J. *Morals and medicine.* Boston: Beacon Press, 1960.
Theological and ethical interpretation of the issues concerning: truthful communication of findings to patient, regulation of conception, artificial insemination, sterilization, and euthanasia.

Gosney, E. S. & Popenol, P. *Sterilization for human betterment.* New York: Macmillan, 1930.
Discusses eugenic sterilization in the mentally ill and results of research in which 6,255 individuals were sterilized in California.

Guttmacher, A. F. (Ed.) *The case for legalized abortion now.* California: Diablo Press, 1967.

Contains 13 brief articles presenting various arguments in favor of more liberal abortion laws. Begins with a history of abortion practices. Public view is presented.

Landman, J. H. *Human sterilization.* New York: Macmillan, 1932.
History of eugenic sterilization movement. Discusses laws and legal decisions in the United States as well as compulsory legal human sterilization.

Abuse in Institutions

In Institutions for the Mentally Ill and Mentally Retarded

Bartlett, F. L. Institutional peonage: our exploitation of mental patients. *Atlantic,* 1964, *214,* 116–119.
Discusses problems of patients working in large institutions with little compensation and treatment. Discusses the danger that the more competent patients will become "good patients," and, consequently, never leave the institution. Article discusses other institutional problems, such as back wards of custodial hospitals.

Blatt, B. & Kaplan, F. *Christmas in purgatory: a photographic essay on mental retardation.* Boston: Allyn and Bacon, 1966.
Discussion, in words and pictures, of treatment of the mentally retarded in institutions.

Blatt, B. The dark side of the mirror. *Mental Retardation,* 1968, *6* (5), 42–44.
Description of conditions in an institution for the mentally retarded.

Blatt, B. & Mangel, C. Tragedy and hope of retarded children. *Look,* 1967, *41,* 96–99.
Portrayal of conditions in institutions for the mentally retarded, particularly emphasizing the "back wards."

Davies, S. P. *Social control of the mentally deficient.* New York: Crowel, 1930.
Account of the development of thought and present status of investigation in the field of mental deficiency. Reviews various methods of treating the feeble-minded, from the beginnings of Itard and Seguin to present tendencies toward sterilization and segregation.

Dix, D. *Memorial to the Legislature of Massachusetts, 1843.* Nutley, New Jersey: Roche Laboratories, Reprint, 1966.
Dorothea Dix's 1843 address to Massachusetts legislature which discusses conditions in jails and asylums throughout the state.

Dybwad, G. Roadblocks to renewal of residential care. In Menaloscino, F., *Psychiatric Approaches to Mental Retardation.* New York, Basic Books (in press).
Discusses problems that must be confronted and solved before society can expect residential care programs for the retarded to improve.

Garber, R. Two Philadelphia psychiatrists and a theory of American psychiatry. *Mental Hygiene,* 1969, *53* (1), 131–140.
Discusses the efforts of Rush, Stricker, Beers, Dix, and Pinel in relation to humane care for the mentally ill.

Goffman, E. *Asylums: essays on the social situation of mental patients and other inmates.* New York: Doubleday and Company, 1961.

Analysis of life in "total institutions" or closed worlds. Describes what institutions make of the inmate, and what he can make of life inside them.

Kanner, L. *A history of the care and study of the mentally retarded.* Springfield, Illinois: Charles C. Thomas, 1964.
An historical perspective of the treatment of the mentally retarded.

Kirkbride, T. *On the construction and general arrangements of hospitals for the insane.* Philadelphia, Pennsylvania, 1854. Nutley, New Jersey: Roche Laboratories, Reprint, n.d.
Provides guidelines for building hospitals to meet the needs and comforts of the disturbed. Discusses the role of employees in the hospital.

Kugel, R. & Wolfensberger, W. (Eds.) *Changing patterns in residential services for the mentally retarded.* A President's committee on mental retardation monograph: Washington, D.C., 1969.
Landmark book discusses residential services for the mentally retarded in the United States and other countries.

Menninger, K. Psychiatrists urged to speak out against "sins" of current scene. *Roche Report: Frontiers of Hospital Psychiatry.* Nutley, New Jersey: Roche Inc., 6 (1), 5–6.
Current sins include commitment to "eternal damnation" through labeling, and silence in the face of dehumanizing conditions.

Norris, D. The born fool: a study of attitudes in recent times. *Forward Trends.* London: 1963–1964, 8 (1).
Historical perspectives indicating the ways society has viewed the mentally retarded.

Pinel, P. *A treatise on insanity, in which are contained the principles of a new and more practical nosology of maniacal disorders,* translated by D. Davis. London: W. Todd, 1806. Nutley, New Jersey: Roche Laboratories, Reprint, 1966.
Discusses Pinel's work at Bicetre, and scientific documentation of his observations.

Rush, B. *Medical inquiries and observations upon the diseases of the mind.* Nutley, New Jersey: Roche Laboratories, Reprint, 1966.
Role of the physician in relationship to his patient. Discusses care and treatment of the "mad" patient, including a description of patient's physical surroundings, use of strait jackets and other forms of physical restraint.

Szasz, Thomas S., Science and public policy: The crime of involuntary mental hospitalization. *Medical Opinion & Review,* May 1968, 24–35.
Discusses commitment to mental institutions, terming it a "crime against humanity" and a deprivation of human rights.

Ullmann, L. P. *Institution and outcome: a comparative study of psychiatric hospitals.* New York: Pergamon Press, 1967.
Environmental influences that may significantly affect the behavior of the staff and, ultimately, the therapeutic goal of the hospital.

Vail, D. G. *Dehumanization and the institutional career.* Illinois: Charles C. Thomas, 1966.
Description of dehumanization which occurs in an institutional setting, discussing the loss of such human attributes as self-awareness, self-esteem, capacity to love, will, and morality. Author compares hospital life to Auschwitz, and asks the reader to remember the now-living dead.

In Prisons and Hospitals

Clemmer, D. *The prison community.* New York: Rinehart and Company, 1958.
Sociological study of the culture of the prison examines both "formal" and "informal" organizations within the prison. Prisoner groups and channels of communication are explored and discussed.

Fox, V. *Violence behind bars: an explosive report on prison riots in the United States.* New York: Vantage Press, 1956.
Study of the prison riot, and its underlying conditions and causes.

Kenny, J. A. Civil rights in medicine. *American Journal of Orthopsychiatry,* 1965, *35 (1).*
Discusses racial discrimination in regard to hospitals and the medical organization, and suggests that the mental health professional should become knowledgeable on "medical civil rights."

Lader, L. Blackest disgrace in American local government: the county jail. *Reader's Digest,* 1959, *74,* 111–114.
Article contains a condemnation of conditions in United States' county jails, describing the filth, brutality, and corruption the author saw.

Martin, J. B. *Break down the walls. American prisons: present, past, and future.* New York: Ballantine Books, 1954.
Presents a study of the prison riot of 1952 in the State Prison of Southern Michigan at Jackson, covering the present condition of the American prison system, the problems, and what might be done to correct the situation.

Menninger, K. *The crime of punishment.* New York: Viking Press, 1968.
Discusses the crime of punishment as the aggravation of more crime. Also, analyzes the war between lawyers and psychiatrists, the public's role in crime, and the injustice of justice.

Menninger, K. The crime of punishment. *Saturday Review,* 1968, *51 (36),* 21–25+.
Article discusses some of the psychological explanations of violence and the wish to hurt others. Author feels that punishment is based on a motive of retaliation, retribution, or perhaps even guilt concerning sublimated desires to commit crimes. Discusses the horrible conditions of prisons, the "treatment" received there, and suggestions for improvement.

Nesse, R. #24933. *Prison exposures.* New York: Chilton Company Book Division, 1951.
Presents an illustrated story of life in a prison, as told by an inmate.

Robinson, L. N. *Jails: care and treatment of misdemeanant prisoners in the United States.* Philadelphia: John C. Winston Company, 1944.
Discusses problems involved in the American jail system, and suggestions for improvement.

Rubenstein, B., & Levitl, M. An approach to humanism in a medical setting: the preceptor program at the Wayne State University School of Medicine. *American Journal of Orthopsychiatry,* 1966, *36 (1).*
Describes an effort to influence the thoughts, feelings, and behavior of groups of medical students by providing special experiences which will offer antigens for the "dehumanizing influences that are found in traditional medical education."

An R_x for sick hospitals. *Newsweek,* 1966, *68,* 57–61.
Points out the fact that one of the biggest obstacles to the implementation of Medicare is the present condition of United States hospitals. The "sick

hospitals" are characterized by inadequate care, dubious treatment, obsolete facilities, overworked staffs. Article makes suggestions for improvement.

Sandu, H. S. The impact of short-term institutionalization on prison inmates. *British Journal of Criminology,* 1964, *45.*
Author describes the prison as providing NO correctional program, but rather inducing negative effects, such as increased hostility, deterioration of self-concept, and increased sexual perversion.

Townsend, Peter. *The last refuge,* abr. ed. New York: Humanities Press, Inc., 1964.
Report of horrifying conditions in some British geriatric wards.

Trasler, G. The social relations of persistent offenders. *Sociological Review,* 1965, *9.*
Because criminal offenders have problems resulting from inadequacies in socialization, the author feels that prisons are not justified in maintaining traditional closed institutions.

In the Schools

Friedenberg, E. Z. Requiem for the urban schools. *Saturday Review,* 1967, *50,* 77–79+.
Describes experiences of Kohn and Kozol in Harlem and Boston, and evaluates their picture of the situation.

Kohl, R. *36 children.* New York: New American Library, 1968.
Experiences of a teacher in a Harlem public school. Discusses what happens when he leaves.

Kozol, J. *Death at an early age.* Boston: Houghton Mifflin, 1967.
Experiences of a teacher in a Boston public school located in the predominantly black community.

Szasz, Thomas S. Psychiatry in public schools. *Teachers College Record,* 1964, *66 (1),* 57–63.
Discusses the diagnostic role of the school psychiatrist as an infringement upon the rights of individuals.

Abuse in the Community

Black ghettos: the American nightmare; a symposium. *Atlantic,* 1967, *220,* 97–110.
Selections from Stokely Carmichael and Charles Hamilton, Robert Coles, M.D., and Jonathan Kozol. Traces development of the ghetto, its conditions, how its residents react to it and the white world surrounding them, as well as aspects of schools in the ghetto.

Brown, C. *Manchild in the promised land.* New York: Macmillan, 1965.
Story of a man who struggles to get out of the Harlem ghetto.

Coles, R. The children of the American ghetto. *Harper's Magazine,* 1967, *235,* 16.
Psychology, strengths as well as weaknesses, of the black children of the American ghetto; effects of attitudes of American liberals on them.

Drew, E. Going hungry in America. *Atlantic,* 1968, *222 (6),* 53–61.
Discusses hunger, starvation, and malnutrition. Presents scientific information that indicates a connection between malnutrition in children and brain damage. Describes the situation in the Mississippi Delta.

Ginsberg, E. *The troublesome presence: American democracy and the Negro.*
London: The Free Press of Glencoe, 1964.
*History of the American Negro to the present day, including the injustices and
inequalities he has faced.*

Harrington, M. *The other America.* Baltimore, Maryland: Penguin Books, 1968.
*Describes poverty in America, and reasons for its existence, including sug-
gestions for improvement.*

Lorenz, K. *On aggression.* New York: Harcourt, Brace and World, 1966.
*Discusses aggression, "the fighting instinct in beast and man which is di-
rected against members of the same species." Describes typical forms of
aggression and methods of controlling it.*

Mendelsohn, J. *The martyrs.* New York: Harper and Row, 1966.
*Personal stories of 16 people slain for racial reasons in the South since the
United States Supreme Court 1954 school segregation decision. In most cases,
the killers either have not been found, or have not been indicted or convicted.*

Montagu, M. F. Ashley (ed.). *Man and aggression.* New York: Oxford University
Press, 1968.
*Analysis of the concept of instinct, a discussion of animal behavior, and a
comparison of human behavior with that of other animals.*

Ottley, R. *Black odyssey: the story of the Negro in America.* New York: Charles
Scribner's Sons, 1948.
*Historical view of the conditions and circumstances of the Negro's life in
America and the social and economic factors that have shaped the Negro's
life.*

Storr, A. *Human aggression.* New York: Atheneum, 1968.
*Describes and analyzes the different ways in which different types of human
beings try to cope with aggression.*

Wiesel, E. *The Jews of silence.* New York: New American Library, 1967.
*Discusses everyday life of three million Jews living in Russia, and subtle
methods of anti-semitism.*

Abuse in the Family

Bettelheim, B. *The empty fortress: infantile autism and the birth of the self.* New
York: Macmillan, 1967.
*Infantile autism, its treatment, and what we can learn from it regarding the
emergence of a self in the normal or abnormal infant.*

Holter, J., & Friedman S. B. Principles of management in child abuse cases.
American Journal of Orthopsychiatry, 1968, *38* (1), 127–135.
*Procedures for a team-diagnostic approach in cases of child abuse. Discusses
sources of information about the family, planning for the future protection of
the child, coordination of various professional services for the family, and the
role of the professional person as an "external superego" for the parents.*

Jones, D. *Children who need protection: an annotated bibliography.* U.S. Department of Health, Education, and Welfare, 1966.
*References to child neglect, including: child abuse, child welfare, maternal
deprivation, protective services, social casework, the courts, and State Legislation.*